Maynooth College is two hundred years old. Age is honourable and achievement is to be honoured, and both age and achievement will be widely celebrated on the bicentenary. The occasion will see the celebration of Maynooth's original purpose, still continued, the training of priests for Ireland. It will also mark the development of that purpose over two centuries, eventually to include third-level education of men and women in philosophy and theology, in the sciences, and in the arts.

To honour in an appropriate way these two hundred years of teaching, members of the college staff are publishing a series of books in a number of academic disciplines. Edited by members of the College Faculty, these books will range from texts based on standard theology courses to interdisciplinary studies with a theological or religious involvement.

The venture is undertaken with pride in the long Maynooth academic tradition and in modest continuance of it.

The
TRIUNE
GOD

For Ciar

Thomas Marsh

The TRIUNE GOD

A Biblical, Historical, and Theological Study

TWENTY-THIRD PUBLICATIONS
Mystic, Connecticut 06355

Twenty-Third Publications
185 Willow Street
P.O. Box 180
Mystic, CT 06355
(203) 536-2611
800-321-0411
Published in association with The Columba Press, Dublin, Ireland.

ISBN 0-89622-631-X
Library of Congress Catalog Card Number 94-78128
Printed in Ireland by Colour Books Ltd, Dublin.

Contents

Abbreviations etc

The *Revised Standard Version* has been used throughout for biblical quotations, except where otherwise indicated.

For biblical references the RSV abbreviations have been followed.

Translation of patristic texts have been taken from W.J. Jurgens, *The Faith of the Early Fathers*, I-III, Collegeville, Liturgical Press, 1970-1979, where available; elsewhere they are taken from various sources.

The following abbreviations are used:

c	circa/about
d	died
D/S	H. Denzinger-A. Schonmetzer, *Enchiridion Symbolorum, Definitionum et Declarationum de rebus fidei et morum*, Freiburg im Breisgau, 1965.
ITQ	*The Irish Theological Quarterly*
N/D	J. Neuner-J. Dupuis, *The Christian Faith in the Doctrinal Documents of the Catholic Church*, London/Sydney, Collins, 1983.
NPNF	*A Select Library of the Nicene and Post-Nicene Fathers of the Christian Church*, Second Series, reprinted Grand Rapids, Eerdmans.
tr	translation

Foreword

This book offers a study of the theology of the Trinity from its origin in biblical history and revelation through the significant periods of its history down the centuries to the state of this theology at the present day. It presents, therefore, a study in breadth rather than depth. There would seem to be a place for such a comprehensive overview of this subject at the moment and the writer hopes that his effort may serve the needs of students and others who seek a general presentation of the topic rather than a specialised discussion of some of its particular aspects. Those who wish to pursue their interest further may consult the literature listed in the bibliography at the end.

Though the work covers a wide range of material, biblical, historical, theological, the writer hopes that, given the task in hand, the study is both accurate and adequate. Given that the study largely concentrates on basic and general trends rather than specific, particular questions, detailed references to scholarly discussion seemed unnecessary. For the sake of readability, therefore, references have been, as far as possible, incorporated into the text and notes have been kept to a minimum. A complete reference for every modern work mentioned may be found in the bibliography.

One important area of the subject which has not been formally treated in the work is the approach of Orthodox theology to the doctrine of the Trinity. Though the Western Church and the Eastern share the same basic dotrine here, each tradition has, since the Middle Ages, undergone a different historical experience and developed a somewhat different approach to the theology of the Trinity. Today both these traditions are engaged in keen dialogue, to their mutual enrichment. The study presented here wishes to concentrate on the approach of the Latin tradition. To have included a formal treatment of the Orthodox theology would both have deflected somewhat from this purpose and over-extended a study which already covers an extensive range. But many fine presentations of the Orthodox viewpoint exist today in English and are readily available to the interested reader.

The author wishes to express his gratitude and indebtedness to Father Dermot Lane, a personal friend and an Irish theological colleague of many years, who very readily agreed to read an earlier draft of the work and made a number of valuable suggestions. The reader may rest assured that the final text has benefited significantly from his advice. Its shortcomings, however, remain totally the author's own.

Thomas A. Marsh
St Patrick's College
Maynooth

Introduction

A God-towardsness is a basic and essential feature of the human being, of being human. There is in the human being a basic orientation which continually directs it to seek to relate to and exist in relationship with a transcendent Absolute, God. When this orientation, this drive, is given expression, there is prayer. In their prayer human beings name and address their God. The structure of human prayer, therefore, discloses the God that is here believed in, who and what this God is. One can truly say: Tell me your prayer and I will tell you your God.

God, however, at least in the Christian understanding, is not a human discovery. The human does not find God, as one might find a hidden or unknown object. On the contrary, God seeks out the human. God discloses God, reveals God to humans. The world as created is already such a revelation, but one which is partial and ambiguous. God's true revelation of God occurs as history, initially and progressively in the history of Israel and then finally and fully in the event of Jesus Christ. In this unveiling of God in history, this historical revelation, God communicates God-self to humanity and seeks to relate humanity to God-self, to evoke response. Divine revelation is community creating. God's self-revelation is not a private and individualistic affair. It is public and community oriented, even if it is mediated through representative individuals: Abraham, Moses, Jesus. This community comes into being through positively responding to God's revealing overture in acknowledging, accepting, putting it into practice. This response is what is called the faith of the community. Faith is the response to revelation, to the God who reveals God. This faith is an all-embracing expression; it colours and affects the whole of life of both the community and its individual members. But this faith is encapsulated and receives its supreme expression in the prayer of the community. Here, in the structure and terms of the community's prayer, we can discern the community's basic understanding of God as revealed. From this basic understanding particular aspects can be drawn out and formulated. When these are put together, one gets a Creed, a confession of faith, a summary statement of basic aspects of the community's belief. So follows the principle: *Lex orandi statuit legem credendi* [Prosper of Aquitaine]; the structure and system of prayer establishes and determines the structure and system of belief statement. This credal confession in turn, according as its particular elements are further reflected on, gives rise to doctrine, official Church teaching. Then finally, the Christian mind, seeking an understanding of this body of doctrine, develops the discipline we call theology, faith seeking understanding.

In studying the Christian understanding of God as Triune, we turn first, therefore, not to the Church's developed doctrine and theology, historically a late arrival on the scene, but to the prayer of the Church. The basic, developed form of the Church's prayer is found in the Eucharistic Prayer. It will be helpful to recall here the structure of this familiar prayer, taking as our model Eucharistic Prayer III and noting in particular the opening address and the concluding doxology.

Opening Address

Father, you are holy indeed,
and all creation rightly gives you praise.
All life, all holiness comes from you
through your Son, Jesus Christ our Lord,
by the working of the Holy Spirit.
From age to age you gather a people to yourself,
so that from east to west
a perfect offering may be made
to the glory of your name.

Invocation of the Holy Spirit; Narrative of the Last Supper; Memorial Prayer; Invocation of the Holy Spirit; Prayer for the Church; Prayer for the Dead.

Concluding Doxology

Through him,
with him,
in him,
in the unity of the Holy Spirit,
all glory and honour is yours,
Almighty Father,
forever and ever.
Amen.

We have here a succinct summary of the whole of Christian faith. The basic structure and emphases of this prayer are clear and simple, yet they deserve and require close attention. One should note first that, though this is a prayer to God, it is addressed solely to the Father, not to the Son or Holy Spirit, though the Son and the Spirit receive significant mention. This structure is determined by the way God has approached humankind in history, in those events which constitute and are called salvation history. This history reveals God as Father, Son and Holy Spirit, but in accordance with a certain order or structure which the divine revelation has involved and which the prepositions 'from', 'through', 'in' express: God has here communicated God-self in a movement from the Father through the Son in the Spirit. The immediate result of God's revelation is a gathered people. Why are they gathered? To make the appropriate faith response to God, the prayer of praise. This prayer, this response to God by the people God has approached, now displays an ascending structure which is in inverse correspondence with the descending structure of God's movement. This is prayer in the Spirit through and with the Son to the Father. This is the basic structure of all Christian prayer, whatever its form, and it is so because of the way God has revealed God-self in God's approach to us.

God's self-revelation and the prayer response of the community of faith present God as the Father who relates to us through the Son in the Spirit and we to God the Father in the Spirit through and with the Son. God is the Father, but Deity here also involves and includes the Son and the Holy Spirit. There is one God, but this one God involves a threeness, a Trinity. This God is a Triune God.

This structure and implication of revelation and Christian prayer was there from the beginning. It is evident, for example, in the statement of Ephesians 2:18: 'Through him [Christ] we both [Jew and Gentile, all] have access in one Spirit to the Father'. Christian prayer in the Apostolic Age had the same triadic or trinitarian structure as prayer today. Faith in God as Triune was implicit but fundamental in Christain faith from the beginning. The typical biblical and Jewish stress on the one God is evident throughout the New Testament. This one God is Yahweh, the God of Israel, the God of Abraham, Isaac and Jacob. But in early Christianity this one God of biblical faith is termed the Father: 'for us there is one God, the Father ...'. [1 Cor 8,6] Yet, the New Testament also understands the Deity to involve the Son and the Holy Spirit. This is to be seen especially in those statements which describe the salvation which has been accomplished by God through Jesus Christ in the Holy Spirit and which is now avaliable in the Church. But throughout the period of the New Testament this understanding of God as Triune remains implicit in the sense that no effort is made or even envisaged at formulating an explicit statement of it, and still less at formulating any theological understanding. One simply finds salvation history statements that God the Father has acted definitively through Christ in the Spirit. Yet acknowledgment of God as Triune is already there awaiting thinking out and spelling out.

Early Christianity is here already committed to a revolution in the Jewish understanding of God. But it will take the Church centuries before it will be in a position to achieve the theological clarification which will enable it to issue its formal doctrinal statement on the Triune God. As usual it will be the emergence of heresy which will force the Church along this road. The great catalyst here will be the views of Arius which will lead to the Council of Nicea in 325 AD and initiate the great fourth century Controversy which in principle will be concluded at the First Council of Constantinople in 381. Over the following centuries, culminating in the great medieval scholastic system, theologians will assemble the doctrinal data established in and as a result of the Controversy into the classical scholastic treatise on the Trinity, the Tract *De Deo Trino*. Today this scholastic presentation is the subject of a critical re-assessment which is underlining some basic limitations in this system. The main thrust of this new interest in the theology of the Trinity is towards rendering the subject less abstract and remote but more actual and relevant to the life of the Church and the Christian. The theology of the Trinity is here seeking to re-occupy its ancient place as the heart and centre of the whole theological enterprise.

This introductory outline of the origin and development of the doctrine and theology of the Trinity dictates the shape of the study presented here. This will begin with a review of the background, origin and emergence of this understanding of God in biblical history and revelation, involving both the Old Testament and the New. It will then follow the history of the doctrine over the centuries, from the early efforts of the pre-Nicene period, through the stormy debates of the fourth century Controversy, the development of the later Latin tradition, down to the scholastic tract of modern times. It will conclude with a review of the theology of the Trinity today and some of the main issues with which this theology is now concerned.

CHAPTER 1

The God of Israel

Israel and Christianity believe in the one, same God. Both are the products of the same salvation history and acknowledge the same God who directs and reveals Godself in that history. Christians too regard themselves as children of Abraham – 'our father in faith'. For Israel this one God is Yahweh, the God of Abraham, Isaac and Jacob. Christianity differs from Israel in that it asserts that this one God is also three – Yahweh, the Father, the Son, Jesus Christ, and the Holy Spirit of God. In this basic assertion of faith, Christianity has accomplished a revolution in the Jewish understanding of God. It explains and claims to justify this revolution by maintaining that salvation history, which in the period of Israel remains on-going and open-ended, achieves in the events of Jesus Christ and the outpouring of the Holy Spirit its fulfilment and completion. In this completion of salvation history the one God of the faith of Israel is revealed as *also* three – a Tri-une God.

It follows from this basic position that Christian faith is an outgrowth of the faith of Israel. This is the background and context everywhere presupposed in early Christianity as recorded throughout the New Testament. The period of origin is fundamental for the understanding of any movement, since it is at this embryonic stage that basic characteristics are asserted and documented. The concept of God in Christian faith is a revolutionary, non-logical development of the understanding of God in the faith of Israel. The Christian concept of God is not a totally new beginning; it has a pre-history in the faith of Israel. This pre-history is therefore essential background for an understanding of the development which takes place in the emergence of Christian faith. To understand Christianity's concept of God as Triune, one must begin with the understanding of God in the faith of Israel. There is both continuity and discontinuity here. Both of these features need to be asserted and highlighted if an understanding of this revolutionary development in Christian faith is to be achieved and justice done regarding it. A study of the Christian concept of

God as Triune must therefore begin before Christianity by going back to the understanding of God in Israel.

The God of Israel
The God who formed and called the People of Israel in their history is the same God in whom Christian faith also believes. Many, indeed most, of the basic features which characterise this understanding of God constitute therefore common ground between Israel and Christianity. Here there is essentially little difference between the Old Testament and the New. And Christian faith always has and always will illustrate its understanding of God almost equally from both Testaments. This common ground applies above all to the conception of God as a God of saving concern and love who guides salvation history to a definitive goal which constitutes redemption for universal human history. God's promise to Abraham which begins the biblical narrative of salvation history stands over and unites both all salvation history and the whole of human history: 'I will make of you a great nation ... and by you all the families of the earth shall bless themselves.' (Gen 12:2-3) The Christian statement 'God is love' (1 Jn 4:8) is essentially an Old Testament statement and emphasis, even if the Christian writer has immediately to add that the ultimate manifestation of this love was when God 'sent his only Son into the world'. But at least in this basic assertion of what God means, Jew and Christian Gentile are at one.

A comprehensive study of the God of biblical faith would have to embrace these attributes which characterise the understanding of God in both Judaism and Christianity. This, however, is not possible in this work devoted as it is to the Christian doctrine of God as Trinity. But it is important to note that Christian faith asserts these attributes of the God which it acknowledges and confesses as Triune. This is an implication of the important summary statement of the Council of Florence in its Decree for the Jacobites (1442 AD) which states that 'everything [appertaining to the three divine persons] is one where there is no opposition of relationship' (*omnia sunt unum, ubi non obviat relationis oppositio*). (N/D 325; D/S 1330) In other words, the only distinctions which Christian faith acknowledges in God are the distinctions of the three persons, Father, Son and Holy Spirit. All other statements made of God, including these attributes predicated of God, refer to God as one without distinction. Though an understanding of the implications of this doctrinal statement will concern us again later in this work, it suffices for the moment to assure us that the attributes asserted of the one God of the faith of Israel in the Old Testament apply fully and equally to the triune God of Christian faith. The distinction of persons in God recognised in that faith does not affect or distribute predication of these attributes.

This understanding of God common to both the Old and the New Testament must remain presupposed in this work. But it is important to note that it is presupposed. In our consideration here of the background in the Old Testament to the Christian concept of God, the concentration will be on the emphatic statement of monotheism which characterises the presentation of God in the Old Testament and the question whether this strong assertion that God is one is in principle compatible with or on the contrary precludes the Christian assertion that this God is also three. Is there direct, irreconcilable contradiction here or is the Old Testament statement open to the qualification which the Christian assertion claims? Is there simply discontinuity here between the Testaments or a balance of continuity and justifiable discontinuity?

The Old Testament presents the faith of Israel as a strict monotheism. Faith in the one, true God who is revealed to them in their history and chose them as God's own people is basic and emphatic in the Old Testament. A few well-known texts suffice to illustrate the point.

> I am the Lord your God, who brought you out of the land of Egypt, out of the house of bondage. You shall have no other gods before me. (Ex 20:2-3)
>
> Hear, O Israel: The Lord our God is one Lord .... (Deut 6:4)
>
> I am the first and I am the last; besides me there is no god. (Is 44:6)

One must be careful, however, how one assesses this Old Testament assertion of the one God. It is very easy to be simplistic here and to see this assertion of the divine Unicity as fundamentally incompatible with the later Christian concept of the divine Triad. This, however, was not the view of the early Christians who, we must remember, were themselves Jewish converts. They saw no conflict between the Jewish assertion of one God and their own specific understanding of God as also a Triad. Yet, a revolution in the understanding of God had undoubtedly taken place. To appreciate what was involved here, we need to look carefully at the concept of monotheism in the history of Israel.

Israel's understanding of God is called Yahwism, from the enigmatic reply which God gives to Moses's question: What is your name? at the incident of the Burning Bush, Exodus 3:14-15. But a critical approach to the texts of the Old Testament shows that

Yahwism was not always the strict monotheism which it certainly
later became, especially under the impact of the great prophets,
8th to 6th century B.C. In Israel's earlier period, though the question is disputed, the attitude seems to have been more open. The
majority of scholars maintain that at this stage, while Israel certainly worshipped one God, this did not involve the denial of the
existence or the validity of the gods of other peoples. Israel's theistic faith at this stage, according to this view, was a Henotheism
rather than a Monotheism, an acknowledgement of one God exclusive to Israel without denying the existence of gods of other
peoples. One might better describe this attitude as a Monolatry,
exclusive worship of one God, a practical rather than a speculative, and certainly not a philosophical, Monotheism. As J. L.
McKenzie has remarked: 'A speculative philosophical monotheism appears nowhere in the Bible.' (*Dictionary of the Bible*, 584)[1]

Later, however, Israel came to see its God, Yahweh, as the one
and only true God and the gods of all other peoples as empty
idols. This is a development especially of Israel's great prophetic
period and it is fully accomplished and given its most forthright
expression in the 6th century document known as Second Isaiah.
(Is 40-55)

Israel's understanding of God was not a human discovery but
was derived from God's revelation of God to them in their history. The most significant moment in the disclosure of the identity
of this God occurred in Moses' encounter at the incident of the
Burning Bush on Mount Horeb described in Exodus 3:1-15. Prior
to this, in the period of the Patriarchs, various names were applied to the God who had called Abraham. The basic name used,
and that on which most of the others were based, was El. This was
a generic name for Deity common among the Western Semitic
peoples to whom Abraham and his clan belonged and from
whom it was adopted. Among these derivatives of El in common
use in the early period was the plural form Elohim which literally
meant the Deities but which was always used in early Israel in a
singular sense. This usage sometimes gives the impression of a
plurality in the Godhead according as the plural noun attracts
other grammatically plural forms. The following well-known text
illustrates the point.

> Then Elohim/God said: 'Let *us* make man in *our* image, after
> *our* likeness ...'. So Elohim/God created man in *his* own im-
> age, in the image of Elohim/God *he* created him; male and
> female *he* created them. (Gen 1: 26-27, emphasis added; cf
> also Gen 3: 22; 11:7)

Christian exegesis has sometimes read into these texts a suggestion of plurality in God, a veiled anticipation of the doctrine of the Trinity. Such an interpretation, however, cannot be allowed. Though the form here is plural, the sense is clearly singular. The plural usage is of purely grammatical significance. El and its many derivatives were generic names and carried with them that sense of remoteness and abstraction typical of such terms. They were not specific personal names and therefore lacked that note of close personal relationship and allegiance which we expect to find in our address to and acknowledgement of God. It is precisely this remoteness and impersonal quality which leads to Moses' question on Mount Horeb.

Revelation of the 'Name': Exodus 3: 1-15
This incident is a theophany, a manifestation of God. The narrative here consists of three sections describing consecutively:
a) The Call of Moses: vv 1-6. God here identifies Godself as: 'the God/Elohim of your fathers, the God/Elohim of Abraham, the God/Elohim of Isaac, the God/Elohim of Jacob'.
b) The Mission of Moses: vv 7-12: 'I will send you to Pharaoh that you may bring forth my people, the sons of Israel, out of Egypt'.
c) Revelation of the 'Name': vv 13-15. Moses now asks: 'If they [the people] ask me his [God's] name, what shall I say?' It is God's reply to this question which here claims our interest and attention. But to appreciate the full significance of the reply, some analysis, not only of text, but of context and background is necessary.

The background which prompts Moses' question is found in the religious culture to which he belonged. This is described by D M G Stalker as follows: 'In early religion it was thought necessary to know the deity's name before cultic relations could be entered upon with him ... and such relations Moses wished to establish. At the same time the name was regarded as indicative of character. The Israelite's question is thus a very practical one. ... According to Egyptian ideas each god had several names. But his real name he kept a secret.' (*Peake's Commentary on the Bible*, 212) This secret name of the god is thus the first key to unlocking the meaning of the text here. The modern reader needs to remember that in the Bible and the general culture from which it sprang and which it in so many ways exemplifies the name of someone had a much stronger significance than is usual with us today. There a name was not a mere identifying label. It expressed the being, personality, power of the person named. It was in a way a definition. Further, in addressing a god, invocation of the proper name was regarded as possessing a quasi-magical power and force; it, as it were, released the power of the god. It was very important, therefore, that people knew the secret or favoured name of the god, because then they could invoke him and obtain benefits from him. Bearing this background in mind, we can now proceed to a consideration of God's reply to Moses's question. This reads as follows.

> God said to Moses: 'I AM WHO I AM. ... Say this to the people of Israel: "I AM has sent me to you." ... This is my name forever and thus I am to be remembered throughout all generations.'

It should first be noticed that God here reveals God's 'Name', not on God's own initiative, but only on Moses's request. Revelation of the 'Name' occurs, as it were, incidentally in the narrative. This is, of course, literary artistry, but it also has its own significance. Though from Israel's point of view, revelation of the divine 'Name' was the climax and the most important aspect of this incident, overshadowing even the liberating mission of Moses, from God's point of view it was secondary and incidental. According to God's intention, this was not the basic and primary purpose of the theophany. This fact has its own implications. But what does the revealed 'Name' mean?

This is a question which has its own problems and is the subject of much scholarly discussion. In the original consonantal Hebrew text, the word translated 'I AM' consists simply of the four Hebrew letters YHWH – hence known as the Tetragrammeton. It can be identified that this word represents some form of the archaic Hebrew verb 'to be', but its exact meaning is far from certain. It is also clear, however, that grammar alone will not unlock the meaning here. For this one has to have recourse to the fuller spelling out of the 'Name' in the statement 'I AM WHO [I] AM', to the background and whole context of this narrative and, indeed, to the theology of the Pentateuch as a whole. One meaning, much favoured in later times, especially among the philosophically minded medieval commentators, can certainly be excluded, namely, the metaphysical explanation, God as the one who simply *is*. This tendency, in fact, appeared as early as the philosophically conscious Greek LXX translation (3rd century BC) which translated our text: *ego eimi ho on* – 'I am the Existent One' – and was given further scope by St Jerome's Vulgate Latin version: *sum qui sum* – the text the medievals commented on. Metaphysical thought, however, is very alien to the Bible and certainly does not represent the meaning here. The solution must be sought elsewhere.

When full recourse is had to the sources indicated, it emerges that the meaning of the term YHWH is really a statement -at least, it requires a statement to express its full meaning. This statement may be rendered as follows: 'I am the one who will be there with you ... in the way I will be there'. In other words, God does not answer Moses' question – at least, not in the way he expected. God does not reveal God's secret, quasi-magical name by which God can be invoked and, as it were, made to operate. In this sense God refuses and rejects Moses' question. God says: 'I am not that kind of God'. Instead, God asserts and commits Godself to a saving relationship with Israel. God will be there with them guiding their history towards its salvific goal. But what that future history is going to involve, what its climax is going to be and how precisely God will be there revealing God in that climax - this God does not disclose. In this sense, God leaves the future open. God is identified here simply by God's promise of future salvation. That is God's 'Name'.[2]

This enigmatic self-identification of God in the incident of the Burning Bush has important implications for an understanding of God's revelation of Godself to Israel of the Old Testament period. God's refusal to disclose God's 'real' name should be noted. God here simply describes God as the one who is the director of salvation history and who will bring it to a climax and conclusion. In effect, God states that that is all Israel needs to know. But further, in saying that that is God's 'Name' for all generations, God is saying that that position is final. God's 'real' name will not be disclosed in human time. God is and will remain throughout all human time the Anonymous One. The implications of this position for all efforts, past and present, to 'name' God will concern us again in this study.

The basic implication of God's reply to Moses, however, concerns the promise and assertion that God is directing and guiding salvation history – and therefore the revelation which that history involves and mediates – into a future and a climax in that future which to human eyes remains undisclosed and hidden. The future path of salvation history remains open-ended – until the climax has occurred. Until then, humans can only wait upon events. But they enter upon that future with the assurance of God's promise that God is guiding the process; God is and will be there with them. The history of Israel is a history of waiting, a night which awaits a dawn. The time will come, however, when the word of God in Isaiah 43: 18-19 will be fulfilled: 'Remember not the former things, nor consider the things of old. Behold, I am doing a new thing.'

Given that God in the last analysis is unknowable to the human mind in that the mind can never fully grasp or define God, and given that the understanding of God in Israel is a process developing from primitive forms but always conditioned by and subject to on-going salvation history, then that understanding itself must ever remain open to such development and further disclosure that future salvation history may involve. In the period of Israel salvation history itself is in process, reaching out towards a divinely appointed climax in the future. Until that climax has been achieved, salvation history remains open-ended and incomplete. Since salvation history is the vehicle which mediates revelation and consequent understanding of God, then that revelation and understanding as presented in the Old Testament also remains incomplete and open to development and future qualification. The understanding of God in the faith of Israel is and can only be the beginning of a sentence. The conclusion remains to be written. There can as yet be no full stop.

This fundamental conditioning of the role of Israel in salvation history must be borne in mind in assessing the Old Testament assertion that there is *one* God. This too is an unfinished sentence. There is certainly no revelation of the Trinity in the Old Testament. But the assertion that God is *one* must nevertheless remain open to possible future qualification.

Transcendence and Immanence

Another feature of God's self-revelation to Israel which has implications for this study must also be considered here. This concerns the dual character of transcendence and immanence which God's presence to Israel and Israel's understanding of God involves.

Israel experienced the God revealed in their history as utterly transcendent to the world. This God is not to be identified with any part, aspect, element of the world. This God is totally above the world, transcendent, Wholly Other as regards it. Yet, this Wholly Other, this utterly transcendent God, is also present in the world and active in history. The world, in fact, is filled with God's presence. And in a special way God is present to Israel in their history, making them the vehicle of the divine saving purpose and guiding their history towards that goal. The God who is transcendent to the world is also immanent in it. The faith of Israel thus brought them very early face-to-face with this great problem of

theism: How is the God who is transcendent to the world also immanent in it? How can God be above and beyond the world and
yet also in it? How can the transcendence and immanence of God
be reconciled?

This problem presented itself to the very unphilosophical mind
of Israel in a very practical way – as a problem of language. How
can one speak in the same language, with the same set of terms, of
a God who is above and beyond the world and yet active in it? To
speak of God in a transcendent way would seem to preclude one
from speaking of God in the same terms as immanent, and vice
versa. This very practical God-talk problem forced an option on
Israel. It had to choose between transcendence and immanence as
the more basic feature and characteristic of its God. One would
have to predominate and control the other. Israel opted for transcendence.

The problem now narrowed itself to the question of how to
speak of the immanent features of the God acknowledged as transcendent. If your God is transcendent and your language describes this transcendence, how can you use this same language to
describe God's immanent aspects? Israel's answer to this problem
was simply: anthropomorphism – it simply pictured God present
and active on earth like a human being. Thus, it spoke of God
walking in the garden in the cool of the evening; of God coming
down from God's abode on high to see the city and tower of Ba-
bel; of God coming down to see and investigate Sodom and Gom-
morah. (Gen 3:8;11:5; 18:21) Israel simply pictured its God in the
form of a human being manifesting human features, speaking of
the face, the hand, the finger of God. But especially, it spoke of the
word (*dabar*) of God and the breath/spirit (*ruah*) of God. These latter concepts, destined to become so significant later in Christian
faith and theology, represent in the Old Testament the power of
the transcendent God going forth and accomplishing in various
ways God's designs on earth. They are anthropomorphic, linguistic devices to describe how God, true to the promise, is 'there
with' God's people, guiding their history.

Closely related to these concepts of the Word and the Spirit is
the theme of the Wisdom of God as developed and presented in
the Wisdom literature. The concept of Wisdom here describes
God's immanence in creation and in human life. This theme is one
of the ways the Old Testament links together the revelation of
God in creation and in salvation history. Another prominent way
it presents this relation is by developing its creation narrative,

Genesis 1-3, and placing it as a interpretative prologue to its whole account of salvation history.

Christian exegesis has often claimed that in these concepts of the Word, Wisdom and Spirit/Breath of God, the revelation of the Trinity is already foreshadowed in the Old Testament. These expressions, in other words, already have there, in some implicit way or other, a trinitarian meaning. Such exegesis by hindsight, however, cannot be allowed, at least as regards what nowadays is called the historical, literal sense. But in fairness, this Christian approach never suggested that the trinitarian meaning was even an implication of the literal sense of these texts. Instead, these exegetes appealed here to the specifically Christian concept of a typical or spiritual/allegorical level of meaning to the Old Testament and propounded this Christian interpretation on this basis. Origen, for example, the great expert of the spiritual/allegorical approach to the Old Testament, was fully aware of the distinction between this approach and that of the historical, literal sense which he also respected. We are entering here on the question of biblical hermeneutics and the different levels of meaning or 'senses' of Scripture which Christian faith has detected in the Bible, especially the Old Testament. This is a topic of great and significant interest. It cannot, however, be pursued any further here. We simply note here that these concepts of the Word and the Spirit of God in the Old Testament are basically literary devices to describe the activity in history of the transcendent God whereby God controls and directs the destiny of the Chosen People.

There is also, however, a deeper implication to these concepts and the immanent activity of God which they describe which merits attention here. This immanent activity of God expresses God's providence, God's guiding presence in history accomplishing the divine saving purpose. It is by means of this providence that God is revealed. Now God's self- revelation to humans is never immediate and direct: 'No one has ever seen God; the only Son, who is in the bosom of the Father, he has made him known.' (Jn 1:18) God's self- revelation occurs always by means of something other than God, through a chosen medium of communication which thereby becomes God's self-expression, sign, sacrament. This consideration raises the question of the relation of God to these chosen media of communication and revelation. This relation admits of degrees, sometimes greater, sometimes lesser. There is, for example, the relation between God and the Prophets and then an obviously closer relation between God and God's

Word and Spirit. God's Word and Spirit go forth from God but in accomplishing their purpose they represent the very presence of God. These degrees of relation between God and God's media of revelation suggest, at least, the possibility of a medium which is both identical with God and yet, being God's medium, also distinct. Were this not so, it would seem that a final, full revelation of God to humans would not be possible. There would, at most, be an infinite, asymptotic series of never-ending closer relationships between God and God's chosen media. There would and could be no conlusion to revelation other than a purely arbitrary stop. God would in very principle be incapable of finally and fully revealing God. Such a situation would seem to make the very idea of revelation absurd. Yet, if a medium of revelation which is both one with God and also distinct is possible, this introduces a complexity and a differentiation into what is meant by 'God' which the word and concept 'one' is not adequate to express. Once again, the very notion of God's self-revelation in history, which is the substance of Israel's experience of itself as God's People, suggests that the Old Testament assertion of the *one* God has about it an openess and complexity which further historical revelation may yet qualify and clarify.

One might add also that the precise meaning of the term 'one' is, surprisingly, not at all clear. When one says 'There is one this …', is the meaning of this statement purely negative, saying simply 'this' is not two or more, or has it also a positive content, adding something positive about 'this'? And if it is adding something positive, what is it? The term 'one' certainly has the negative sense mentioned, denial of plurality, but it is not at all clear what further positive sense it can have. It is at least very difficult to see how the unity asserted in the term 'one' must also exclude all form of complexity. Unity and complexity are not incompatible.

The monotheism of Israel certainly has a strong negative sense. Israel here distinguishes its acknowledged God from 'the gods many' of the pagan peoples surrounding it throughout its history. Perhaps there is also a contrast here between the simplicity of the Creator God and the compositeness and multiplicity which characterises all created things. But it would surely be going too far to maintain that the assertion that God is one excludes all complexity within that one God. Perhaps the fact that the faith of Israel compels it to speak of the Word *of God* and the Spirit *of God* proceeding forth *from God*, perhaps this fact contains a hint of just such a complexity. Perhaps – though tell it not in Gath! – the nowadays much maligned spiritual exegesis of these texts did have a point after all.

Our discussion here of the revelation of God to Israel and the understanding of God in that faith has concentrated on the strong assertion that there is *one* God. Revelation in the period of Israel is determined by its source which is salvation history. Since this history is here still in process and open to future development, the revelation which it mediates is also by definition incomplete and subject to future qualification. This open, provisional character of Old Testament revelation applies also to the assertion of the *one* God. While it is inconceivable that this statement will be nullified, it must nevertheless remain open for the moment to possible future qualification. It still remains to be seen how God will finally be 'there' and what this final involvement of God in history will mean for our understanding of God.

Notes

1. For a recent discussion of this issue, see Andrew Mayes, 'The Emergence of Monotheism in Israel', in J. M. Byrne, ed., *The Christian Understanding of God Today*, Dublin, Columba Press, 1993, 26-33.

2. Discussion of this important passage may be consulted in the standard commentaries and in the standard works on the theology of the Old Testament. The interpretation followed here is based especially on the study of the passage in Henry Renckens, *The Religion of Israel*, London, Sheed & Ward 1967, chapter 3, 'The God of Israel', 97-139.

CHAPTER 2

The God of Early Christianity

Through him we both have access in one Spirit to the Father.
Eph 2:18

The basis and foundation of the revolution in the biblical understanding of God which occurs in Christian faith is the belief that
salvation history, and the revelation of God which it involves and
mediates, has been accomplished and achieved in the life, death
and resurrection of Jesus of Nazareth and in the outpouring of the
Spirit of God which climaxes these events. God's promise of salvation which underpins the history of Israel is now fulfilled. Since
salvation history is the vehicle of revelation and since our ultimate knowledge of God depends upon and comes from revelation, this completion of salvation history means that *now* God is
fully revealed and may be fully known. The sentence which God
had begun in the words to Moses at the Burning Bush, the divine
'Name', is here completed. We now know what was meant when
God said: 'I am the one who will be there with you – in the way I
will be there.' What did this completion of salvation history involve for the understanding of God which had characterised the
faith of Israel? And how was the new understanding of God
which now emerged given expression and witnessed to in early
Christian faith? These are the two questions, Foundation and Witness, which here claim our attention.

Foundation: Salvation History Completed

In the vision of Christian faith salvation history reached its climax
and completion in the two events which we may summarily call
here the event of Christ and the event of the Spirit. It must be noted, however, that these events brought with them no special language explaining themselves. These two events had brought this
new faith community into existence and made it what it was.
From their experience of these events, the first Christians were
convinced that God had here fulfilled the divine promise to Israel.
But these events provided no language to describe and explain
the 'new thing' which God had now accomplished. For this the
early Christians could only go back to the language of the promise

as contained in the Old Testament and its symbols. In terms of salvation history, Israel had been a pilgrim people on the road, a people on Journey towards Journey's End. The first Christians saw themselves as the people of Journey's End. But the only language they possessed to describe their situation was the previous language of Journey, of promise as foretold but yet unfulfilled.

Events had now, however, outpaced this language and rendered it inadequate in principle for their purpose. They were, therefore, faced with the daunting task of creating a new language which would in some more adequate way express the novelty of their new-found faith. The New Testament is the record of how they progressively set about this task over the best part of a century and what their achievement was. It might also be noted here that the almost exclusive concentration of modern New Testament exegesis on the historical-critical method and the corresponding high status accorded this approach, has brought with it a strong bias, all the more influential for being largely unconscious, towards earlier stages of this developing tradition and its more primitive forms of thought. The resulting tendency is to regard these earlier stages as somehow the more authentic expressions of Christian faith and to see later more developed thought as in some measure or other a declension from pristine purity. This attitude is an inversion of right hermeneutical principle. The creation in early Christianity of a new conceptual system and language to express the new faith has to consist of a development from more primitive to more developed forms of thought. This process will require time and, occasionally, flashes of genius. But it means that we must look to the later rather than the earlier stages of this process for the more adequate and authentic statement of Christian faith. It further implies that one should not set earlier and later stages of New Testament thought over against one another as somehow necessarily incompatible. One will have to expect later forms both to incorporate earlier and yet transform them in some original way. A deeper insight of faith is developing through this process and seeking expression at a deeper level.

This process of developing insight, which will have its final and finest achievement in the statement and theology of the Fourth Gospel, begins with the far simpler statement which the first Christians deliver to their fellow Jews in the aftermath of the event of Pentecost. St Peter's Pentecost sermon as given in Acts 2, and making all allowance for certain later features which can be detected in it, is rightly regarded as providing a good outline of this early Christian kerygma.[1] The climax and conclusion of this speech states: 'Let all the house of Israel therefore know assuredly that God has made him both Lord and Christ, this Jesus whom you crucified.' (v 36) This identification of the risen, exalted Jesus with the awaited Messiah/Christ means that the Messianic Age with all its Blessings has now been inaugurated. As foretold by the Prophets, the crowning, sealing element of these Blessings would be the universal outpouring of the Spirit of God. (cf Joel 2:28-29; Ezek 36:24-27) Peter accordingly points to and presents the event of Pentecost morning as the fulfilment of this prophecy and the sure sign that the Messianic Age has dawned: 'Being therefore exalted at the right hand of God, and having received from the Father the promise of the Holy Spirit, he has poured out this which you see and hear.' (v 33)

Peter's remarks here, stating the early Christian kerygma, are based on the acknowledgment that the foundation events of Christian faith to which he refers mark the fulfilment of God's promise to Israel. This, indeed, is how he begins his sermon: 'This is what was spoken by the prophet ....' (v 16; cf Acts 3:18, 24) He then identifies these events in terms of the language and symbols of the promise, the description of the New Age given in the prophets. The inauguration of this new and final period in salvation history was associated in the thought of Israel with the appearance of a figure of this End-Time who, though variously described, was most popularly regarded as the Messiah, a new King of the line of David. The other prominent feature which would mark the dawning of this Age and help to identify it was, as has been said, the outpouring of the Spirit of God. Indeed, according to well-known texts of Isaiah (11:1-2; 42:1; 61:1-3), this gift would first appear as an endowment of the Messiah himself. For Peter and his companions, who constitute the inaugural Christian community, events have now perfectly matched and given effect to the symbols of the prophetic portrayal. Here Jesus of Nazareth is identified and confessed as the Messiah/Christ who by the victory of his death and resurrection inaugurates the End-Time, Salvation Time, with its final gift, the outpouring of the Holy Spirit, 'the promise of the Father'. (Acts 1:4) Prophetic symbol has issued in reality of history.

This early statement of Christian faith is couched in the language of the prophetic portrayal, the language of the promise and the journey. This was the only language at the disposal of the first Christians and the language that was most serviceable to them in their efforts to bring their novel message to the attention of their fellow Jews. It will soon be evident, however, that this language of the past will not be adequate to encompass and express the meaning of the present with all its novelty. Fulfilment has surpassed and superseded promise and requires a language connatural and appropriate to itself. The task of creating this new language begins almost immediately and continues throughout the period of the New Testament. But from the very beginning and by virtue of the acknowledgment in faith of the foundation events themselves, a new and revolutionary understanding of God is being proposed which demands and will continue to demand ever more explicit expression. This new understanding is imposed by the events themselves; an appropriate language to express it will have to be created. What this new understanding of God means and involves is the question which must now claim our attention.

The basis of the Christian understanding of God lies in the acknowledgment that God has fulfilled God's promise of salvation and brought salvation history to conclusion through Jesus of Nazareth confessed as the Christ and in the outpouring of the Spirit. With these events God has said God's final word and declared who and what God is. The understanding of God which develops from this basis concerns, therefore, these three references, God, Jesus Christ, the Spirit of God, and the relationship between them. Exposition of this understanding involves consideration of each of these terms and their meaning in the New Testament.

God the Father

In the New Testament the expression *Ho Theos*/The God, following Jewish Greek usage, signifies Yahweh, the God of Israel, the God of Abraham, Isaac and Jacob. All the features and attributes which characterise the understanding of God in the Old Testament are exemplified here also. In this sense the New Testament is most certainly speaking of the same God as the Old. Accordingly, it can occasion no surprise that the New Testament also contains and continues the emphatic biblical assertion that this God is *one*: 'for us there is one God, the Father' (1 Cor 8:6); 'there is ... one God and Father of us all'. (Eph 4,6) One has to endorse, therefore, the conclusion of Karl Rahner: 'This confession of the *one* God runs through the entire New Testament.' ('Theos in the NT', *Th Inv*, 1, 100) The force and implication of this assertion must not be lost on us. It means that for early Christianity, too, Yahweh, the one God, sums up and represents all that the term 'God' means and involves. Any further statement about God which Christian faith may wish to make, must be both compatible with this assertion and an explication of it.[2]

But already in the quotations just cited, Christian faith has made a further and profoundly significant statement. It has described Yahweh, the one God, as 'Father'. What is the significance of this epithet as used of God? The use of the term 'Father' for God was not an invention of the New Testament. It occurs also in the Old. But the startling contrast in the incidence of this usage between the Testaments marks a major shift in emphasis and understanding. In the Old Testament it is estimated that the term 'Father' is used of God fifteen times. In the New Testament it is found in the Gospels *alone*, and on the lips of Jesus, one hundred and seventy-five times! In Matthew 5-7, the Sermon on the Mount, it occurs fifteen times. What is the significance of this new emphasis? The reluctance of the Old Testament to use the term 'Father' for God is explained both by the fear of introducing mythological ideas of divine paternity, so common in the ancient Near East, into Israel's understanding of its God and also by reverence for the transcendent character of Yahweh. To the ears of Israel, use of such a term would have sounded too familiar, lacking in reverence. The few times the term is used of God, the usage is clearly a metaphor, an image employed to express some aspect or aspects of God's relationship with God's people. It is never here a name for God. In particular, the term expressed the absolute authority of God over Israel and especially God's saving concern and loving tenderness towards them. As so used, the image is obviously borrowed from and expresses the patriarchal culture which Israel shares with the whole ancient Near East. Its background lies in the status of the one who is head of the family, clan, tribe, and guardian of its welfare.

It is important to note that the 'fatherhood' attributed to God here refers to God's exclusive relationship with Israel as the Chosen People. God is not called 'Father' here in virtue of being the Creator of all things, visible and invisible, and thereby 'Father' of all humans. God is simply 'Father' of Israel because God has chosen this people to be the vehicle of God's saving purpose in history. The image of fatherhood expresses some basic aspects of this relationship between God and Israel. In choosing Israel as God's People, God calls them to observe God's commands, to obey God's Law. Israel is here required to respond to God with the obedience a son is expected to show towards the commands of his father. Corresponding to the notion of God as 'Father' of Israel, therefore, stands that of Israel as 'Son' of God. (Ex 4:22; Deut 14:1-2; Hos 11:1) Essentially, therefore, this 'Father-Son' image expresses the covenant relationship between God and Israel.

The comparative statistics of the usage of the term 'Father' for God in the Old and New Testaments show that a startlingly new way of understanding God is taking place in early Christian thought. Here, the term 'Father' is the most frequent and the most characteristic expression for God. There is indeed evidence of an increasing tendency to use this term of God in Judaism in the first century A.D. But this confined and embryonic development cannot explain the strong Christian predilection for this term. This has its source in Jesus' own characteristic way of speaking of and addressing God. Further, the expression which Jesus favoured here was not the more generic term 'Father' but the much more intimate term 'Abba' – the familiar term within the family for the father corresponding in our usage to terms such as 'Papa'. The debate concerning how original this usage was to Jesus in the Judaism of that time need not concern us here. What is certain is that this was the way of speaking of and addressing God characteristic of Jesus. Later Christian usage, therefore, has its source here and represents a continuation of Jesus' own personal God-language.[3]

The term 'father' is a relational term: a person is a father in relation to his children. The Synoptic Gospels, on the basis of the most stringent application of the historical-critical method, show that Jesus had an awareness of a relationship with God that was unique and exclusive to himself and which he expressed in terms of the father-son image. Though the primary emphasis in Jesus' consciousness of a special 'sonship' of God lies in his obedience to God, its classical biblical meaning, this emphasis does not capture or exhaust the full significance of his claim to a unique and exclusive relationship with God. As a Jew among Jews the most he could claim here was a greater degree of obedience, not a new kind of relationship. To express this hidden depth of meaning the biblical expression 'son of God' will have to be given a new and revolutionary meaning. The first Christians will see Jesus' claim to a unique 'sonship' vindicated by God himself in the Easter events. They will then begin the endeavour to bring to expression this hidden meaning in the way they will develop the title 'Son of God' for Jesus, an endeavour which will be a primary concern of the christology of the New Testament which now gets under way. For the moment, however, our attention must focus on what this recognition of the exalted status of Jesus involves for the understanding of God.

The terms 'father' and 'son' are reciprocal terms: one implies and points to the other. If Jesus, therefore, is acknowledged as

'Son of God' in some special and unique sense, then the corrolary of this is also acknowledged: God is 'Father' of Jesus in a correspondingly special sense. A new meaning has here emerged in the biblical understanding of God as Father. In the Old Testament this title referred to God's election of and saving relationship with Israel; now it signifies God's special relationship with Jesus of Nazareth. If it was God's relationship with Israel which ultimately enabled them to recognise who God was, which defined God for them, now for the early Christians, God is finally revealed and defined in and through God's relationship with Jesus. For Christian faith, God is 'The God and Father of our Lord Jesus Christ'. (Rom 15:6; 2 Cor 1:3;11:31; Eph 1:3; Col 1:3; I Pet 1:3) Commenting on this expression in 1 Peter 1:3, J.N.D. Kelly correctly notes: 'it crystalizes the essence of the gospel. Christian worship is not directed to Deity as such, but to the God whom Christ has revealed and whose Son in a unique sense he is.' (*The Epistles of Peter and of Jude*, 47)

Christian faith identified what God had accomplished in Jesus of Nazareth as God's ultimate 'being there with you', the completion of salvation history. This identification implied and was based on a recognition of a special relationship between God and Jesus which early Christian thought, developing here a basic theme in Jesus' own self-understanding, expressed especially in terms of the 'Father/Son' image. For early Christianity God, in bringing salvation history to a completion, had ultimately revealed God as 'the Father of the Lord Jesus Christ'. Henceforth in Christian thought this would now be God's 'Name'. With this, Christian faith had accomplished a revolution in the understanding of God in Israel. But what this new understanding of God involved and implied, how to formulate it and saveguard it from error – this was a task for the future. The subsequent history of trinitarian theology is the record of how this task was undertaken and accomplished.

Jesus, the Christ, the Son of God

The new meaning to the term 'Father' for God which emerged in Christian faith was a way of expressing the relationship between God and Jesus of Nazareth which was basic to that faith. A particular understanding of Jesus also followed from the perception of this relationship. To speak of God as the Father of Jesus in a special sense meant also speaking of Jesus as the 'Son of God' in a special sense. Accordingly, development of this expression as a title exclusive to Jesus began very early in Christian thought.[4]

Basic to Christian thought from its inception was the conviction that Jesus of Nazareth was the Figure of the End-Time in and through whom God had fulfilled God's promise to Israel, the eagerly awaited Messiah, the Christ. But, basic as this title was for Jesus in Christian faith, it did not and could not say of him all that that faith wished to say. To make good this deficiency, the Christian mind sought out and developed many other titles and images for Jesus. Of these one of the most significant was the title 'Son of God'. In developing and applying this title to Jesus, Christian faith was basing itself upon the consciousness of a filial relationship with God which Jesus himself had displayed. We have already noted the biblical background and usage of this expression and its function there as an image to express the obedience to God required of Israel and the King of Israel. This same meaning continues to characterise the application of this title to Jesus throughout the New Testament. It here expresses especially his 'obedience unto death' whereby God's saving purpose was accomplished. But Christian faith also wished to say much more than this. It wished to say something about the special and unique character which it recognised in Jesus' relationship with God. In order to do this it had to make the title 'Son of God' exclusive to Jesus. It thus came to use this title of Jesus in an absolute way. Jesus was not merely 'son of God' but 'the Son of God', 'the only Son', 'the only-begotten Son'. This development makes explicit the implication of Christian faith already mentioned, namely, that Jesus' relationship with God is different in kind, not merely in degree, to that of all other human beings. Jesus is the Son of God; others can relate to God only by divine favour, by grace, through acknowledging Jesus as the Christ of God, the Son of God, the Lord. By so relating to Jesus they are granted participation in his relationship with the Father.

There is now, therefore, a new basis of relationship with God, a New Covenant replacing that of Mount Sinai. This New Covenant, which ushers in the Messianic Age with all its Blessings and in which all humanity is called to participate, is Jesus Christ. This is the Good News of Salvation which brings the community of Christ's followers, the Church, into existence and sets it on its missionary road.

Fundamental to an account of itself and its foundation which the Church is required to give, both to itself and to others, is therefore a christology, a statement of who Jesus Christ is. In setting about this difficult task, however, the Church discovered that the concept and title 'Son of God' alone, even when absolutised, was

not fully adequate to plumb the depths of meaning which it perceived to Jesus and wished to express. The human associations of
the concept and its metaphorical character set limitations to its
value here. Even when the concept was most finely sharpened, a
plus of meaning remained unexpressed. Early Christian faith,
therefore, invoked the aid of many other biblical images and titles
to supplement the basic and central description of Jesus as Son of
God. Of particular importance here was the title 'Lord' ascribed to
Jesus by his followers from a very early stage. To appreciate the
significance of this title, one must remember that these early
Christians lived in a world which was very familiar with 'lords'
and above all the great lord, Caesar Augustus. It is in this context
that St Paul remarks:

> For although there may be so-called gods in heaven or on
> earth – as indeed there are many 'gods' and many 'lords' –
> yet for us there is one God, the Father, from whom are all
> things and for whom we exist, and one Lord, Jesus Christ,
> through whom are all things and through whom we exist. (1
> Cor 8: 5-6)

The final achievement of this effort within the New Testament
period and literature comes with the highly developed christology
of the Fourth Gospel. We turn now, therefore, to consider this
statement, the New Testament's last word, as it were, on Christ,
but noting also the basis upon which the statement rests and
which it shares with all the rest of the New Testament, even the
earliest strata.

Christian faith claims that the accomplishment of final salvation as promised by God to Israel was achieved in Jesus of Nazareth who henceforth is confessed in that faith as the Christ, the
Son of God, the Lord. Jesus, however, is not the mere instrument
of that salvation. If he was simply that, he could, when the work
was done, have been cast aside and largely forgotten. The work
accomplished, he would have no further role to play. But Jesus
was himself this salvation, not a mere agent of its delivery. 'There
is salvation in no one else, for there is no other name under heaven
given among men by which we must be saved'. (Acts 4:12)

To the biblical mind salvation, like creation, is something
which only God can do. Like creation, salvation defines God,
declares who and what God is. God is salvation. But if it now
emerges that Jesus, in and through the events of his human career,
is salvation, then it has to follow that now and finally Jesus defines and expresses God. *Somehow*, he is one with God. He belongs
to the definition of God. Yet, Jesus is not Yahweh, the Father.

Christian faith achieved its clearest and most developed statement of these deep insights in the Fourth Gospel. In John 10:30,
Jesus states: 'I and the Father are one'. The unity of Father and Son
which this text proclaims and primarily and directly intends is
undoubtedly a dynamic one rather than an ontological, though
the latter is an implication. Jesus is one with the Father because he
is the Father's definitive act of salvation and revelation. Were this
not so, salvation could not be said to have been accomplished.
Jesus, therefore, defines God and so he is one with the Father. He
is the human face of God. C.K. Barrett's comment on this text in
the *Peake Commentary* is perceptive: 'say "Jesus" and you have
said "God"' – adding: 'essential relationship is also implied'.

The dynamic unity of Father and Son which is asserted here
cannot, when ultimately considered, be conceived as an evolving
one, something which comes to be. Such unity with God is not
and cannot be an achievement. It has to be located in the eternal
being and existence of God. It was this consideration which pro-
pelled early Christian faith to develop its concept of the pre-
existence of Christ. This concept was a logical implication of the
basic faith position that God had acted definitively in Jesus Christ.
It now enabled the Fourth Gospel to put the coping stone on the
early Christian understanding of Christ and of God. The Evangelist opens his Gospel with the famous, anthem-like words:

> In the beginning was the Word, and the Word was with God
> [Ho Theos], and the Word was God [Theos]. ... And the
> Word became flesh and dwelt among us.

The Evangelist, to give expression to the deep insights of faith
which now concern him, has here called to his aid the Old Testament concept of the *dabar Yahweh*, the Word of God, especially as
this had been interpreted in the Wisdom literature and, as in the
Alexandrian Judaism of Philo, identified with Wisdom. Contemporary, developed Jewish thought has provided him with the conceptual and linquistic tools to construct his statement. But these
concepts, as they are here applied to Jesus, are reinterpreted and
transformed. Jesus is not reduced to them but rather gives them
their new meaning and content.

In this new and bold statement of Christian faith, the concept of
Incarnation, towards which earlier New Testament thought had
been groping its way, is given explicit expression: 'the Word was
made flesh'. With this development the revolution in the Jewish
understanding of God is also explicit. For the Word who becomes
flesh is the Word who in the beginning was with God/Ho Theos
and was God/Theos. The application here of the term Theos to

the pre-incarnate Word is, as commentators ancient and modern remind us, predicative. It signifies an attribute, not a personal name. It might even indeed be translated here as 'divine' were it not that such an abstract term would be foreign to the thought of the New Testament and too loose in meaning to capture the sense here. As already noted, the New Testament, following Jewish Greek usage, reserves the expression Ho Theos for Yahweh, the Father. This expression is here, therefore, a personal name for the Father which the Father does not and cannot share with anyone else, not even the Son. The subtle and supple character of ancient Greek, however, was able to provide a distinction here, by the inclusion or omission of the definite article with Theos, which modern language versions are unable to match. According to this usage, Theos with the article refers to and is a personal name for the Father; applied to Christ without the article or anarthrously, Theos both distinguishes Christ from the Father and also asserts what later theology, having developed an abstract, ontological language, will call the true divinity of Christ. The revolution in the biblical understanding of God, which later trinitarian theology will explicitly formulate, is here therefore in view.

The thought of the New Testament is totally concerned with and dominated by the narrative of salvation history as accomplished and achieved in Jesus Christ. The form of thought and expression which such a narrative requires and demands is a dynamic or functional one. It is primarily and centrally concerned with what God *does*, rather than with what God *is*. It simply wishes to *narrate* the definitive deeds of God in Jesus Christ in a logical sequence which climaxes and culminates in the resurrection and the outpouring of the Spirit. The only unity it envisages in this sequence of discrete events is that of God acting here throughout accomplishing God's saving purpose. This eventually leads New Testament thought to assert explicitly the unity, but not the identity, of Jesus with the Father. The final stage of this developed thinking is achieved in the Fourth Gospel. Hence the confident application here in the opening words of the noun Theos/God to Jesus while still clearly preserving the distinction between him and Ho Theos/The God – the Father. Perhaps among modern English versions, the translation of the NEB comes closest to capturing the sense of the Greek: 'The Word dwelt with God, and what God was, the Word was'.

This christological understanding presented in the Fourth Gospel is distinctive of that document. It is certainly the most sophisticated and developed christology of the New Testament. This, however, does not mean that it is at variance with or contradicts earlier strata of New Testament thought. The divinity of Christ which this Gospel so boldly asserts in its own terms is also to be found in earlier documents, though presented in different ways and in less developed forms. It is to be seen, for example, in the title Kurios/Lord, the title of Yahweh in Greek-speaking Judaism, but used of Christ from a very early stage in Christianity; in the absolute use of the title 'the Son [of God]'; and in a variety of other, sometimes very subtle, ways. On this issue, the Fourth Gospel represents the achievement of early Christian thought in its most developed form. But however one assesses the novelty of Johannine christology and however more explicit here the recognition of Christ's divinity, the basis of the assertion is the same as in the earlier and indeed the earliest forms of Christian thought: the finality of God's saving action in Jesus Christ who himself is this act.

In this admission of the unity, but not identity, of Jesus Christ with the Father, this recognition of the divinity of Christ, Christian faith has accomplished a revolution in the Old Testament and Jewish understanding of God. The 'Name' which God revealed to Moses was a promise which said: 'I will be there with you – in the way I will be there'. Jesus Christ is the fulfilment of this promise, the way God is ultimately and finally there, the completion of salvation history - and of the sentence God began but left unfinished at the Burning Bush.

In the Fourth Gospel Jesus, in the great and defiant 'I AM' formulas of chapter 8 (vv 24,28,58), appropriates the divine 'Name' to himself: 'Before Abraham was, I AM'. Commenting on 8,24, C.K. Barrett notes: '"Am" … indicates the eternal being of Christ, and thereby places him on a level with God'. (*Peake*, 854) Again, however, it is important to note that the basis of this appropriation is soteriological: Jesus claims the divine 'Name' because he is the definitive saving act of God, the way God is ultimately and finally there. Darkly and mysteriously, this final 'being there' of God occurs in human history in the death of Jesus on the Cross: 'When you have lifted up the Son of Man, then you will know that I am he'. (8:28) It is in the event of the Cross that God finally completes the sentence begun in Exodus 3:15, fulfills his promise, is 'there'. St John and St Paul are at one in this basic, profound assertion: 'God was in Christ reconciling the world to himself.' (2 Cor 5:19)

The Spirit of God
The narrative of salvation history which the New Testament presents, and the implications of which it constantly preaches,

culminates in the event which it describes as the gift or outpouring of the Holy Spirit, the Spirit of God (Jn 20; Acts 2). This is not an aftermath event, a consequence of completed salvation history. It is the culminating event of that history and, with the event of Christ, constitutes the foundation of the community of Christian faith, the Church. It is, therefore, an event of fundamental importance for the coming into being and understanding of Christianity. As such. this event is also loaded with significance for the understanding of God which now emerges in Christian faith.

The theme of the Spirit of God, *ruah Yahweh*, is not an invention of the New Testament. It has an expansive background in the Old, a background which is always presupposed whenever the theme is mentioned in the New. To understand the significance of the event of the Spirit for Christian faith, therefore, some consideration, however summary, of this theme in the Old Testament is necesary.[5]

The concept of the Spirit of God makes its appearance in the literature of Israel in the context of the settlement in the land of Canaan. In this context, the expression represents a symbol for transient manifestations of God's power breaking into history guiding the destiny of God's people. In its transient, come-and-go way, this power manifests itself in the charismatic leaders of Israel called Judges, in warriors such as Samson, and especially in those itinerant groups of seers or prophets called in Hebrew *nebiim*. Israel will later attempt to develop the idea of an abiding presence of the Spirit. For example, it is said of David, following his anointing by Samuel, that 'the Spirit of the Lord came mightily upon David from that day forward'. (1 Sam 16:13) The problematic history of Israel, however, will cancel all such efforts to institutionalise the presence of God's Spirit. Rather, the prophets, in their portrayal of the Messianic Age, will project this notion of an abiding presence of the Spirit into the future and present it as the crowning, sealing gift of the Messianic Blessings. (Ezek 36:26-27; Joel 2:28-29) The universal and abiding outpouring of the Spirit of God will be a sign that the Messianic Age has dawned.

Meanwhile, in post-exilic Judaism the *ruah Yahweh* came to be associated almost exclusively with the charism of prophecy. The Spirit here is understood and presented as 'the Spirit of prophecy'.[6] Moreover, Judaism now also developed the notion of 'the quenched Spirit': prophecy had ceased in Israel because God had withdrawn God's Spirit on account of the sins of the people. The voice of God was no longer to be heard in the Land; the most one could hope to hear would be a distant echo of God speaking, a *bath qol*, 'the daughter of a voice'. The Spirit of God, however, will return to Israel with the coming of the Messiah and this dramatic return will be a sure sign that the New Age has arrived.[7] This is the background which gives meaning to the Gospel narrative of the descent of the Spirit upon Jesus at his baptism. This is the return of the quenched Spirit to Israel in the person of the Messiah signaling the dawning of the Messianic Age. The basic structure of the Christian account of salvation history is already indicated here: God is bringing salvation history to a conclusion and a completion in these two events, the appearance of the Messiah and the gift of God's Spirit. Significantly, this account of the final, decisive action of God involves reference to the Father, the Son and the Holy Spirit.

The concept of the Spirit which first appears in early Christianity is that of the prophetic Spirit, the prevailing concept in contemporary Judaism. The clearest evidence of this is the way the Spirit is understood and presented in Acts of the Apostles. Here, the Spirit is the One who enables forceful preaching of the Gospel and accompanies and confirms that preaching with powerful signs. But, as with early christology, so also here in pneumatology Christian faith soon found this level of thought too shallow to say what it felt necessary to say of the Holy Spirit. The pioneer in developing a new way of understanding the role of the Spirit in Christian life was, as in so many other areas, St Paul. In the early Church the Holy Spirit, conceived of as the Spirit of prophecy, was associated especially with the charasmatic gifts which were then so prominent a feature of Christian life. St Paul shared this understanding but experience of factions developing in the young community at Corinth forced him to think more deeply about the gift of the Holy Spirit and to develop a new, more comprehensive pneumatology. The fruits of this endeavour feature prominently in his subsequent Letters, 1 and 2 Corinthians, Galatians, Romans.

The source of Paul's new development lay in his retrieval of another biblical concept of the *ruah Yahweh* according to which the Spirit represents the *life-giving* power of God. In the Old Testament this function is attributed to the Spirit in the Genesis account of creation: 'the Spirit of God was moving over the face of the waters'. (Gen 1:2) But since creation is a *semel pro semper* or once-forever act of God, this function of the Spirit does not recur in the life of Israel. The classical concept of the Spirit in the life of Israel is that of the in-breaking Spirit of prophecy. When, however, the prophets come to describe the future age as a *new* creation, they reintroduce this concept of the life-giving Spirit who will be the agent of this renewal and the source of its new life. (Ezek 36:26-27; 37:14; Is 32: 13-19; 44:3-4) From this context St Paul now retrieves this notion of the Spirit as life-giving and from this basis proceeds to develop a new, more comprehensive pneumatology.

The theme of the Holy Spirit is a prominent feature of all the major, genuine Pauline Letters, though he gives his finest and most complete statement in Romans 8, the *locus classicus* of Pauline pneumatology. Basic to his developed thought is the notion of the Spirit as life-giving – 1 Corinthians 15:45; 2 Corinthians 3:6; Romans 8:2. Invoking this concept enables him to see and describe Christian existence as a new life and to present the Spirit of God as the source and principle of this new life in both the community and its individual members. Christian life is 'the fruit of the Spirit'. (Gal 5:22-23) But this new life is also essentially *Christian* life, a graced sharing in Christ's relationship with the Father, a sharing in his sonship. This dual perception of Christian life as at once both life 'in Christ' and life 'in the Spirit' enables St Paul to achieve his synthesis of christology and pneumatology, to relate together organically the two foundation events of the Church, the event of Christ and the event of the Spirit. The life of Christ as extended to and shared in by Christians is life 'in the Spirit'. But the life of Christ is his relationship with the Father and the Father's relationship with him. The conclusion and deep insight of this Pauline theology is that the life of God which is the relationship of the Father and Son is the Spirit of God. The basic statement of Christian faith with its triadic reference, the kerygma of salvation accomplished by God, the Father, through Jesus Christ, the Son, and in the gift of the Holy Spirit, here achieves significant clarification. The life of God is the life of the Father shared with the Son and this life is the Spirit of God who in and through the victory of Christ is now poured out on all his followers and in and from them is available to all human beings, Jew and Gentile, slave and free. This is the Gospel as Paul now understands it, the Gospel which has become the driving-force of his life and for which he fights both within the Church and without.

That this developed theological insight of St Paul was not readily understood in the Church even in his own time is clear from his own statements. Pauline theology, in the true sense of that term, does not begin to make a real impact on Christian thought generally until Irenaeus at the end of the second century. The reference in 2 Peter 3:15-16 to the letters of 'our beloved brother Paul' in which 'there are some things hard to understand' is not the only indication in the New Testament that the Church of this period had diffi-

culty following the thought of St Paul. Yet there is also evidence
that Pauline thought had made an impact within the early Church
even outside the strictly Pauline circles. Pauline influence can be
detected in the Johannine literature, though absorbed and re-
worked in accordance with that distinctive system of thought and
given a typical Johannine stamp. A particular instance of this is
the concept of the Spirit as life-giving. In John 6,63, 'it is the S/
spirit that gives life, the flesh is of no avail', the term pneuma/
spirit involves a typical Johannine *double entendre* embracing the
contrast spirit-flesh and the Spirit of God. The Pauline concept of
the life-giving Spirit is therefore in view here and asserted. (Note
also Jn 3:5-6,8; 7:37-39; 20:22-23)[8]

Throughout the Fourth Gospel also, the gift of salvation which
Jesus has achieved and made available, the fruit of his victory, is
described as new life. But again, this new life is first and foremost
the relationship between the Father and Jesus, the Son. Participation in this relationship is the new life which the victory of Jesus
makes available.

Though this theme pervades the Fourth Gospel, it is the special
emphasis of chapter 17, the Priestly Prayer of Jesus which is so
powerful a summary of the Evangelist's whole message. Jesus
here prays to the Father that his followers throughout the ages
may share in the unity which exists between the Father and himself: 'that they may all be one, even as you, Father, are in me, and I
in you, that they also may be in us ...'. (v 21) This life, this sharing
in the unity of Father and Son, is the manifestation of God's
'Name', (v 6) and this 'Name' is the relationship of love between
Father and Son: 'I have made known to them your Name ... that
the love with which you have loved me may be in them, and I in
them'. (v 26) Here, as in 1 John 4:8,16, God is defined as love, the
love which is the relationship between Father and Son and which
the redemptive work of Christ has made available on earth. But in
the Fourth Gospel, as in St Paul, this fruit of Christ's redemptive
victory, this new life, is the Spirit of God poured forth. This is the
theme of Jesus's words at the Feast of Tabernacles in John 7,
where the image of water slaking thirst – 'living water' – is, as
elsewhere in the gospel, a symbol of life: 'Jesus stood up and pro-
claimed: "If any one thirst, let him come to me and drink ...."
Now this he said about the Spirit, which those who believed in
him were to receive; for as yet the Spirit had not been given, because Jesus was not yet glorified.' (v 39) The same understanding
appears in 1 John 4:13: 'Here is the proof that we dwell in him

[God] and he dwells in us: he has imparted his Spirit to us.' (NEB)
Here again, St John re-presents and develops the thought of St
Paul: 'God's love has been poured into our hearts through the
Holy Spirit which has been given to us'. (Rom 5:5)

Conclusion

The message of the New Testament is a narrative, a statement that
God has accomplished final salvation in the events of Jesus Christ
and the outpouring of God's Spirit. This final act of God, this completion of salvation history, consists, according to the deepening
insight of Christian faith, in God's communication of Godself, of
God's very life, to God's creatures. Creation is here redeemed, restored to its original purpose. But this life of God which is now
made available, this life which *is* God, consists of the relationship
of love between the Father and the Son which is the Spirit of God.
The final act of God, precisely because it is the *final* act of *God*,
involves God's full self-disclosure, God's full and final self-
revelation, God's 'Name' now and forever, 'for all generations'.
This final divine 'Name' involves the triadic reference: Father,
Son, Holy Spirit. For Christian faith this is how God is now and
henceforth known.

This understanding of God which now takes root in Christian
thought is not a theological understanding. It is a statement of
what God has done and who God is revealed to be in what God
has done. It is and remains a narrative-statement of salvation history. But this salvation history statement is and must always be
the source and criterion of all theological effort to probe and systematise the implications of this understanding, to develop, in
other words, a 'theo-logy', a discourse concerning God on the basis of what God has revealed of God-self. The New Testament,
even in its final pages, does not attempt or even envisage this task.
This is a task for the future. The New Testament is satisfied to
state and preach the Good News which this kerygma is.

Through him we both have access in one Spirit to the Father.

The Witness of Faith

The triadic understanding of God which is discerned in Christian
faith is given expression and witnessed to in that faith in many
and various ways. The New Testament, constituting a record of
that faith in its formative stages, expresses this understanding,
implicitly or explicity, on every page. I propose here to select and
outline three of the main forms of that witness. These are: The

Narrative of Salvation; The Structure of Early Christian Prayer;
Early Credal Formulas.

The Narrative of Salvation

The Christian message is a Good News, the Good News of salvation accomplished by God. God accomplished this salvation in
and through Jesus of Nazareth whose earthly career concluded
with his death on the Cross, but was followed by his resurrection
and the outpouring of the Holy Spirit. The Christian message is
essentially a statement, a narration, of these events. It began as a
very basic, succinct statement : Jesus died and was raised by God.
This is the early Christian kerygma, the public announcement of
the epochal events which, for Christian faith, constitute the events
of the End-Time. Soon, however, this bare statement undergoes
expansion. The statement of Jesus's death is developed into an account of his arrest, trial, execution – the Passion Narrative of the
Gospels; the statement of his resurection is filled out with accounts of his appearances as the Risen One. The Passion Narrative
raised the question why Jesus was condemned and executed.
What was his offence? This question could only be answered by
some account, however summary, of his public career or ministry,
of what he had publicly said and done. This was provided by an
account of his public life, of those events which took place 'beginning from the baptism of John until the day when he was taken up
from us'. (Acts 1:22)

Though Jesus's baptism by John marked the beginning of his
public ministry, it obviously did not explain the origin of Jesus.
His personal story did not begin here. Matthew and Luke, therefore, incorporate into their Gospels an Infancy Narrative which
recounts the conception and birth of Jesus. Even this, however,
does not adequately explain the origin of Jesus for Christian faith.
The Fourth Gospel, therefore, places this origin 'In the beginning
... with God'. With this starting point the New Testament's narrative of salvation history accomplished in Jesus Christ is complete.

It is not the aim of the New Testament, and especially here the
Gospels, in presenting this narrative and telling this story to write
a biography of Jesus in the modern sense of that term. Though
they are certainly concerned with 'what actually happened', they
are much more concerned with the *significance* of 'what actually
happened'. This deeper level of meaning, however, is not available to eyesight, and still less to the language of eyesight, the language of eyewitness. This level is discernible only to the eyes of
faith. It is concerned with what God is doing and accomplishing

in and through these events of history. To give expression to this
the positive science of history is inadequate. What mainly concerns us here, however, is to note the understanding of God
which this narrative of God's saving action presents. This action
involves not only God, Ho Theos/the Father, but also the Son of
God and the Holy Spirit. It involves this triadic reference and understanding of God and it cannot be recounted otherwise. It must
suffice here to indicate briefly this triadic character of God's action at the key, pivotal moments of the narrative.

This triadic reference appears very clearly at the beginning of
the story – in the angel's words to Mary in the Third Gospel.

> The Holy Spirit will come upon you, and the power of the
> Most High will overshadow you; therefore the child to be
> born will be called holy, the Son of God. (Lk 1,35)

We meet the same reference again in the Baptism scene which
opens the public ministry of Jesus: the heavens open – the Holy
Spirit descends upon Jesus – the voice of God (the Father) is heard
saying: 'This is my beloved Son'. (Mt 3:16-17; Mk 1:10-11; Lk 3:21-
22) From this moment Jesus's life is Spirit-directed and Spirit-
empowered – a point emphasised especially by St Luke in whose
Gospel the Holy Spirit is a major theme. (Lk 4:1,14,18-21; Mt 4:1;
Mark 1:12) During the ministry and in the Fourth Gospel at the
Last Supper, Jesus promises his followers that on the achievement
of his own work the Father will send the Holy Spirit upon them:
'you shall receive power when the Holy Spirit has come upon
you'. (Acts 1:8) This promise is fulfilled following the resurrection
of Jesus, when he has been 'glorified'. (Jn 20; Acts 2) With these
climactic events the narrative of salvation accomplished is complete. The End-Time, the Time of Salvation, has arrived. The Messianic Community enjoying the Messianic Blessings has come into
being. Henceforth it can be said: 'Through him we both [Jew and
Gentile – all] have access in one Spirit to the Father'. (Eph 2:18)

Our interest in this summary review of the Christian narrative
of salvation lies in the understanding of God which it involves,
presents and witnesses. God here means Yahweh, the one, true
God of Israel. But this one God has now in these final events of
salvation disclosed Godself as the Father of the Son, Jesus Christ,
and the Sender of the Spirit. For Christian faith this triadic reference is essential to the understanding of the God whose saving action in Christ and in the Spirit is the foundation of that faith.
Christian faith bears witness to this understanding in the story
which it tells and ever re-tells, its narrative of salvation accomplished.

Early Christian Prayer

The New Testament frequently includes snippets of Christian prayer and hymns. This prayer material enables us to discern not only the spirit but also the structure characteristic of Christian prayer in its very origin. This prayer form is certainly an adaptation of Jewish prayer, but with a significant difference and development. Prayer always expresses the understanding of the god addressed; it names its god. The Christian adaptation of Jewish prayer is determined by the new understanding of God which has emerged in Christianity. In the way it names and addresses God, in its basic structure, early Christian prayer reveals this understanding.

Christian prayer is based on and represents a continuation of Jesus' own characteristic form of prayer. In his prayer Jesus addressed God as Abba – his intimate Father. When asked by his disciples to teach them to pray, that is, to enable them to pray like himself, he taught them the Our Father. This becomes and remains the basis of all Christian prayer which in its basic structure is always, implicitly or explicitly, addressed to the Father. We obtain an insight into the nature of early Christian prayer by noting a phrase which occurs frequently in the New Testament and which speaks of praying to God the Father 'calling on the name of Jesus' (Acts 9:14,21; 1 Cor 1:2; Rom 10:12; 2 Tim 2:22) We find a similar expression in the Fourth Gospel where Jesus several times tells his followers to make their prayer 'in his name'. (14:15f; 15:16; 16:23,26) What is being inculcated here is that Christian prayer is prayer to the Father in union with Jesus Christ, prayer with and through Jesus Christ. Christian prayer is a sharing in the prayer of Christ the Son to God the Father, that prayer which expresses the relationship of the Son to the Father. The same notion underlies the well-known text of Hebrews 7:25, which indeed may be regarded as indicating the basis for this prayer practice: 'He is able for all time to save those who draw near to God through him, since he always lives to make intercession for them'. The central image of Christ in Hebrews is that of our High Priest who gathers up all our prayers and makes them part of his own. From its very origins Christian prayer is prayer to the Father in, with and through Jesus Christ. It will be sufficient here to select a few texts to illustrate and underscore this point.

> Let us thank God ... through our Lord Jesus Christ. (1 Cor 15:57)
>
> I thank my God through Jesus Christ for all of you. (Rom 1:8)

To the only wise God be glory for evermore through Jesus
Christ! Amen. (Rom 16:27)

Whatever you do, in word or deed, do everything in the
name of the Lord Jesus, giving thanks to God the Father
through him. (Col 3:17)

Further attention to the prayer material of the New Testament
enables us to discern there another, further dimension. In the
Fourth Gospel Jesus refers to the coming time 'when the true wor-
shippers will worship the Father in S/spirit and truth'. (Jn 4:23)
We meet here again typical Johannine *double entendre*: *pneuma*
here certainly includes in its reference the Spirit of God. Christian
prayer is also prayer in the Spirit. Here once again the Fourth Gospel is reproducing and re-echoing Pauline thought and themes.
For St Paul the Christian exists *in the Spirit*. The Spirit, as it were, is
the Christian's natural environment, as air for the human or water
for the fish. This environment, this existence in the Spirit, is existence in the presence of God. With the coming of the Holy Spirit,
'Heaven was opened' (Mt 3:16; Mk 1:10; Lk 3:21): God's presence,
the Temple which is not built by human hand, is available to all.
The outpouring of the Holy Spirit upon the community of Jesus'
followers makes this community the Temple of the Holy Spirit,
the Temple of God: 'a dwelling-place of God in the Spirit'. (Eph
2:22; cf 1 Cor 3:16-17; 6:18-20; 2 Cor 6:14-16) Existing in the Spirit,
the Christian is united to Christ and is able to share in Christ's
prayer to the Father.

The Spirit you have received is ... a Spirit that makes us
sons, enabling us to cry 'Abba! Father!' (Rom 8:15 NEB)

Because you are sons, God has sent the Spirit of his Son into
our hearts, crying, 'Abba! Father!' (Gal 4:6)

There is thus a triadic structure to Christian prayer from its very
origin. This is prayer *to* the Father *through* the Son *in* the Spirit:
'Through him we both have access in one Spirit to the Father'.
This structure reveals the understanding of God whom the prayer
acknowledges and addresses. God here involves reference to
Father, Son and Holy Spirit.

Early Credal Formulas

The New Testament contains many short formulas which crystal-
ise and summarise the basic tenets of Christian faith. These formulas are short confessions of faith in God and God's saving
work. They are the beginning of what will later develop into the
full-blown Creeds of the Church. Like the later Creeds, but in
much more summary form, these formulas state the Christian un-

derstanding of God on the basis of the saving work God has accomplished. They name God as so understood in Christian faith. In them we find that the Son and the Holy Spirit belong with the Father to this naming, this understanding of God. Some of these expressions are very brief one-member formulas, such as 'Jesus is Lord/Son of God'. Others have two members or references: they mention both God the Father and Jesus Christ. Thus 1 Corinthians 8:6: 'For us there is one God, the Father ... and one Lord, Jesus Christ ....' This format is common in greetings and prayers, which in this matter are closely related to the confession formulas: 'Grace to you and peace from God our Father and the Lord Jesus Christ' (Rom 1:7); 'May our God and Father himself, and our Lord Jesus, direct our way to you'. (1 Thess 3:11) It can be seen from these formulas that for the New Testament God cannot be fully or properly named without reference to Jesus Christ. Christ, the Son, belongs to the reference, the naming of God, the statement who God is.

When this early Christian confession of faith in God attains its full development, it appears as a three-member formula: there is reference to Father, Son and Holy Spirit. Ephesians 2:18 is a simple and clear example of this form of statement: 'Through him we both have access in one Spirit to the Father'. The blessing which concludes 2 Corinthians also presents this triadic structure: 'The grace of the Lord Jesus Christ and the love of God and the fellowship of the Holy Spirit be with you all'. (2 Cor 13:14) In fact, one is liable to find this type of triadic reference to God in any passage of the New Testament which is concerned with didache or teaching, as the following quotation, 1 Corinthians 6:11, illustrates.

You were washed, you were sanctified, you were justified, in the name of the Lord Jesus Christ and in the Spirit of our God. Commenting on this verse, C.K.Barrett notes: 'The quite unconscious Trinitarianism of the concluding words should be noted: *the Lord Jesus Christ, the Spirit, our God.* Trinitarian theology, at least in its New Testament form, did not arise out of speculation, but out of the fact that when Christians spoke of what God had done for them and in them they often found themselves obliged to use threefold language of this kind.' (*The First Epistle to the Corinthians*, 143 – emphasis original)

But the most important text which presents this triadic reference to and understanding of God is undoubtedly Matthew 28:19. There the risen Jesus commissions and commands his disciples: 'Go therefore and make disciples of all nations, baptizing them in the name of the Father and of the Son and of the Holy Spirit'. This text certainly reflects the developed baptismal practice of the early Church. The context is that of preaching the Gospel, conversion, Christian initiation. In its earlier form baptism was probably administered 'in the name of Jesus Christ', that is, into relationship with and allegiance to Jesus Christ, Christian discipleship. Soon, however, this bare and purely christological reference was seen to be inadequate. Relationship with Christ also involved relationship with the Father and with the Holy Spirit and these too had to be mentioned explicitly. Baptism relates the initiate to God as God is finally revealed in the completion of salvation history in Christ. This relationship involves relationship with the Father, the Son and the Holy Spirit. Once again we find that the full Christian statement of God involves this triadic reference and understanding. It is very probable that the baptismal practice which this text reflects involved a confession of faith consisting of simple credal questions and answers such as one finds later in more developed form in the initiation ritual of Hippolytus' *Apostolic Tradition*, c. 215 A.D.

In these three-member formulas we see that the Holy Spirit too belongs to the early Christian naming and understanding of God. Reference to God is incomplete unless it includes mention of the Son and the Holy Spirit. The triadic understanding of God as Father, Son and Holy Spirit in early Christianity comes to light and is witnessed to in these expressions. This is the understanding of God confessed in the embryonic Creed, taught in Christian catechesis, expressed in Christian prayer.

One might sum up what this amounts to in the following way. If all reality were divided by a vertical line into two sections representing God-reality and non-God-reality, the New Testament would place Christ, the Son, and the Holy Spirit with the Father on the God side of the line. The conclusion of J.N.D. Kelly in his study of this material in the New Testament is fully justified: 'The impression inevitably conveyed is that the conception of the threefold manifestation of the Godhead was embedded deeply in Christian thinking from the start.' (*Early Christian Creeds*, 23)

Conclusion

A new and distinctive understanding of the God of Israel emerges with the birth of Christianity. This understanding continues the emphatic assertion of Israel that there is one God, Yahweh. Christianity, too, is an emphatic monotheism. But this one God is now seen and understood as the Father of the Lord Jesus Christ, the

Son of God, and the Sender of the Spirit. The one God is also *some-how* a Triad. This understanding is not the result of a logical pro-cess of reasoning applied to the faith of Israel. It is the product and fruit of the experience of the Events of the End Time as under-stood in Christian faith. In these Events the history of Israel has been completed and its promise achieved. In this completion of salvation history God is finally and fully 'there with' God's peo-ple. The occurrence of the End Time, therefore, involves God's final, full self-disclosure. This final self-disclosure reveals the one God as also *somehow* a Triad. Christianity's distinctive understand-ing of God is rooted in its faith experience of the End Time Events.

This understanding of salvation history leads early Christianity to a re-reading of the history of Israel in the light of the End which has occurred. This is no new experience within the faith of Israel. Throughout her history Israel had constantly re-read and re-interpreted her past in the light of the present. What is new here is the note of finality. God has now spoken God's final word, per-formed God's final deed. But God's final word and deed can only be – God-self. But if this final word and deed is Jesus Christ, the Son, and the Holy Spirit, then the Son and the Spirit belong to the full reference which God is, belong to the definition of God. This is the revelation of the Tri-Une God.

Notes

1. On the early kerygma, see especially C.H. Dodd, *The Apostolic Preaching and its Developments*, London, Hodder & Stoughton, 1963 Edition, "The Primitive Preaching", 7-35.
2. Rahner's magisterial essay still remains the best discussion of this question.
3. On this whole question concerning the use of the term 'Father' for God in the Old Testament and the New, see J. Jeremias, *The Prayers of Jesus*, London, SCM, 1967, and R. Hamerton-Kelly, *God the Father: Theology and Patriarchy in the Teaching of Jesus*, Philadel-phia, Fortress Press, 1979.
4. For the background, early history and meaning of the title 'Son of God' applied to Jesus in the New Testament, see M. Hengel, *The Son of God: The Origin of Christology and the History of Jewish-Hellenistic Religion*, London, SCM, 1976.
5. For a fuller discussion of the theme of the Spirit in early Christ-ianity and its background in the Old Testament and Judaism, see the article by the author, 'The Holy Spirit in Early Christian Teaching', *ITQ*, 45 [1978], 101-116.

6 On this see G.F. Moore, *Judaism in the First Centuries of the Christian Era*, 1, Cambridge, Mass., 1927, 237, 421. The concept of the Spirit in the Palestinian Targums, which Moore here discusses, goes back to and derives from a pre-Christian position.

7. See W. Forster, *Palestinian Judaism in New Testament Times*, London, 1964, 4-5.

8. See J. McPolin, 'The Holy Spirit in the Lucan and Johannine Writings: A Comparative and Complementary Study', *ITQ*, 45 [1978], 117-131.

CHAPTER 3

The First Theology: Before Nicaea

The triadic understanding of God as Father, Son and Holy Spirit which the New Testament displays is not the product of theological reflection. It is rather the largely unreflective reaction to the impact of the revelatory experience of Jesus Christ and the coming of the Spirit. This is a pre-theological position determined by the experience of accomplished salvation history and coming to expression in the mind and language of Christian faith. This position asserts that God is both one and three, a Tri-une God. The matter, however, will not be able to rest there. Deep questions lie hidden in the assertion of a Triune God. These questions did not surface in the period or the literature of the New Testament. There they lie hidden beneath the surface, implicit in the living faith. But the time has to come when these questions will break that surface and assert themselves. Then the effort will have to begin to find answers.

The basic question which is at issue here may be stated in various ways. How can God be both one and three? How can the triadic statement of God be reconciled with the biblical and also Christian assertion that God is one? If there is one God and this one God is the Father, how can the Son and the Spirit also be truly God? Christian faith has inherited from Israel the assertion that there is one God – and continues that assertion. Moreover, this one God is the Father – 'there is one God and Father of all'. (Eph 4,6) In early Christianity, and indeed well into the fourth century, the expression 'the one God' may be described as a personal name exclusive to the Father. The Christian mind was therefore faced with the task of reconciling this inherited way of thinking and speaking of God with what it now wished to say of God as Triad. This required developing a new conceptual system and an appropriate, new language for God – no easy task!

It was also an unavoidable task, and this for many reasons. In the Christian mind faith will seek understanding. The questions lurking in the Christian statement of God will eventually manifest themselves and provoke an intellectual effort to find answers. Further, Christianity, becoming conscious of its distinct identity over against Judaism on the one hand and Paganism on the other, but with a mission to both, will be obliged to explain its understanding of God to both and point out and justify the differences. This will require on the part of Christian faith an effort to clarify for itself its own distinctive understanding of God. Again, as Christianity develops, the need to distinguish between orthodoxy and heresy will arise and become an urgent task. Throughout the history of the Church, it will be the rise of heresy which will provoke the definition of orthodoxy. But identifying heresy requires being able to state and explain why this position is heretical, being able to point out where the dividing line between heresy and orthodoxy is. This is seldom an easy task since the issues are often very subtle. Heresy often wears the face of orthodoxy. As the word itself implies, it is often simply a partial, over-selective orthodoxy. Detecting heresy can therefore be a difficult and subtle matter. This was especially true in the early period of the Church when a guiding body of official Church doctrine had not yet come to exist. All these reasons were operative in gradually provoking the Christian mind to undertake the task of clarifying its distinctive understanding and statement of God and, once it had begun, continued to fuel this effort over the centuries.

We will be concerned in this chapter with the way this effort of *fides quaerens intellectum* got under way in the course of the second century and with following its path through to the eve of the great controversy of the fourth century. We are concerned here, therefore, with the history of Christian thought on the question of God over the period from the close of the New Testament to the Council of Nicaea, roughly from around 100 AD to the first appearance of Arianism about 318 AD. The review offered here will concentrate on the writings of the second century Apologists and then the later pre-Nicene theologians. It will therefore basically consist of these two parts. But before proceeding with this programme, it will be helpful for completeness sake to notice briefly the approach to our topic displayed by earlier writers, the so-called Apostolic Fathers.

This literature, the earliest, extant non-canonical Christian literature, belongs roughly to the period c. 100 to 150 AD. There is as yet little sign here of a *theological* approach to the question of God. In form and content this writing, consisting mainly of letters and sermons, is really a continuation of the New Testament itself. It is a writing within the Church addressed to the Church, not to those

outside. The understanding of God found here is very similar to
that in the New Testament itself. There is one God, the Father -
but Jesus Christ and the Spirit of God also belong to the full divine
reference, the reference which states fully who God is on the basis
of the experience of salvation history. As in the New Testament,
this statement appears especially in prayer and credal-type formulas. The following short excerpts from the Letter of Clement of
Rome to the Church in Corinth, dated c. 98 AD, and the Martyr-
dom of Polycarp, usually dated c. 155 AD, must suffice here to indicate this similarity.

> Do we not have one God, one Christ, one Spirit of grace
> poured out upon us? (*1 Clement*, 46,6)

> Through whom [Jesus Christ] be glory to you [the Father]
> with him and with the Holy Spirit, both now and through
> ages yet to come. Amen. (*Martyrdom of Polycarp*, 14,31)

There are, however, some significant points beginning to
emerge concerning the Triad in this literature which are worthy of
note. The expression 'the one God' continues here, as in the New
Testament, to denote God the Father. But the title 'God/Theos',
and even sometimes 'Ho Theos', is now much more frequently
used of Christ. The opening words of II (Pseudo-) Clement, c. 150
AD, may be regarded as typical: 'Brethren, we must think of Jesus
Christ as God (Theos).' But perhaps the most interesting feature
of this literature is that reference to the Holy Spirit has become
both infrequent and, where it does occur, unclear and insignificant in meaning. Reference to the Spirit in this writing is normally
found embedded in traditional formulas of prayer, ritual, credal
statement. It is more the repetition of an inherited traditional formula, a learnt-off formula, than a meaningful expression of living
faith. Here again, this literature reveals itself as a continuation of
the later phases of New Testament thought where, the Johannine
literature apart, the theme of the Holy Spirit has faded dramatically in significance. This situation, this odd neglect of the role and
status of the Holy Spirit, will continue to characterise theology of
the Trinity, though with some significant exceptions, until the later phases of the fourth century controversy. Some of the conse-
quences of this neglect of the theme of the Spirit are, indeed, still
with us.

The Apologists[1]

Around the middle of the second century a new genre of Christian writing begins to make its appearance. This is the Christian

Apology, written by a group of writers known accordingly as the Apologists. This literature is a public defence of and argument for Christianity written by educated Christian converts from paganism. It is a literature addressed not directly to the Church itself but to those outside it, directed especially at the imperial authorities and often indeed addressed to the Emperor himself. Its background is the context of Christianity as a proscribed or illegal religion in the Roman Empire liable at any moment or in any place to active persecution. As well as answering various calumnies circulating in pagan society concerning Christianity, these writings maintain as their main thesis that there is no legal ground for the proscription of Christianity because Christianity possesses and presents true knowledge of the true God and the highest principles of ethical conduct. In other words, Christians, if the truth was acknowledged, are the best citizens the Empire has. 'More than all other people', writes Justin Martyr, the most prominent of these writers, 'we are your helpers and allies in maintaining peace'. (1 Apology, 12) We find here the first real effort of intellectual Christianity to engage pagan culture – the prevailing thought system of the Hellenistic and Roman world. Prior to becoming Christians, these writers were themselves products and representatives of this culture and therefore knew it from inside. Conscious of the prevailing philosophies of the time, especially Platonism and Stoicism, they maintain that Christianity is the highest and true philosophy, embracing whatever is true in these systems but also correcting and purifying their errors. The Apologists are thus committed to finding a bridge between Christian faith and pagan philosophic thought. Some of them, such as Justin Martyr, display a high estimation of Hellenistic philosophy, even to the point of seeing in it an *evangelica praeparatio*.

In presenting their case for Christian faith as the true philosophy and religion to pagans, the basic issue for the Apologists was the question of God. To put forward a convincing case for the Christian understanding of God to educated pagans, two things were required of them. They had first to do some hard thinking themselves about what this understanding was and then they had to find some bridge to or connecting link with pagan thought to enable it to grasp this concept. Beginning with St Justin Martyr (d. c. 167 AD), they found this bridge or link in the Logos notion of pagan philosophy. In ordinary Greek the term *logos* could mean either the inner thought of the mind or this thought as outwardly expressed in words. The term, however, also had a special or technical meaning in Greek philosophy, especially in Platonism and

Stoicism, the two most influential philosophic schools in the early centuries of the Christian era. Since these two philosophies, or some combination of them, – for the attitude at this period was very eclectic _ constituted the *lingua franca* of educated thought at this time, the Apologists had no alternative but to adopt this medium of discourse if they wished their case to win a hearing from the public they addressed.

There was, however, a major problem here. Pagan philosophy, in any of its forms, was an inadequate, in many ways a dangerously inadequate, medium within which to express the *Christian* understanding of God. To have recourse to this medium inevitably meant running the risk of reducing Christian faith to this level of discourse, of presenting the faith as just another form or variation of prevailing philosophic thought. Yet, there was no way out of this dilemma for these writers but to attempt the task and run the risk. Some of them, indeed, such as Tatian and later Tertullian, were conscious of the problem and roundly condemned and repudiated the alien philosophy in which, nevertheless, their own thinking continued to be steeped. With these writers, therefore, Christian faith for the first time moves out of its congenital world of biblical thought with all its categories and attempts to clothe itself in a new dress. However admirable and inevitable this new venture was, this effort to address and engage the outside world on its own terms, Christian faith could not but emerge from this encounter with wounds and battle-scars. Indeed, it may be said that the history of the Christian understanding of God from here on is simply a record of the effort to identify and heal these wounds. A foundation is being laid here on which the future will build but, having built, will then find itself involved in a long process of correction and reconstruction. Since it is these early Apologists who first lay this foundation, and thereby in many ways determine the parameters of the future debate, it is important to pay close attention to the content and implications of their bold endeavour. Since this endeavour centres round their adaptation of the Logos concept in Hellenistic philosophy, it is necessary first to say a brief word about the meaning of this concept in Platonist and Stoic philosophy at this period.[2]

Stoicism was a materialist, pantheist philosophy which understood the universe to consist of an original fiery substance which contained within itself a principle of rationality. This principle imposed a rational order upon the original, shapeless substance which explains the harmony of the universe and everything in it. Stoicism called this pervading principle Logos and it is what this philosophy understands as Divinity or God. As pervading all things, Stoicism described this principle as *logos spermatikos*, 'the seminal or pervasive logos'. The *logos spermatikos* attained its highest form in the rational soul of the human being. Here Stoicism made a distinction which the Apologists, beginning with Justin Martyr, were to adopt and use in their efforts to understand and explain the Divine Triad. This was the distinction between the *logos endiathetos*, 'immanent reason', the thought within the mind, and the *logos prophorikos*, the thought as outwardly expressed. The use of this distinction by the Apologists to explain the relation between God the Father and God's Word/Son was to have a profound influence on later efforts to develop a trinitarian theology. It was also to be the source of many of the problems which that theology created for itself.

Platonic philosophy in this period, Middle Platonism as it is usually called, represents a development of the thought of Plato with a stronger theistic and religious emphasis. Here Plato's Supreme Being, The Good or The One, is more recognisablly God. Further, the Demiurge or Architect of the Universe which Plato had spoken of in the *Timaeus* was now described as the Mind (Nous) or Logos of God and this philosophy, again here attempting to develop Plato, could also speak, however vaguely, of a third divine-like entity, a World Soul or Psyche. This Triad represented a descending hierarchy of First Principles or divine Beings in which the second and third members served as intermediaries between the utterly transcendent, supreme God and our world of sense experience. The Logos here was even described as a 'second God' and 'Son of God'. Stoicism could also speak of a similar Triad, though in this pantheist philosophy these terms would have a somewhat different meaning.

This Triad of the philosophers, this language of the divine World as consisting of God, Logos, Psyche, was too similar to the Christian Triad, God, Son, Pneuma, to pass unnoticed by these early Christian theologians. Moreover, Philo, the Jewish philosopher of Alexandria (d. c. 50 AD), and perhaps others before him, had already pioneered an accommodation between the world of biblical thought and that of Hellenistic philosophy. Philo identified the Logos of that philosophy and the Word of God of the Bible. Though Philo spoke of the Logos in very personal terms, after the manner of the presentation of Wisdom in the Book of Wisdom, this was literary device. The Logos here was not a personal divine Being distinct from Yahweh, the God of Israel, but rather a symbol for the providential activity of God in creation and salvation history, especially the Word of God which spoke in the theophanies of the Old Testament and in the prophets. The Fourth Gospel, therefore, broke a thought-barrier with its daring and totally original assertion that Jesus Christ was the Logos Incarnate. This idea of Incarnation, of the transcendent God somehow entering truly and fully into the world of human experience, this idea marked a radical break with all previous efforts, Jewish or Hellenistic, to relate God and this world. Stoicism solved this problem by adopting the easy solution of pantheism – the world itself simply was God. Platonism established the connection by asserting a descending chain of being from the transcendent God through certain lesser intermediaries down to the world of human reality and experience. At a popular religious level Gnosticism took this solution to extremes by propounding a bewildering plethora of intermediaries. Jewish biblical thought maintained the transcendence of God, but, seeing the world as God's total, free creation, understood it as governed by divine providence through interventions of God's power from on high. Jewish philosophers like Philo attempted an accommodation between this notion of providential relationship and the intermediary notion of Platonic thought. Christian faith asserted the 'scandalous' solution of Incarnation. God's providential relationship with Israel through her history culminated in the sending of God's Son into the world as one truly and fully human: 'the Word was made flesh and dwelt among us'. The accommodation of biblical faith with Hellenistic philosophy outlined by Philo, and, apparently, endorsed for Christianity by the Fourth Gospel, proved too tempting for the early Apologists in their effort to offer a public defence of their faith and gain for it intellectual respectability. Following the apparent cue of St John's Prologue, they confidently identified Jesus Christ with the Logos dimly perceived and spoken of in pagan philosophy.

The advantages of this approach from the Apologists' point of view seemed obvious. It enabled them to give Christian faith universal significance and substantiate its universal claim upon both Jew and Gentile. The Logos which pervaded all reality and achieved its highest expression in the human mind or reason had become incarnate as Jesus Christ and now claimed the allegiance of that mind, the obedience of faith. At a time when the universal Christian mission was growing in achievement and confidence, implementing the mandate of the Lord 'Make disciples of all nations', the attraction of this approach to cultured and enthusiastic pagan converts was obvious. That they were also taking within the house of faith something of a Trojan Horse was beyond the limit of their vision.

Indications of future problems, however, begin to emerge when one examines the implications of this attempted fusion of Athens and Jerusalem for the triadic understanding of God in Christian faith. The situation can be best appreciated, perhaps, by presenting first an outline of the *position* of the Apologists on this issue and then the *problem* which this position entailed.

The Position

The first emphatic statement in the understanding of God presented by the Apologists is that there is *one* God. This one God is the Father. 'We proclaim ourselves atheists', writes Justin, 'in respect to those whom you call gods, but not in regard to the most true God, the Father ...' (*1 Apol* 6) 'We acknowledge one God' writes Athenagoras of Athens, 'unbegotten, eternal, invisible ...' (*Supplication for the Christians* 10) 'He alone is God', writes Theophilus of Antioch. (*To Autolycus* 1,6) This statement is a continuation of the emphatic biblical assertion of monotheism common to both the Old and the New Testament. It was also a statement acceptable to the educated pagan public of the period, for Hellenistic philosophy too asserted a one supreme God, even if it could also accommodate many, lesser intermediary divine beings. The expression 'the Most High God' (*Ho Theos Hypsistos*) was common to both the Bible and pagan religious philosophy and appears frequently in the writings of the Apologists. The term 'monarchy', meaning monotheism, which was to become so important a term in later Christian writers, makes its first appearance here. (Justin, *Dialogue with Trypho* 1,3; Tatian, *Address to the Greeks* 14,1; Theophilus, *To Autol* 2,4; 2,35; 2,38]

This assertion of the one true God, the Father, is the first statement of the Apologists in their presentation of the Christian understanding of God. It is an absolutely basic statement. Any further statement about God which this understanding may wish to make must be both reconcilable with this assertion and in some way an explication of it. It is important to be clear what this assertion involves. It is especially necessary to note that the expression 'the one God' does *not* mean here what it will later mean in developed trinitarian theology. There the divine unity will mean the one divine nature. Here it means simply and totally God the Father. The Father sums up and is the total Godhead, all that God is, all that 'God' means. This is the meaning which the term 'monarchy' already has in this literature.

The Apologists follow this statement that God is one with the statement that this God has communicated Godself to humans in creation and salvation history through the Son and the Spirit. Here we meet again the Christian triadic statement of God as consisting of Father, Son and Holy Spirit. The source and background of this statement is now traditional: the narrative of salvation history issuing in doxology and credal formulas. The following selection of texts must suffice to illustrate how central this reference is to the Apologists' understanding of God.

> We reverence and worship him [God the Father] and the Son who came forth from him ... and the prophetic Spirit. (Justin, *1 Apol* 6)
> Who, then, would not be astonished to hear those called atheists who speak of God the Father and of God the Son and of the Holy Spirit, and who proclaim their union in power and their distinction in order? (Athenagoras, *Supplic* 24)
> The three days before the luminaries were created are types of the Triad: God, his Word, and his Wisdom. (Theophilus, *To Autol* 2,15)

This last quotation, from Theophilus of Antioch, has the distinction of being the first occurrence in Christian literature of the term Triad [Gk *Trias*] which from now on will become the technical term for God as Three and will soon be translated into Latin by Tertullian as *Trinitas*, thus giving us the English word Trinity.[3] Justin Martyr also, it might be remarked, shows that the triadic baptismal formula of Matthew 28,19 is now standard practice in the Church. Christian converts in Rome in the mid second century are baptised 'in the name of God, the Lord and Father of all, and of our Saviour, Jesus Christ, and of the Holy Spirit'. (*1 Apol* 61)

The first, and rather obvious, question which now arises is how these writers envisage the relation between the Son and the Spirit and the one God, the Father. Modern commentators often describe the thought of the Apologists on this issue as 'confused'. This is an ungenerous and inaccurate assessment, and one which invokes the developed thought of a later period, which these writers made possible, as a judgement upon that of an earlier. One must readily admit that the thought of these writers on this deep and important issue, which they are the first to address, is not fully worked out, but remains incomplete both conceptually and linguistically. And, as earlier remarked, they are deliberately clothing their thought in the alien language of those outside the faith whom they are here addressing and attempting to convince. Their position on this issue, therefore, is characterised by a certain imprecision and a lack of total clarity and coherence as a result of which, as we shall presently see, seeds of future problems lie embedded in their statements. Nevertheless, it remains true that what these writers wish to say, as distinct from the inadequate way in which they say it, is reasonably clear.

In identifying the trend of the Apologists' thought here, one should first note the clear distinction which they make between God and everything else, between God and what is not God. God is eternal; everything else has had a beginning and has been brought into existence by God from non-existence. God, writes Theophilus, 'created everything out of that which did not exist; for nothing is coeval with God'. (*To Autol* 2,4) Given this clear distinction, the question now is where to place the Son and the Spirit – with God the Father or among the things created. Here the Apologists do not hesitate: the Son and the Spirit belong to the reference 'God', they are not to be placed among things which have a beginning, which have been brought into existence by God from non-existence, creatures.

In attempting to explain this position, the concentration of the Apologists rests on the status of the Son. As regards the Spirit, they simply take it for granted that, since the Spirit is the Spirit *of God*, the matter is obvious and requires little further argument. The status of the Son is of far greater import for them. A basic argument for Christianity rests on the assertion that the preexistent Son of God has become incarnate as Jesus Christ for the salvation of the world. As the Founder of their religion, Christians take and bear his name. 'From him', writes Justin, 'we have received our name as Christians.' (*1 Apol* 12) But how is the relation of the Son to the one God, the Father, to be understood and presented? The Apologists summarily dismiss any suggestion that this relationship can be conceived after the manner of human birth, in terms of human fatherhood and sonship, even if this comparison has inevitably to be invoked in attempting to describe this relationship. Beginning with Justin Martyr, they find another way of presenting this relationship. They identify the Son as the Logos of God dimly recognised and spoken of in pagan philosophy but who has truly revealed itself as this Logos when speaking in the theophanies and prophets of the Old Testament and who now finally has become fully human as Jesus Christ.

This identification of the Son with the Logos is the Apologists' trump card in their effort to achieve for Christianity public intellectual respectability. However, this move only renders more acute the question of the status of the Son and his relation to the

Father. For if the Son is the Logos of God existing alongside God
the Father, and himself also truly called God, how can the attribute 'one' be maintained when speaking of God? Are there not
now two Gods – at least? The Apologists answer this question by
invoking the Stoic distinction between 'the immanent word/
thought' (*logos endiathetos*) and 'the expressed word/thought' (*logos prophorikos*). The Logos always existed in and with God the
Father as God's immanent Mind and Thought [*logos endiathetos*].
When the Father willed to create, he first uttered or expressed this
Thought/Logos which now comes to exist alongside him as his
expressed Logos (*logos prophorikos*). Though two distinct successive stages of existence are here attributed to the Logos, it is the
very same Logos who subsists in both. The second stage comes
about simply through God's will and purpose to create, which
God does by expressing this intention, that is, by uttering this Lo-
gos/Thought. The expressed Logos of this later stage, however, is
the same as the eternal, immanent Logos of the earlier. The following passages illustrate this notion of the Apologists.

> God [the Father] existed in the beginning. ... He was alone.
> ... and with him was the Logos himself who was in him ....
> By his simply willing it, the Logos springs forth ... the first-
> begotten work of the Father. We know him to be the begin-
> ning of the world. (Tatian, *Address* 5)
> God, having his own Logos internally in his very organs, be-
> got him, emitting him along with his own Wisdom [=the
> Spirit] before all things. He had this Logos for a helper in the
> things which he made, and through him were all things
> created. (Theopilus, *To Autol* 2,10)
> The Logos of God, which also is his Son, ... always exists in-
> ternally in the heart of God. Before anything was created he
> [the Father] had this Counsellor, being his own Mind and
> Thought; and when God wished to create what he had de-
> cided upon, he begot this uttered Logos, the First-born of all
> creation, not emptying himself of the Logos, but having be-
> gotten the Logos, and conversing always with the Logos.
> (Theophilus, *To Autol* 2,22)

In applying the Stoic distinction to the successive stages which
they envisage for the Logos, the Apologists tend, perhaps not fully consistently, to associate the Logos becoming Son of God with
the second stage, from the moment the Father utters, 'brings
forth', his Thought. This utterance is the generation of the Logos
as Son. Though a linguistic factor, the association of the putting
forth of thought in word with the 'birth' of the word, may be

influential here, the fact remains that dating the existence of the Logos as 'Son of God' only from this moment creates a problem for the theology of the Apologists. Yet, their major interest and emphasis in appealing to the distinction of the immanent and expressed word lies in the assertion of the identity of the Logos in both stages. The Logos who exists eternally as the Mind or Thought of God the Father is the same Logos who is God's agent in creation, the expression of his providence in salvation history and truly incarnate as Jesus Christ. The Apologists show their concern to emphasise this identity and continuity of the Logos through the successive stages they envisage by rejecting any idea that the generation of the Logos meant any separation from God, a separation which could only mean that God's being was divided and that salvation history was the work of someone less than God.

> He [the Logos] was begotten by communication, and not by a cutting off; for what is cut off is separated from the original substance; but that which proceeds from something by communication ... does not diminish that from which it is taken. For just as from one torch many fires are lighted, and the light of the first torch is not lessened by the igniting of the many torches, so also the Logos, proceeding from the power of the Father, has not rendered the Progenitor wordless. (Tatian, *Address* 5; cf Justin, *Dial* 61; Theophilus, *To Autol* 2,22)

The Apologists are much less concerned with the theme of the Holy Spirit than with that of the Logos. This reflects the low state of Spirit theology at this period. The Spirit here is not a living theme but rather a formal reference which cannot be completely ignored. It receives mention from these writers because it is part of the traditional triadic statement of God. There is no effort on their part to develop a significant pneumatology in any way comparable to the Logos christology which is their main interest and focus. The thin pneumatology which they do present is a primitive one which reflects and re-presents that characteristic of Late Judaism which Early Christianity inherited and which pervades a document such as Acts of the Apostles. One looks in vain here for even an echo of the Pauline theology of the life-giving Spirit animating the life of the Church and the Christian. In this literature the Spirit of God is understood as the prophetic Spirit who inspired and spoke through the prophets, inspired the writing of Scripture and still acts as an inspiring force in Christian witness. This is a concept of the charismatic, prophetic Spirit, the Spirit as source of occasional extraordinary phenomena rather than source of ordinary Christian life. (cf Justin, *1 Apol* 6; 13; 43; Tatian, *Address* 13; Athenagoras, *Supplic* 7; 9; 10; Theophilus, *To Autol* 1,14; 2,10; 3, 12)

Though the description of the activity of the Holy Spirit as the Apologists present it could easily be regarded as that of an impersonal supernatural force, again reflecting here the biblical and Jewish source of the concept, the association of the Spirit with the very personal Father and Son in the triadic statement of God ensures that the Spirit also is understood as personal. But the concept of 'person' as applicable to the Triad, which will later be so central in trinitarian discussion, is not as yet a topic of any theological interest. This aspect of the Holy Spirit, therefore, remains here at a very underdeveloped stage. The Apologists accept, on the basis of the traditional triadic statement of faith, that the Father, the Son and the Holy Spirit are really distinct. They encounter a problem, however, in trying to distinguish between the activity of the Logos and that of the Spirit in salvation history. The source of this problem lies in the Old Testament which can appeal interchangeably to both the Word of God and the Spirit of God as the inspiring source of prophetic revelation. This problem is more acute for the Christian mind precisely because of the clear distinction between the Son and the Spirit which Christian faith imposes. The Apologists do not succeed in resolving this problem. They do not even attempt to advance a solution. Theophilus of Antioch does indeed distinguish between the Word of God and the Wisdom of God and uses the latter as a synonym for the Spirit: 'The three days before the luminaries were created are types of the Triad: God, his Word, and his Wisdom'. But, apart from reflecting the influence of the Book of Wisdom and its identification of Wisdom and the Spirit (cf 1,6; 7,22; 9,17), the distinction, though later accepted by Irenaeus and some others, is rather artificial and has little real biblical basis. The distinction does not appear in the other Apologists who generally identify Wisdom with the Logos/ Word of God (cf Justin, *Dial* 61; 100) and often present the Logos as the source of inspiration and revelation in the biblical prophets. 'It is the Divine Logos' writes Justin, 'who moves them [the prophets]'. (*1 Apol* 36) But Justin can also speak in the same work of 'the Holy Spirit who predicted through the prophets everything concerning Jesus'. (*1 Apol* 61) Here again we meet an example of the underdeveloped state of pneumatology characteristic of the period and the lack of interest which the Apologists display in attempting any significant development. The theme of the Holy Spirit is not a high priority on their theological agenda.

The Apologists are, however, committed to mention of the Spirit because of the triadic statement of faith and therefore feel a need to account for the mission and role of the Spirit in salvation history. The concept of the Spirit of prophecy serves their purpose here since it provides them with an expansive biblical background upon which to call. But they also attempt to parallel the coming forth of the Spirit from God with the coming forth of the Word as Logos Prophorikos. Thus Athenagoras, having mentioned the coming forth of the Logos, continues: 'The Holy Spirit also, who works in those who speak prophetically, we regard as an effluence of God, flowing out and returning like a ray of the sun'. (*Supplic* 10; cf also Theophilus, *To Autol* 2,10) Thus, through the Logos/Son and the Spirit, both of which express God's very being, the one God, the Father, communicates Godself to creatures in creation and salvation history.

One further emphasis in the Apologists' description of the Triad deserves mention. The traditional ranking of the references – Father, Son, Spirit – is consistently preserved by them. But in their insistence that the Father is the origin of the Son and the Spirit and expresses Godself in and through them, they give special prominence to this ranking and give it a special, indeed a technical, name, 'order' (Gk *taxis*). Thus Athenagoras speaks of 'God the Father and of God the Son and of the Holy Spirit' and of 'their power in union and their distinction in order (*taxis*)'. (*Supplic* 10) It is this notion which enables Justin to speak of the Son holding 'a second place' and the Spirit 'a third'. (*1 Apol* 13) His language here is simply an expression of this acknowledged *taxis*. This term and concept, appearing here in Athenagoras for the first time, is destined to have a long and influential history in Greek patristic theology.

The Problem

A review of the Apologists' achievement in developing and presenting an understanding of the Christian concept of God to their pagan public has to take note of both its strengths and its weaknesses. The basic problem confronting them was how to reconcile the triadic statement of God, which according to Christian faith accomplished salvation history entailed and revealed, with the equally emphatic assertion of that faith that God is one. In their effort to make this enigmatic position understandable to educated pagans, they concentrate their attention on the figure of Jesus Christ acknowledged in Christian faith as the preexistent Son of God. For their purpose they adopt and press into service the well-

known Stoic distinction of the thought within the mind, the inner
thought, and the thought as uttered forth, the expressed thought.
From all eternity there is in God the Mind/Thought/Logos of
God. When deciding to create, God expresses, brings forth, this
Thought/Logos who now, precisely as *God's* Logos, the expression of God's will and power, accomplishes God's purpose and
finally becomes truly human as Jesus Christ. From the moment
that God utters, 'brings forth', this Logos, the Logos may also be
called 'Son of God'. In a similar if less prominent manner the
Apologists attempt to explain the figure and mission of the Spirit/
Breath of God. Something of the force of their statement may be
gathered and something of its achievement assessed from the following passage from Tatian.

> God existed in the beginning. But we have been taught that
> the beginning is the power of the Logos. For the Master of
> the universe, who himself is the foundation of all, insofar as
> no creature was yet made, was alone. But inasmuch as he
> was all power, he was the foundation of things visible and
> invisible; and with him was the Logos himself, who was in
> him, and who sustains all things by a rational power. By his
> [God] simply willing it, the Word springs forth; and the
> Word, not proceeding in vain, becomes the first-begotten
> work of the Father. We know him to be the beginning of the
> world. He was begotten by communication, and not by a
> cutting off; for what is cut off is separated from the original
> substance; but that which proceeds from something by com-
> munication, and which accepts the choice of arrangement,
> does not diminish that from which it is taken. For just as
> from one torch many fires are lighted, and the light of the
> first torch is not lessened by the igniting of the many torches,
> so also the Word, proceeding from the power of the Father,
> has not rendered the Progenitor wordless. (*Address* 5)

The Apologists, it should be noted, maintain the true divinity
of the Logos, and correspondingly of the Spirit, in a number of
ways. The Logos is originally and eternally the immanent
Thought of God and retains this status in and throughout its
'expressed' stage, since this expression or generation does not involve any separation from God. Neither the Logos nor the Spirit is
a creature, something brought into existence by God from non-
existence; they do not have a beginning, but belong to the eternal
being of God. In their roles in salvation history they activate and
give expression to the will and power of God. The Apologists conceive divine being or divinity in dynamic, not in ontological or

essentialist, terms: God is 'all power' and the one will and power of God continues to operate in the Logos and the Spirit. 'We assert' writes Athenagoras, 'that there is a God, and a Son who is his Logos, and a Holy Spirit, united in power'. (*Supplic* 24) For this reason he can speak of 'the Father and the Son being one. Since the Son is in the Father and the Father is in the Son by the unity and power of the Spirit'. (ibid 10)

Despite the impressive achievement of the Apologists in presenting their case – and, given the circumstances in which they wrote, it is impressive – they have also succeeded in creating a major problem for the Christian understanding of God as Triune. They are, in a way, victims of their own success. Since they represent the first intellectual effort of the Christian mind to address this question, they also thereby lay the foundation and determine the parameters and terms of future discussion of the issue. The next generation of theologians will gratefully inherit their presentation and attempt to develop it, only to find themselves confronted by the problem which this presentation entails. It is important, therefore, to be clear on what this problem exactly is.

The main interest and emphasis of the Apologists lies in explaining how God has approached humankind in creation and salvation history as Father, Son and Holy Spirit and saved it. But they are also concerned to emphasise that it is 'the one God, the Father' who throughout this activity is approaching us and saving us. To justify and reconcile these two positions, it is clearly necessary to clarify the relation between the Son and the Spirit on the one hand and 'the one God, the Father'. It is precisely here, at this crucial point, that the Apologists play their trump card by invoking and adopting the distinction of *logos endiathetos* and *logos prophorikos*, the thought within the mind and this thought as outwardly expressed. However, it is also this distinction which now creates their problem.

Identifying Jesus Christ as the Logos Incarnate, the Apologists can present him as eternally one with God as his Mind or Thought. And they can also present his role in creation and salvation history as this Thought/Logos outwardly expressed, Logos Prophorikos. This second stage or state of the Logos, however, has a beginning. It is not eternal. It takes place at a particular moment which therefore divides the 'history' of the Logos into two phases, into a 'before' and an 'after'. This moment is described as that when the Father utters his Logos, when the Logos proceeds forth from the *will* of the Father. It is also the moment of the 'bringing forth' or 'generation' of the Logos from the Father and

therefore it is from this moment, and only from this moment. that
the Logos can properly be called 'Son of God'.

The problem with this position is a double one. Following this
expression or generation, the Logos clearly subsists as a personal
being distinct from the Father, occupying, as Justin says, 'a second
place'. But prior to this, as *logos endiathetos*, as God's eternal immanent Mind or Thought, was the Logos then also a subsistent being
distinct from the Father? When one speaks of God's immanent
Mind/Thought, is one not simply referring to an *attribute* of God,
God's rationality, which is in no real way distinct from God and
can be so spoken of only in a figurative sense, like the literary per-
sonification of the Wisdom of God in the biblical Wisdom literature? The Apologists do not address this basic problem which
their enthusiastic endorsement of the Stoic distinction has imposed upon them. Perhaps they felt that within the terms they
were using the question was unanswerable, and so better ignored.
In reading them, however, one gets the impression that, if pushed
on the issue, they would take refuge in the concept of the incomprehensibility of God. On this last point, at least. they would find
themselves in total accord with Hellenistic philosophers of every
persuasion.

The second side of the Apologists' problem reinforces the first.
The Apologists mark the bringing forth or generation of the Logos
as a 'beginning' (Justin, *Dial* 61; Theophilus, *To Autol* 2,10) and
describe the expressed Logos as 'the first-begotten work of the
Father' (Tatian, *Address* 5; *Athenagoras*, Supplic 10), as the 'first-
born of God, of all creation' (Justin, *1 Apol* 53; Theophilus, *To Autol* 2,22). It is true that what the Apologists mean by this use of 'beginning' and 'first' is that the Logos is the origin of creation, the
One 'through whom all things are made', and that they never
countenance the idea that the Logos itself is a creature. 'He is the
first-begotten of the Father' writes Athenagoras, 'not as having
been produced (=creature) ... but as coming forth'. (*Supplic*, 10)
But they also strongly insist that this 'coming forth' of the Logos
has been determined by the *will*, the free decision, of the Father.
(Justin, *2 Apol* 6; *Dial* 61; 100; Theophilus, *To Autol* 2,22) This
creates the suspicion, to say the least, that the existence of the
Logos as a distinct subsistent being dates only from the moment
of the implementation of this decision, the generation of the Logos
as Son. This suspicion is increased by the use in this context, for
the first time, of the fateful text of Proverbs 8: 22, later so beloved
of the Arians and the cause of so much heart-searching to the orthodox: 'The Lord made me the beginning of his ways'. (Athena-

goras, *Supplic*, 10) When one recalls the Apologists' strong insistence on the eternal God as one, alone, having nothing coeval with himself, and when one notes their failure to clarify the status of the immanent Logos as anything other than an attribute or aspect of the one God and their insistence that the Logos only becomes 'Son of God' from the moment of his utterance forth, the impression is easily conveyed that the Logos comes into existence as a distinct being only from this moment. One can certainly vindicate the Apologists of any subordinationist *intention* in their portrayal of the Logos and the Spirit. But their adoption of the *logos endiathetos\logos prophorokos* distinction has ensured that, despite their best intentions, a subordinationist implication is there and can be logically deduced from their position. This distinction, which up to a point they find so serviceable, in the event also prevents and precludes them from finding a distinction within the one God to justify what they wish to say of God as three in salvation history. In this presentation the impression is easily conveyed that God in God's eternal being is a strict Monad who following God's decision to create unfolds into and *becomes* a Triad. This is the problem deeply embedded in the theology of the Apologists. Yet, as the first Christian thinkers to address the question of God as one and as three, they have also determined the context and set the terms of future discussion. Later generations of theologians in inheriting their theology will also inherit their problem. For many of them the logic of the subordinationist implication will seem too obvious and prove too tempting. In the endeavours of Christian theology, the Stoic distinction will yet show itself a sorcerer's apprentice.

Later Pre-Nicene Theology

The generation of writers who immediately succeed to and carry forward the theological enterprise of the Apologists cover a period which runs from the end of the second century to around the middle of the third. They comprise Irenaeus of Lyons (d. c. 200), Hippolytus of Rome (d. c. 235), Tertullian of Carthage (d. c. 235), Origen of Alexandria (d. 254/5), Novatian of Rome (d. c. 258). These writers inherit the theological position of the Apologists and most of them accept its general terms and attempt to develop it further. Our concentration here will be on this development. The writers who will particularly claim our attention are Irenaeus, Tertullian and Origen, for theirs is the contribution of greatest significance.

First, however, it may be helpful to say a brief word about the genre of Christian literature of this period. Although some of these writers also write apologies for the Christian religion, notably Tertullian and Origen, this form is not the main literary preoccupation of the period nor is it where the thinking of these writers on the question of God is most prominently presented. This is found rather in their anti-heretical works which constitute the bulk of this literature and represent the main concern of these writers. Their purpose here is to warn Christians against erroneous teaching by exposing it for the heresy which it is. Here again, therefore, we meet a literature which is written within the Church and addressed to the Church.

The heresies concerning God which have become prominent at this period and which these writers combat represent two opposite extremes, Monarchianism or Modalism on the one hand and Subordinationism on the other. Monarchianism asserted that there is only one God, and explained the distinct references of the Triad, Father, Son, Holy Spirit, as simply different names for this one God in the different forms or modes (hence Modalism) in which God has revealed Godself in salvation history. It was prepared to follow the logic of its position and even countenance the statement that it was God the Father who suffered on the Cross (Patripassionism). The distinctions of the Triad according to this position are merely verbal, not real. It solved the problem of God as Three simply by denying any reality other than verbal to these references. It maintained, according to Tertulian, that 'one cannot believe in one only God in any other way than by saying that the Father, Son and Holy Spirit are the very selfsame Person'. (*Against Praxeas* 2) In ancient times this position was often referred to as 'the teaching of Sabellius' (Sabellianism) after the name of one of its main exponents. Today this teaching is usually called Modalist Monarchianism to distinguish it from another form termed Dynamic Monarchianism. Dynamic Monarchianism maintained that the one God was a strict Monad whose power (*dynamis*) descended upon and operated in the man Jesus who, in himself, was nothing more than this, a 'mere man' (*psilos anthropos*). At this time this position was seen as basically a christological aberration, but its implications concerning an understanding of God were obvious. In maintaining a strictly monadic view of God, it effectively denied any real meaning to the concept of God as Triad.

Subordinationism represents a form of thought which asserts that there is one Supreme Being or God but which can also accommodate many or few lesser divine figures who serve to mediate

between and relate the transcendent God and this world of experience. It was especially attractive to those minds who felt that this
God could not be directly linked with or involved in this evil
world of matter. Hellenistic philosophy, as we have noted, especially in its Platonist expression, presents this conceptual character. Subordinationism as a Christian heresy confronted the writers of our period above all in those Gnostic systems which pur-
ported to be Christian, indeed the purest form of Christianity.
Gnosticism, an umbrella term embracing many diverse types, had
its basis and origin, like so many religious philosophies, in the
postulate of dualism, the assertion of two original, opposite principles, spirit (good) and matter (evil). It explained the immersion
of spirit, the human soul, in matter as due to a series of descents
from the Heavenly World of the Supreme God, the Pleroma,
involving a descending series of lesser divine-like beings called
aeons. Salvation for the spirit consisted in release from its involvement with matter through the appearence of a Saviour-figure who
gave it knowledge (Gk *gnosis* – hence Gnosticism) of its situation
and how it had come about. Christian Gnosticism, which also presented many forms, attempted to give this religious philosophy a
Christian accommodation. Here, the Saviour-figure who delivered the saving *gnosis* was Christ, a spiritual, docetic being from
the Heavenly World who was usually distinguished from the
man Jesus upon whom he descended either at his birth or baptism
and from whom he departed before his passion and death.
Though its orthodox critics were concerned with many other aspects of Gnostic teaching, the Gnostic portrayal of a non-incarnate
Christ who was a divine emanation or aeon inferior in being to the
Supreme God was a particular challenge to Christian faith which
these writers felt obliged to meet and expose.

The contrasting understanding of the divine Triad presented
by Modalism and Subordinationism confronted the theologians
of this period with much more explicit views on this issue than
was the case with the Apologists. These writers were now called
upon anew to assert and clarify the specific Christian understanding of God as both one and three. In meeting this challenge they
re-present the thought of the Apologists which they have inherited but in doing so find themselves forced to re-think and develop
it. It is this effort at development which is significant and which
here must claim our attention. Sufficient may already have been
said, however, to raise the suspicion that the terms and parameters of the Apologists' presentation may not be adequate for
the task now on hand. The mould which they imposed upon this

issue may yet have to be broken and replaced before real progress
may be possible.

Irenaeus of Lyons

We begin our examination of the thought of these later pre-
Nicene theologians on God and the Triad with the earliest of these
writers, Irenaeus of Lyons. He is significant not merely because he
is the first but much more because his writings, widely available
both in the original Greek and very early Latin translation, were
immensely influential throughout the whole Church then and later. His works extant today consist of the voluminous *Against the
Heresies* and the much shorter, more pastoral *Demonstration of the
Apostolic Preaching*.

In Irenaeus, as in all orthodox Christian writers from now on,
statements that God is One and also a Triad are commonplace. It
may be important, however, to stress again that here, as throughout the pre-Nicene period and long after, the 'one God' is the
Father: 'He alone is found to be God ... he alone is Father' (*Ag Hers*
2,30,9); 'there is one God the Father' (ibid 5,18,2). Of Irenaeus'
plentiful reference to God as Triad, the following passage must
suffice: 'The Church ... has received from the Apostles and from
their disciples the faith in one God, the Father almighty ... and in
one Christ Jesus, the Son of God ... and in the Holy Spirit'. (ibid
1,10,1; see also the basic summary of Christian teaching, Irenaeus'
Rule of Faith, *Dem* 6, the first occurence in patristic literature of
this summary form of doctrinal statement.) Mention might also be
made of his witness to the triadic form of baptism. (*Dem* 3;7;100) It
is very probable that the practice he refers to consisted of the credal questions put to the candidate during the rite of immersion: 'Do
you believe in God the Father? – Do you believe in Jesus Christ,
the Son of God? – Do you believe in the Holy Spirit of God?'.

Irenaeus devotes far more attention to the respective roles of
the Son and the Spirit in salvation history than do the Apologists.
This emphasis reflects his pastoral concern to instruct the faithful
and to warn them of the distortions of the heretics, that is, for him,
the Gnostics. He is, in fact, the first writer to use the term 'Economy' to describe God's activity in creation and salvation history.
This term is derived from a combination of two Greek words:
oikos, meaning 'house', and *nomos*, meaning 'law', 'regulation',
'system of administration'. The combined word, therefore, means
literally the running, the administration of the house, so giving
us, in an extended sense, the meaning of the word in ordinary
usage today. In Irenaeus the term means God's providential

administration of God's 'house' of creation through God's saving activity in salvation history by means of the Son and the Spirit. In later Greek theology the word will become a technical term for the culmination of this activity, the Incarnation. Irenaeus emphasises the intimate relation of the Son and the Spirit with the Father and with one another in this activity by the striking image of describing them as the Father's 'two hands'. (*Ag Hers* 4, pref 4; 4,20,1; 5,1,3; 5,5,1; 5,6,1; *Dem* 11)

An exposition of Irenaeus' general christology is not required in this study. Some aspects, however, of the way he conceives and presents Christ are relevant to an understanding of his concept of the divine Triad. The basic themes he parades are familiar from the Apologists but he develops them in his own characteristic way. Like the Apologists, he describes Christ as the Logos of God who is the Son of God. The Logos was the Father's agent in creation, spoke through the prophets and finally became incarnate as Jesus Christ. 'He became' writes Irenaeus, in a statement which has echoed through the ages, 'what we are to enable us to become what he is'. (*Ag Hers* 5, pref) The role of the Logos in salvation history is developed by Irenaeus in terms of the Johannine theme of Christ Revealer of the Father and the Pauline theme of Christ the Second Adam, Restorer of broken humanity. 'The Father of our Lord Jesus Christ', he writes, 'is revealed through his Logos, who is his Son' (ibid 2,30,9)'; and again, in another famous phrase, 'What is invisible in the Son is the Father, and what is visible in the Father is the Son'. (ibid 4,6,6) The redemptive work of Christ as the Second Adam he describes in another striking expression: 'the recapitulation (*anakephalaiosis*) of all things in Christ'. (ibid 3,16,6; passim)

The most striking feature of Irenaeus' theology of the Triad, however, lies in his pneumatology. We have already noted the primitive, underdeveloped state of this theme in the Apologists. This situation begins to change dramatically with Irenaeus. The occasion and stimulus for his interest in this theme is clear. The Gnostic sects, especially those such as the Valentinians who seem to have been closest to the Church in teaching and practice, seeing themselves as the saved elite within the general Christian body, since they alone possessed and could deliver the true, saving Gnosis, identified this Gnosis with the gift of the Spirit which, accordingly, they claimed that they alone possessed and could confer in their initiation rites. Sealed with this gift, they were the saved, the true Spirituals/Pneumatics, to be distinguished from ordinary Christians, the Psychics, who still had some hope of salvation,

and from the rest of humankind, the Materialists/Hylics who had
no such hope. At a time when the Church's consciousness and understanding of the Spirit had fallen dangerously into the background, this was indeed to occupy vacated high ground. Irenaeus
was the first churchman to diagnose the situation clearly and see
the danger. His answer was to retrieve and develop a significant,
ecclesiological theology of the Holy Spirit.

The source to which Irenaeus returned to find his theology of
the Spirit was St Paul. Surprising as it is to us, he is the first second
century writer to show an interest in this source and to give prominence to Pauline themes and ideas. Indeed it can be said that he
introduces Paul to the post-New Testament Church. The concept
of the prophetic Spirit, prominent in the Apologists, is repeated in
Irenaeus. But his special contribution lies in his retrieval and rein-
troduction of the Pauline concept of the Spirit as life-giving: 'The
Spirit of the Father purifies the human and raises him/her to the
life of God' (*Dem* 6); the Spirit 'renews humans from their old
ways into the newness of Christ' (*Ag Hers* 3,17,1); the Spirit oper-
ating through baptism 'leads us on to the life of God' (ibid 3,17,2).
Irenaeus realises the ecclesiological significance of this concept of
the Spirit and, following St Paul, is able to link it organically with
the Church. The Church 'constantly has its youth renewed by the
Spirit of God ... Where the Church is, there is the Spirit of God;
and where the Spirit of God is, there is the Church and every
grace'. (ibid 3,24,1) Here it is the Church itself, and not the Gnostic
sects, which possesses the Spirit and is empowered to confer this
gift. The Spirit, he declares, is Truth, that is the true Gnosis, and
those who have received the Spirit in the Church are the true Spir-
ituals/Pneumatics. (ibid 3,24,1; 5,10,1) Irenaeus is here effectively
re-occupying the high ground. The development of pneumatology which he here initiates will have lasting influence, even if recognition of its significance will be a slow and gradual process.

That Irenaeus acknowledges the divinity of the Son and the
Spirit is clear from his whole exposition. Even though the Father
is 'the one God', he has no hesitation in calling the Son 'God' also:
'The Father is God, and the Son is God, for whatever is begotten of
God is God' (*Dem* 47); 'He [Christ] is himself in his own right God
and Lord...' (*Ag Hers* 3,19,1) That the Spirit is similarly divine is
taken for granted both by reason of the name, 'Spirit *of God*' and
'*Holy* Spirit' – *Holiness*, it should be remembered, is a biblical
name for God – and also because of the divine works which the
Spirit performs. The question is how Irenaeus envisages the rela-

tion of the Son and the Spirit to the Father. How does he reconcile the assertion of God as Three with the assertion of God as One?

The statements of Irenaeus which throw light on this issue mainly concern the relationship of the Son to the Father. Like all orthodox writers until the end of the fourth century controversy, he largely takes for granted that whatever way this relation is understood will apply also, *mutatis mutandis*, to the Holy Spirit. Throughout this whole period the main focus is certainly on the relation and distinction of the Father and Son. In the case of Irenaeus, it must also be borne in mind that his eye is always centred on the position of the Gnostics and their theory of divine emanations, a series of heavenly figures, the aeons, who. inferior in being to the Supreme God, separate from God in a descending scale down to the human spirit/soul imprisoned in this world. His great and constant concern is to distinguish between and contrast the Christian understanding of the divine Triad with this Gnostic theory of separating descending emanations.

Given this context and concern, it is no surprise to find that Irenaeus links the being and activity of the Son and Spirit as closely as possible to the Father. His image of the Son and Spirit as the 'two hands' of the Father is clear evidence of this. But the evidence he can draw upon to illustrate this close link has of necessity to be the divine activity in creation and salvation history, the activity of God in the 'Economy' as he would put it, the divine operation *ad extra* as theology will later describe it. This activity is documented for the human mind both in the experience of existence itself and in the biblical record of salvation history. Irenaeus never pretends to have access to the being of God in itself, the eternal, immanent being of God. Such access is not available even to the believing mind; it is shrouded and covered by the mystery and incomprehensibility of God. Irenaeus' texts are rich therefore in their description of the activity of God through the Son and the Spirit in creation and history. The act of creation constitutes a definite limit here behind which it is not possible to penetrate, except by speculative inference. The question, however, arises and persists: is this agency strictly that of *God* or of figures, divine if you will, but yet inferior in status and being to the one, supreme God? Irenaeus' very rejection of the Gnostic thesis forces this question to the forefront. Can he substantiate his rejection of this thesis in any way other than by identifying the Son and the Spirit with the Father? One can see the temptation of the Modalist position.

Irenaeus, however, is no Modalist. For him the distinctions of Father, Son and Spirit are very real and very clear. He will even assay a demarcation of the activities of the Three in salvation history, though seeing them as combining to form an organic whole and unity: 'The Spirit prepares the human through the Son of God, the Son leads him/her to the Father, and the Father gives him/her incorruption in eternal life'. (*Ag Hers* 4,20,5) But he is also clear that the references 'Son' and 'Spirit' must truly represent the eternal God and belong to the eternal being of God. The Father, he states, who 'alone is found to be God ... is revealed through his Logos who is his Son . ... The Son, *always* co-existing with the Father, of old and from the beginning, always reveals the Father ...'. (ibid 2,30,9 – emphasis added) In another passage he writes: 'God had no need of others to make what he had already determined of himself to make, as if he had not his own hands. For with him *always* are the Logos and the Wisdom, the Son and the Spirit ...'. (ibid 4,20,1 – emphasis added) Irenaeus' description in these passages of the Son and the Spirit as 'always with' and not 'other to' the one God, the Father, reveals his perception that the distinctions of the Triad revealed in the economy of salvation must somehow represent distinctions in the eternal one God, the Father. His problem is both how to conceive such distinctions and how to distinguish them, however conceived, from the Gnostic theory of emanations, a notion of sparks which fly off from an original fire. He points out the difference and the distance he wishes to establish between himself and the Gnostics when he writes: 'They transfer the generation of the uttered word/logos of humans to the eternal Logos of God, attributing to him a beginning of utterance and a coming into being in a manner like to that of their own word. In what manner, then, would the Logos of God – indeed, the great God himself, since he is the Logos – differ from the word of men, were he to have the same order and process of generation?' (ibid 2,13,8)

Irenaeus here rejects the applicability to the Christian understanding of the Logos of the Stoic distinction of *logos endiathetos\logos prophorikos*. This distinction is too favourable to the position of the Gnostics for his liking. His only alternative is to find real distinctions within the eternal being of God, which would still leave untouched the basic assertion that there is only one God, the Father. His efforts at developing such a position are discernible in his rejection of any suggestion that the Logos had 'a beginning', 'a coming into being', from his insistence that the Logos always was Son of God and did not become such only at the moment of utterance forth for purposes of the Economy, differing here both from the Apologists before him and most pre-Nicene theologians after him, and from his insistence that the Logos/Son co-existed *always* with the Father. One can see the way he is pushing his thought in his comment on John 1:3: 'All things were made through him, and without him was made nothing'. On this text he writes: 'From *all* there is no exception; the Father made *all* things through him [the Logos], whether visible or invisible, whether of sense or of intelligence, whether temporal and for a certain dispensation or eternal and through the ages'.([ibid 1,22,1; emphasis must be regarded as original) It is obvious from this statement that Irenaeus will not allow the Logos to be conceived as a creature or inferior emanation from God in any sense whatsoever. The Logos/Son belongs to the eternal being of God.

Those scholars are correct, therefore, who maintain that Irenaeus asserts the eternal generation of the Son. The question remains, however, how he understands this eternal generation, this eternal distinction within the one God. He is able to appeal here to the well-known idea of the Logos as the Mind and Thought of God. 'God', he writes, 'being altogether Mind and altogether Logos, utters what he thinks and thinks what he utters. His thinking is his Logos, and his Logos is his intelligence, and the Father is that intelligence comprising all things'. (ibid 2,28,5; cf also 1,12, 2) Irenaeus here is not simply repeating the well-worn idea of the Logos as God's eternal, immanent Thought. He is dimly perceiving and attempting to articulate the notion that this concept may yield a real distinction within the one God which yet will not imperil or destroy the cherished divine unity. He is not, however, able to give this concept clear, conceptual content and logical justification. In the end, therefore, he appeals to the mystery and incomprehensibility of God. 'If someone say to us', he writes, "How is the Son produced from the Father?" ... we answer him that no one understands that production or generation ... which in fact is indescribable'. (ibid 2,28,6) Answers to questions of this kind 'we must leave to God'; to do otherwise 'would indeed be the greatest impiety'. (ibid 2,28,2) In the last analysis, the fact of the matter is: 'The Father is incomprehensible'. (ibid 4,20,5)

The thrust and direction of Irenaeus' thought is clear. Yet his final failure to complete his programme by developing clear distinctions within the one God leaves his theological enterprise unfinished. He has, however, advanced the thought of his predecessors in a very significant way. He has pointed theology in a significant direction and theology will yet, by following that direction, develop his 'unfinished symphony'.

Hippolytus and Tertullian

The theological enterprise initiated by the Apologists and carried forward by Irenaeus was now inherited by a new generation of theologians in both the Greek East and the Latin West. This geographical and linguistic distinction now begins to be for the first time a significant factor in Christendom. Prior to the end of the second century, and apart from an early Aramaic-speaking base, Christendom, East and West, had possessed a *lingua franca* in Greek. Hippolytus in Rome still writes in Greek in the early decades of the third century. At the same time, however, Tertullian in North Africa, though bilingual, writes most of his works in Latin. And by the mid-century Novatian in Rome also writes in Latin. From this period on, Latin will be the language of Christianity in the West, Greek in the East. This language difference will yet add its own element of confusion to theological discussion of the meaning of God in Christian faith.

Though these theologians are still much concerned with the threat of Gnosticism, they now also find themselves confronted by the opposite position, that of Modalism. Modalism, as we have seen, solved the problem of God as one and three by reducing the Triad to merely verbal distinctions. Father, Son and Spirit were simply different names for the one God. The most significant contribution of Hippolytus and Tertullian to trinitarian theology occurs in their anti-modalist works, Hippolytus in his *Against Noetus*, Tertullian in his *Against Praxeas*. In rejecting the modalist position these writers emphasise strongly the real distinction of Father, Son and Holy Spirit. They even introduce a special, common term to describe the figures of the Triad: they are three 'Persons'. This is the first use in theology of this term to describe God as Three. The Greek term used by Hippolytus here is *prosopon*, the Latin of Tertullian *persona*. Both terms had the same basic meaning. The Greek term *prosopon* basically meant the face and thence the actor's mask which procaimed his role and character, his distinctive individuality. The corresponding term and direct translation of *prosopon* in Latin was *persona*. Both terms, therefore, conveyed the idea of a particular, distinct individual. By introducing and using these terms in this context both writers were underscoring and emphasising against the Modalists the reality of the distinctions in the Triad, Father, Son, Holy Spirit.

Both writers, however, begin their exposition of the Christian understanding of God not with this assertion of the Trinity but with that of the Unity: there is one God, the Father, and originally this one God was 'alone': 'before all things God was alone'. (Tertullian, *Ag Prax*, 5: cf Hippolytus, *Ag Noet*, 10) For both writers this 'aloneness' of the one God expresses the Christian doctrine of creation from nothing and marks the absolute distinction between God and creation. For both writers proceed immediately to emphasise that this divine Unity has a complex character and contains distinctions within itself. 'Though alone', writes Hippolytus, 'he [God] was multiple, for he was not without his Word and his Wisdom'. (*Ag Noet* 10; Hippolytus, following Tatian and Irenaeus, equates the Wisdom of God and the Spirit of God.) Similarly Tertullian: 'Before all things God was alone ... He was alone, however, in the sense that there was nothing external to himself. But even then he was not really alone, for he had with him that Reason [*ratio*] which he possessed within himself, his own Reason'. (*Ag Prax* 5: Tertullian uses both *ratio*/reason and *sermo*/speech to translate the Greek term *logos*.)

When God willed to create, God did so by expressing the Word (and the Spirit) and this 'expression', this sending forth, is the generation of the Word who henceforth may now also be termed the Son of God – though Hippolytus prefers to reseve this term for the Word Incarnate. 'When he willed', writes Hippolytus, 'he made known his Word, through whom he created all things. ... He begot the Word as author, counsellor and fashioner of those things which have been made. Since he had this Word within himself, invisible to the created world, he made him visible'. (*Ag Noet* 10) For Tertullian this is the moment when God said 'Let there be light' (Gen 1,3) and he marks this transition in the 'history' of the Word from being 'within' God to being 'sent forth' by the temporal expression: 'Then, therefore...'/*Tunc, igitur* .... (*Ag Prax* 7) This is the moment of 'the perfect generation of the Word' who here as Son 'was made the first-begotten, since he was begotten before all things; and the only-begotten, because he alone was begotten of God, in a manner peculiar to himself, from the womb of his own heart'. (ibid)

It is for the purpose of creation, therefore, and the history of salvation which it inaugurates, that the one God extrapolates and expresses forth from God's complex unity the Word and the Spirit. In this 'Economy' – Hippolytus and Tertullian gratefully accept Irenaeus' term and concept – the one God is revealed as Trinity - Father, Son and Holy Spirit.

It is from and because of creation and salvation history that the distinctions, eternally 'invisible' and implicit in the one God, become 'visible' and explicit and identifiable as Son of God and Spirit of God. Tertullian especially, with his capacity for clear, precise expression, reflecting surely his Roman legal background, clarifies the meaning and relation of these distinctions, and thereby makes a lasting contribution to trinitarian theology. He describes the Three as 'Persons', distinct individuals, 'capable', as he puts it 'of being counted'. (*numerum ... patiuntur, Ag Prax* 2; *Against Praxeas* was written in 213 and, though the question is disputed, is probably somewhat later than *Against Noetus*, in which case Tertullian is very probably here adopting and translating Hippolytus' term *prosopon*.) Though discussion still continues concerning the precise meaning of this term 'person' for Tertullian, it is clear that it signifies and emphatically asserts the reality of the distinctions in question. The term constitutes and sums up Tertullian's response to and rejection of the modalist position. But if Tertullian here avoids the Scylla of Modalism, he does so only at the expense of finding himself veering towards and facing the Charybdis of Subordinationism. In adopting the perspective of the Economic Trinitarianism of the Apologists and Irenaeus, he has also inherited their problem, the problem imposed by this approach of how to avoid making the Word/Son and the Spirit subordinate in being to the one, true God and therefore, in effect, creatures of God.

Tertullian's answer to this problem, which he saw very clearly, was to assert the identity of divinity between the Father, Son and Spirit, a divinity, however, which the Father communicated to and shared with the other two. The three Persons, therefore, constitute 'the Trinity of one divinity'. (*Modesty* 21) This communicated one divinity, Godness, that which makes God to be God, Tertullian terms the substance of God. Thus, the Son and the Spirit share 'in the substance [divinity] of the Father'. (*Ag Prax* 3) Christ, proceeding forth from God, the Father, 'in that procession is generated, so that he is Son of God, and is called God from unity of substance with God'. (*Apology* 21) There is here 'no division of substance, but merely an extension ... that which has come forth out of God is at once God and the Son of God and the two are one'. (ibid) The Three 'are *unum*/ one in substance, not *unus*/one in person, as it is written, "I and the Father are one", in respect of unity of substance, not singularity of number'. (*Ag Prax* 25)

Tertullian's finest statement of his understanding of the God-question occurs in his *Against Praxeas* 2. It will be helpful to quote it here as a summary of his mature thought.

> The perversity [of the Modalist Praxeas] considers that it has possession of the pure truth in thinking it impossible to believe in the unity of God without identifying the Father, the

Son, and the Holy Spirit; failing to see that the one may be all in the sense that all are of one, that is through unity of substance; while this still safeguards the mystery of the economy, which disposes the Unity into a Trinity, arranging in order the three Persons, Father, Son, and Holy Spirit, though these are three not in quality, but in degree, not in substance but in form, not in power but in manifestation; of one substance, one quality, one power, because God is one and from him those degrees and forms are assigned in the name of the Father, Son, and Holy Spirit. How they admit of plurality without division the following discussions will show.

Tertullian, incorporating and building upon the thought of Hippolytus, made a lasting contribution to the Christian understanding of God as one and also three. His achievement lay in constructing a formula whereby this dipolar understanding of God could be logically understood, expressed in language and thus justified. Adopting this formula, the Christian could speak confidently of God without fear, at least, of logical contradiction. 'Plurality without division' sums up this understanding, where 'plurality' means the three persons and 'without division' signifies the unity of substance, the unique Godness which all Three share.

In hammering out and defending this formula, however, Tertullian does not abandon the hierarchy, the *taxis*, which the Christian understanding of God ever involves. For him, as for all before him and for many long after him, there is one, original God who in generating the Son becomes Father of the Son and in sending forth his Spirit unfolds into a Trinity. This is once again the Economic Trinitarianism of the Apologists and Irenaeus, though now clarified and sharpened by more precise concepts and terminology. Tertullian stoutly reaffirms the tradition which asserts there is one God and this one God is the Father. The unfolding of this one God, this Monad, into Triad or Trinity which the Economy of creation and salvation history occasions, does not involve any division of Godness or divine substance, but rather, as he puts it, 'an extension'. (*Apol* 21) In sum, Tertullian is a classic upholder and expounder of Economic Trinitarianism: in the Economy the original divine Monad unfolds into a divine Triad.

It would be well, however, to note here that Tertullian has now given *two* meanings to the expression: the one God – namely, the Father, the hitherto traditional meaning, *and* the one divine substance. This new direction, and indeed ambivalence, of meaning is not the least significant of his contributions to the ongoing discussion of our subject. Tertullian's formula of the One and the

Three has provided Christian faith with a logical language to state
its distinctive understanding of God. But in giving two meanings
to the reference 'one', Tertullian has also introduced, however innocently, a basic confusion here which, as we shall have occasion
to notice later, will not in the event be altogether happy.

The basic thrust of the theological enterprise of Hippolytus and
Tertullian was to combat the developing threat of Modalism and,
on the basis of Scripture, tradition and reason, to expose this position as new-fangled and heretical. Since later Church teaching
was to fully endorse and vindicate this endeavour, it seems surprising to us today to find that at the time this 'new theology' was
not welcomed and, in fact, was regarded with deep suspicion.
Earlier, the Logos theology of the Apologists, and the Economic
Trinitarianism which it involved, seems to have provoked a mod-
alist-type reaction, at least in the Church in the West. The developed Trinitarianism of Hippolytus and Tertullian, with its sharpened emphasis on the distinctions in the Triad, met with a similar
reaction. 'The simple, indeed,' writes Tertullian, 'who always constitute the majority of believers, are startled at the Economy, on
the ground that their very rule of faith withdraws them from the
world's plurality of gods to the one only true God.' (*Ag Prax* 3)
Clearly, talk of three divine persons seemed to many at the time to
call in question, at least, the basic tenet of faith that there is only
one God. Reaction took the form of a strong emphasis on the assertion of divine unity, but without any adoption or endorsement
of the new theology of a divine Triad. Nor was this reaction confined to the simple faithful. Church authority at Rome, in the persons of the contemporary popes Zephyrinus and Callistus, seems
to have shared it also.

Modern textbooks often describe this Roman reaction as 'monarchian', but since they also frequently describe Modalism itself
as Monarchianism, following here a tendency of Tertullian himself, the impression is easily conveyed that the Roman position itself was, in the strict sense, modalist. But however similar these
positions may be at first sight, this was not the case. Strictly
understood, the term 'Monarchianism' simply states that there is
one, sole God, a basic statement of Christian faith. But for Christian faith, this statement is incomplete, since it has to proceed further and assert that this one God communicates with us through
the Son and the Spirit who also, therefore, belong to the divine reference. For Modalism the monarchian statement is complete in itself, the terms Father, Son and Spirit being simply different names

for the one God. It seems clear that what frightened the contemporaries of Hippolytus and Tertullian was not the acknowledgement of the distinction between Father, Son and Spirit, but rather the description of this distinction in terms of three *persons*. Somehow this language seems to have suggested a separation between the members of the Triad incompatible with the controlling assertion that God is one and, perhaps, too close an accommodation with pagan polytheism and Gnostic emanationism.

This also explains another peculiar feature of Latin trinitarian theology. This theology, though enthusiastically endorsing Tertullian's language of one divine substance, for a long time, indeed until well into the fourth century and even later, avoids and displays a deep suspicion of the language of person in this context. It will, in fact, only be converted to this usage by the clarification and vindication of similar language in Greek theology by the Cappadocian Fathers. This will be the reason for much of the misunderstanding and confusion on the part of Latin theology over what Greek theology was saying for much of the later controversy.

Final verdict on the adequacy of the trinitarian theology of Hippolytus and Tertullian has to be determined by the measure of its success in addressing the problem endemic to Economic Trinitarianism as initiated by the Apologists, namely, the status of the Word and Spirit as immanent in God prior to their extrapolation as distinct persons in the Economy. In the eternity of God and prior to their emergence as distinct persons, are the Word and Spirit anything more than references to immanent attributes of God devoid of distinct subsistence? Though both writers emphasise strongly that the Word and the Spirit belong to God and will never contemplate placing them on the same level as creatures, they fail nevertheless to assert distinct existence of the Word and Spirit prior to the Economy. In fact, they do not even attempt to do so. Inheriting and accepting the theological perspective of the Apologists, they accept also the basis of that perspective, the distinction between the immanent Logos and the expressed Logos. Since they do not question the system within which they operate, *a fortiori* they do not question the basis of that system. As with the Apologists, the Stoic distinction is still here an imprisoning straitjacket.

Recognising this limitation, however, should not blind us to the achievement of these writers, and especially Tertullian. Economic Trinitarianism has been developed here to the limits of its capacity, even to the point where both its strengths and its inadequacies begin to become recognisable. Tertullian has forged new tools of thought and terminology and created a language with which one may speak coherently of God as both one and three. This will yet prove a sound investment and pay handsome dividends.

Origen of Alexandria

Turning to Eastern and Greek theology in the third century is to find oneself confronted by the dominating figure of Origen of Alexandria (c .185-254/5) A sign of contradiction even in his own lifetime, Origen's thought has remained down to the present day the subject of varied interpretation. This applies especially to his theology of God as Trinity. Here he has often been seen, sometimes even by the same writer, as both the father of Arianism and of fourth century orthodoxy – a mind-boggling achievement!

It is neither possible nor necesary to give here even a summary biography of this great Christian scholar or to describe his wide theological enterprise. The concentration here will be confined to the basic and significant aspects of his theology of the Trinity. Yet some general remarks on the work of Origen and on the present state of Origen scholarship will be helpful.

Most of Origen's literary output consists of biblical commentaries and homilies. This is not the kind of writing which lends itself to systematic statement of theological issues. To discern Origen's thought on any particular topic, one has to collate various references scattered over his vast corpus of works. Fortunately, however, Origen also wrote a work in which he outlined his general theological thought and approach. This is the work usually entitled in English *On First Principles*. Though this work discusses a wide range of doctrinal issues, the first and foremost of these is the triadic understanding of God. From this discussion and related references elsewhere, a good idea can be formed of Origen's trinitarian theology. Yet, here more than in any other area, Origen has been the subject of differing and even contradictory interpretations down to the present day.

There are many reasons for this curious situation, but the basic problem in both ancient and modern times has been the adoption of a faulty approach towards establishing the actual text of Origen's works which then created the problem of understanding an uncertain text. Fortunately, recent Origen scholarship is engaged in rectifying this flawed methodology and as a result a new, more coherent and more convincing understanding of the great Alexandrian's thought is emerging.

The outstanding feature of Origen's thought, which above all characterises him, is his independence and originality of mind, a rare quality at any time but especially in the world of ancient Christianity where strict adherence to tradition was particularly prized and any apparent departure from it aroused immediate suspicion. Though clearly well read in the Christain literature available in his time, Origen is never content simply to repeat his predecessors. In his Preface to *On First Principles* he outlines the Rule of Faith as he has learnt it in the church of Alexandria. This for him is a fixed teaching handed down in the churches from the Apostles and not open to dispute. But this teaching leaves many questions unresolved and therefore open to speculation. The probing mind of Origen seizes eagerly on this grey area and attempts to throw light upon it. This is a work of speculation, a theology of research as it has been called, a theology in process. The viewpoints Origen advocates here, when he does commit himself to a viewpoint, are always tentative and provisional – until something more convincing is proposed. In this sense he is the humblest and least dogmatic of theologians. The originality of his mind, his erudition, the range of ideas he is able to envisage and hold in tension, all this ensures that he is able to break out of the stereotypes of his time and chart a new course. This is a mind whose thought transcends that of its contemporaries and its time. But the measure whereby it achieves this is also the measure whereby its own time, and subsequent ages also, fails to keep pace with it. There is an elusive universality to the thought of Origen which makes it attractive in every age, yet allows it to belong to none.

Turning now from these general comments to Origen's theology of God as Trinity, one notes first the traditional and basic assertion that there is one God who is the Father of the Lord Jesus Christ and the Sender of the Holy Spirit. The first statement of the Rule of Faith is 'that God is one, who created and set in order all things and who, when nothing existed, caused the universe to be – This just and good God [is] the Father of our Lord Jesus Christ …'. (F *Prins* Pref 4; tr Butterworth; so throughout) This one God is 'the fount from which the one [the Son] is born and the other [the Spirit] proceeds'. (ibid 1,2,13) Commenting on the opening verse of the Fourth Gospel, Origen explains that this one God is there called The God/Ho Theos because as God-in-Godself [*Autotheos*] God's divinity is God's own, not derived, whereas the Logos is called simply God/Theos because his divinity, though real and true, is derived from the s upreme God. (*Comm John* 2,2,12-18)

Yet this one, supreme God in generating a Son and breathing forth the Spirit also constitutes a Trinity, Father, Son, Holy Spirit. This is the triadic understanding of God which Christian faith confesses and which forms the basis of its explanation of salvation as now accomplished. The term Trinity/Trias occurs a number of times in the writings of Origen. The three members of the Triad he describes as three *hypostases*: 'There are three Hypostases, the Father and the Son and the Holy Spirit'. (*Comm John* 2,10,75) The term is applied also to the Son and the Spirit individually. (*Comm John* 1,24,151; *F Prins* 1,2,2; 1,1,3) The term does not have in Origen, however, the precise connotation it will later attain in the course of the later controversy. In Origen's time and for long after the word could have different, though closely related, shades of meaning. But for Origen in this context it signifies the distinct and individual existence of the members of the Triad. It corresponds in him, therefore, to *prosopon* in Hippolytus and *persona* in Tertullian. But *hypostasis* in one of its shades of meaning could also refer to the being or substance of something and etymologically it was identical with the Latin term *substantia*. Origen's use of this term, therefore, to describe God as three carried with it seeds of semantic and theological confusion which unfortunately would yet be all too fully realised.

Origen is now faced, like all his predecessors, with the question how to describe the being of the Son and the Spirit in relation to the Father, the source from which they derive. Here especially he displays his originality by breaking with his predecessors and asserting explicitly the eternal generation and existence of the Son and procession of the Spirit. In describing 'how the unbegotten God becomes Father of the only-begotten Son', he writes: 'This is an eternal and everlasting begetting, as brightness is begotten of light'. (*F Prins* 1,2,4) 'The term everlasting or eternal', he later explains, 'properly denotes that which had no beginning of existence and can never cease to be what it is'. (ibid 1,2,11) Origen sums up this concept of the eternal generation and distinct existence of the Son in a simple, succinct formula: 'there never was when he was not'. (ibid 1,2,9; 4,4,1 bis; *Comm Romans* 1,5) This is the formula which Arius will later directly contradict. Similarly, eternal, distinct existence is also predicated of the Holy Spirit: 'The Holy Spirit would never have been included in the unity of the Trinity, that is, along with God the unchangeable Father and with his Son, unless he had always been the Holy Spirit'. (*F Prins* 1,3,4)

In asserting eternal, distinct existence of the Son and the Spirit, Origen has here rejected the applicability to the Trinity of the Stoic distinction of the immanent and expressed Logos. In doing so he has also effectively abandoned the approach of Economic Trinitarianism with which his predecessors had struggled and which this distinction had imposed. The triadic distinctions which others had recognised and acknowledged in and from the Economy of Salvation, Origen sees as belonging to the eternal being of God. This is a major and radical break with previous, and by now traditional, trinitarian theology.

The question persists, however, how to describe the status or being of the eternal Son and Spirit vis-a-vis the Father, the one God. Origen is at one here with his predecessors in emphatically rejecting any idea that the Son or the Spirit can be described as creatures, brought into existence from non-existence. Yet, their being is derived from the Father and they exist distinct from the Father. Origen's answer to this question is, in effect, that the divinity of the Father, that which makes God to be God, is communicated fully and eternally to the Son and the Spirit. Though Origen has no precise, established terminology at his disposal to express this idea – such terminology will only be hammered out in the course of the future controversy – he effectively conveys the point in a number of other ways. It emerges from the distinction which he constantly observes and asserts between the substantial, absolute being and attributes of the Son and the Spirit and the accidental, contingent being of creatures. For example, the Son is immutable, omnipotent, Son not by adoption but in nature, the Spirit is always holy, not made holy. (F Prins 1,2,4; 1,2,10; 1,3,3) It is implied in his concept of pre-existent Wisdom, his basic and primary christological concept, who is eternally the perfect reflection of the Father. He appeals also to the language of nature and substance to express the relation of Father and Son. This relation 'pertains to the nature of deity'; the Son is 'a Son by nature'; this relation consists of 'the unity of nature and substance common to a father and son'. (F Prins 1,1,8; 1,2,5; 1,2,6) That Origen, despite the implications of the last illustration, does not conceive the relation of Father and Son in generic terms, a nature common to members of a class or category, is clear from the fact that God, and therefore the Godness of that God, is not merely one but unique and therefore cannot be multiplied among members of a class without destroying or diluting itself. Godness or divinity for Origen is not a common noun. To think otherwise would be to adopt

'the absurd fables of those who imagine for themselves certain
emanations, splitting the divine nature into parts, and in so far as
they can, dividing God the Father'. (ibid 1,2,6) The Son, on the
contrary, is begotten from the Father's own substance. (ibid 4,4,1)
In sum, when one takes into account all the references of Origen
to the relation of the Son and the Spirit to the Father, justice is only
done to his understanding by recognising that for him the divinity
of the Father is eternally and fully communicated to the Son and
the Spirit.

In this connection it is intriguing to note that the term *homoousios*, the later touchstone of Nicene orthodoxy, occurs once in a
trinitarian context in the extant works of Origen. This, however, is
in a fragment of the *Commentary on Hebrews* preserved in a Latin
translation of Rufinus and since there is no independent check on
this translation, the suspicion that the word, though occurring in
its Greek form, may have been Rufinus' own insertion cannot be
disproved. But whether or not the term here is authentic, it does
nevertheless express Origen's understanding of the relation of the
Son and Spirit to the Father.

This conclusion is reinforced when one looks at the way Origen
conceives this communication of divinity. The images of light
from the sun, water from the source, familiar since the Apologists,
occur again. Origen's favourite image for the generation of the
Son is that of light proceeding from the sun. As usual with him, he
adduces scriptural evidence for this preference, Hebrews 1:3, Colossians 1:15, Wisdom 7:25-26. In Colossians and Hebrews Christ
is called 'the image of the invisible God', 'the brightness of his glory
and express image of his substance'. For Origen, however, these
New Testament texts simply reproduce and re-echo the passage
in the Book of Wisdom where pre-existent, eternal Wisdom, Origen's primary christological concept, is described as 'the breath of
the power of God, a pure effluence of the glory of the Almighty,
the brightness of eternal light, unspotted mirror of the working
and power of God'. (*F Prins* 2,1,5; 2,1,9) But when he seeks a more
precise analogy in human experience to describe the Son's generation and the communication of divinity it involves, his thought
turns to the immanent processes of the mind, the act of will proceeding from the mind yet remaining within it. 'As an act of the
will', he writes, 'proceeds from the mind without either cutting
off any part of the mind or being separated or divided from it, in
some similar fashion has the Father begotten the Son'. (ibid 1,2,6;
cf also 4,4,1) He contrasts this immanent process with that of the

Gnostic theory of emanations emerging and separating from God: 'the absurd fables of those who imagine for themselves certain emanations, splitting the divine nature into parts and dividing God the Father'. (ibid 1,2,6)

A special word deserves to be said on Origen's theology of the Holy Spirit. The discussion of this topic in *On First Principles* (1,3,1-4; 2,7,1-4) constitutes the first specific tract on the Spirit in patristic literature. This is a document which will later significantly influence and be re-echoed by both Athanasius and especially Basil of Caesarea in his classic work *On the Holy Spirit*. Origen's discussion of the Spirit is based totally on the biblical revelation. Neither reason alone nor pagan philosophy, he asserts, possess any knowledge of the Spirit of God. (*F Prins* 1,3,1) In his Rule of Faith he states that 'the Holy Spirit is united in honour and dignity with the Father and the Son' (ibid Pref 4), a statement which implies the divinity of the Spirit and equality with the Father and Son. It is a statement which will later form the basis of Basil's argument for the divinity of the Spirit and through Basil will be incorporated into the Creed of Nicaea at the Council of Constantinople in 381. Like the Son, the Spirit also has origin in and from the Father. Though in the Preface to *On First Principles* he leaves open the question whether this also might be a generation, he never elsewhere endorses this position. In the *Commentary on John* he maintains that the Spirit proceeds from the Father through the Son. (2,10,77) But most of his discussion of the Spirit is devoted to the role of the Spirit in Salvation History. Here he witnesses again to the classic and standard concept of the Spirit in the early Church, that of the prophetic Spirit who inspired the Prophets and Apostles, is the source of biblical inspiration and who continues to activate the witness of Christians through his gifts. The passage of the New Testament from which Origen derives in particular his vision of the working of the Holy Spirit is 1 Corinthians 12,4-7, the Spirit as the source of gifts in the Christian community and its members. The supreme gift of the Spirit, 'the peculiar grace and work of the Holy Spirit' (*F Prins* 1,3,7), is grace, holiness. The Spirit is above all the Sanctifier. In highlighting the sanctifying role of the Holy Spirit, Origen is developing the programme of Irenaeus in retrieving and reintroducing the Pauline concept of the life-giving Spirit. The influence of Irenaeus, indeed, is very detectable in many aspects of Origen's theology. Through Origen this Pauline pneumatology will later exercise great influence on Athanasius and Basil of Caesarea and through them will make a lasting contribution to trinitarian theology.

Origen concludes his discussion of the Trinity in *On First Principles* with a discussion of the respective roles of the three Persons in Salvation History. This is the area which later scholastic theology will term *opera divina ad extra*. For Origen the culmination of this whole activity is the sanctifying work of the Holy Spirit. He attributes distinct roles here to each of the Persons, thereby disagreeing, as many modern theologians do, with a strict understanding and application of the scholastic principle of appropriation. Yet he maintains that it is the one God who is active here throughout and that this threefold activity witnesses to the unity of the Trinity. 'Here', he writes, 'we are most clearly shown that there is no separation in the Trinity, but that this which is called the "gift of the Spirit" is ministered through the Son and worked by God the Father. ... This is the testimony we bear to the unity of Father, Son and Holy Spirit'. (1,3,7-8)

Though the overall thrust and intention of Origen's theology of the Trinity is reasonably clear, difficulties can arise, judged by the standards of later orthodoxy, when some of his statements are taken and judged in isolation. This concerns especially the 'subordinationist' status of the Son which certain texts seem to imply at first sight and which forms the basis of the Subordinationism so often attributed to Origen. The following must suffice here as an example: 'We, who maintain that even the sensible world is made by the Creator of all things, hold that the Son is not mightier than the Father, but subordinate. And we say this because we believe him who said: "The Father who sent me is greater than I".' (*Against Celsus* 8,15) Taken on its own, this text seems clear, explicit and final. One must, however, be more cautious before resting in this final judgement. It needs to be remembered that Origen is writing at a time when a system of precise concepts, and a corresponding precise language to express these concepts, did not yet exist in trinitarian theology. The language available to him wherewith to express his thought is therefore fluid, not fixed and precise. In this situation, a certain licence in expression must be expected and allowed for. Further, it is important always with Origen not to judge any text in isolation. The whole corpus of his writings have to be taken into account and each statement placed alongside other related statements before one is in a position to really interpret his thought. Terminology also creates a particular difficulty here. There is the confusion which then existed between the verbs and their derivatives, *gignomai*, to come to be, and *gennao*, to give birth. As *gennao* was at this time often spelt with one 'n', the perfect participle passive of both verbs often had the same form, though differing in meaning: *genetos* could mean either having come to be or begotten, born. Where Origen used *genetos* of the Son in the sense of 'begotten' later interpreters, ancient and modern, often took him to mean 'having come to be, created'. Moreover, *genetos* in the sense of having come to be is susceptible of two meanings, origin simply or coming into existence from non-existence. Origen, who insists so strongly on the eternal existence of the Son and on the fact that he is not a creature, when using *genetos* in this sense of the Son clearly means eternal origin simply, not a beginning of existence. A clear distinction, however, between these two meanings did not emerge until the next century.

In the light of these and other factors, Origen, in the text quoted as in other similar texts, has to be understood as referring to the Son's eternal origin from the Father and not to the temporal origin of a creature. The 'subordination' in view here, therefore, is one simply of origin, a totally orthodox concept, and an acknowlegement again of the trinitarian *taxis*.

Origen's contribution to the developing trinitarian theology of the pre-Nicene period is considerable and significant and in all kinds of subtle ways will exercise an influence on the great debate of the next century. The basis of his contribution lies undoubtedly in his abandonment of the Economic Trinitarianism of his predecessors, based on his refusal to be seduced by the distinction of the *logos endiathetos\prophorikos*, and his emphatic assertion that the distinctions in the divine Triad belong to the eternal being of God and do not arise simply from the Economy. Here again he has accepted and effectively developed the direction of Irenaeus' thought. His language of three Hypostases, matching that of Hippolytus and Tertullian, provides Eastern Greek theology with a way of describing God as Three, though in many quarters this expression will for long remain either unknown or unacceptable. His appeal to the immanent processes of the mind to illustrate the eternal generation of the Son, another idea developed from hints in Irenaeus, will live on and eventually stimulate some of St Augustine's most profound, if also in ways debatable, thought on the understanding of the Trinity. Origen has no fixed, precise term for the divinity, the Godness, which the Father communicates to the Son and the Spirit. As with so much trinitarian theology, this is a development of the future. But his understanding of this, as with all the other pre-Nicenes, is dynamic rather than essentialist, the power of God flowing from Father to Son to Spirit and thence outward to operate in creation and salvation history.

In comparison with the other pre-Nicene theologians, Origen placed the theology of the Trinity on a new level. That was his achievement. But, as remarked earlier, the measure in which he transcended the mind of his own and later times, was also the measure in which these times failed to understand him and ended by misinterpreting him. His theological enterprise was very personal, very much his own. Few, outside the circle of his own students, could fully assimilate it in all its breadth and depth. Universally acknowledged for his erudition and scholarly acumen, he became the subject of selective and erroneous interpretation. His influence can be discerned on conflicting sides in the great controversy of the following century. His theological legacy, therefore, through no fault of his own, was an ambivalent one. But he had ensured, at least, that he could never be ignored.

Conclusion

In the history of trinitarian theology the pre-Nicene period tends to be approached simply as an introduction to the great controversy of the fourth century and assessed and judged in terms of the extent to which it produced and fashioned the ideas and forces which there came into conflict. It is often seen and presented simply as a backdrop to the real drama. This is unfortunate. Though the seeds of later conflict are certainly being sown here and the deeper origin of the later controversy must be placed here, nevertheless, this period also deserves to be listened to for its own sake. If it lacks the precision of theological concept and terminology which the Controversy will eventually produce, it displays another virtue, a freedom of expression and illustration which speaks immediacy and actuality and ensures that the voice of the living faith is heard in the theology. This is a virtue which later trinitarian theology, for all its orthodoxy, will seldom be accused of.

It is the pre-Nicene period which first faces and takes up the task of articulating the specifically Christian understanding of God. Its basic statement of faith has two clear poles: there is one God; but this one God, in entering human history to redeem and save it, displays a threefold character, Father, Son, and Holy Spirit. The distinctions named in this Triad are real, not purely verbal. For Christian faith, therefore, God is both One and Three. The question for theology is how to reconcile and explain these two apparently conflicting attributes of God. This question quickly reduces itself to that of how to conceive the relation of the Son and the Spirit to the Father, the one God. Two easy but opposing solutions to this question quickly present themselves: Modalism, which denies that the triadic distinctions are real and sees them as purely verbal; and Subordinationism, which so reduces the status of the Son and the Spirit as to deny them true divinity and thus leaves the unique divinity of the Father fully intact. Both these positions, when appearing in extreme and explicit form, are quickly identified as heretical and rejected. But, in the absence as yet of any established, canonised doctrinal formulation, a certain oscillation between these two poles is discernible and acceptable. The theologians of this period are all resolutely anti-modalist. Their central interest lies in asserting that salvation, the solution of the human predicament, has been finally accomplished in the event of Jesus Christ and the Spirit and from this vantage point explaining all history and all reality. Since God, and God alone, can be the author of final salvation, and not any intermediary, however exalted, what meets us humans in Christ and the Spirit is this one God. Yet, Christ and the Spirit are not simply other names for God; there is a real distinction. These theologians, therefore, are committed to acknowledging the reality of the triadic distinctions while still maintaining the assertion that there is one God. The basic question is how to conceive the relation between the Son and the Spirit to the one God, the Father. Both identity and distinction have to be asserted here. The problem is how to understand this and how to express this understanding in the prevailing language.

It is in this context that the Apologists press into service the distinction between the immanent Word and the expressed Word and on this basis attempt to explain the relation of the Son to the Father. The Father has eternally within him his Logos or Thought; when he wills, he expresses forth this immanent Word as his agent in creation and salvation history. This expression of the immanent Word is the generation of the Son who now exists distinct from the Father. A similar process of expression is presumed for the Spirit, but discussion of the Spirit is not a prominent topic in this period. This use of the Stoic distinction was a useful device for the Apologists in their efforts to communicate with their pagan contemporaries, but it created problems for their theology of the Trinity. In this perspective, the Word/Son and the Spirit would seem to come into existence as distinct beings only when God wills it and for the purpose of the economy of creation and salvation. Prior to this the Word and Spirit seem to mean simply eternal, immanent aspects or attributes of God and to lack distinct, personal existence. The one God here seems to unfold into and become a Trinity at the moment of the economy. As distinct existents, the Word and the Spirit are not here eternal but, rather, products of the will of God, subordinate, dependent, in fact, creatures, however exalted. If this is so, then God precisely as God has not yet fully entered human history and salvation cannot be said to be finally accomplished. The Christian Gospel would here seem to be threatened at its very basis.

The Apologists were not conscious of all the implications which their introduction of the Stoic distinction involved. They are, however, aware of its limitations and strive to overcome them. Irenaeus, in particular, is uncomfortable with this perspective and seeks earnestly, though ultimately unsuccessfully, to envisage the triadic distinctions as existing eternally in God. Meanwhile, Tertullian, himself an adherent of Economic Trinitarianism, provides a language wherewith to speak of God as One and Three: God is one substance existing in three persons. He is not able, however, to explain clearly the meaning of these concepts and Latin theology will long remain suspicious of this language of three persons in God.

Theology at this stage had arrived at something of an impasse. Little progress was to be expected by continuing to travel the same road. A new direction was required. This is what Origen provided. He abandons completely the perspective of Economic Trinitarianism and attributes the triadic distinctions to the eternal being of God and speaks of them as three Hypostases. He is careful, however, to preserve the traditional hierarchic order or *taxis* in God: the one God, in eternally expressing God's Wisdom, generates the Son and breathes forth the Spirit. God is eternally Trinity. Origen's theology, however, is not easy to understand and it quickly becomes the subject of selective and erroneous interpretation. His influence, therefore, will be contradictory in its results.

A glimpse of the understanding of God as Trinity in the later stages of the pre-Nicene period is provided by the correspondence between the bishops of Rome and Alexandria, both named Dionysius, in the 260s AD. The bishop of Alexandria, an early student of Origen, in combating certain modalist tendencies within his jurisdiction, had spoken of God as three Hypostases but had also used some illustrations of the relation of the Son to the Father which suggested a subordinationist understanding. He described the Son of God as 'alien in *ousia* from the Father, just as the planter of the vine is to the vine, and the shipbuilder is to the ship'. (Athanasius, *Opinion of Dionysius*, 4 – tr Hanson) Dionysius of Rome, on the matter being reported to him, wrote to his colleague at Alexandria to protest against this teaching. He particularly objected to the language of three Hypostases as used of God and insisted, apparently, that the Son be regarded as *homoousios*/ 'of one substance' with the Father, an influence here perhaps of Tertullian's language of 'one substance'. In reply, the bishop of Alexandria admitted and apologised for his careless use of the unhappy illustrations and showed himself prepared to accept, though apparently with some hesitation, the term *homoousios*. Evidence for this affair is only available to us from later quotation and has to remain somewhat vague. But it seems reasonable to conclude that at this stage the language of three Persons/ Hypostases for God is still regarded with suspicion in many parts of the Church and that the term *homoousios*, introduced perhaps as a counter-emphasis, has already appeared on the theological map, though its meaning is far from clear and its acceptability far from general.

As we approach the end of the pre-Nicene period, theology of the Trinity may be briefly described as follows. The Church believes and confesses one God who in the Economy of Salvation is revealed as Father, Son and Holy Spirit. Theology has engaged in the speculative task of attempting to articulate a coherent understanding of this position of faith. Some of its statements have met with ready acceptance, others, such as the language of three persons, are regarded in many quarters with deep suspicion. This theological endeavour has been largely a speculative one, undertaken by private individuals and has not as yet received any official endorsement. It has to convince simply on the basis of its own merits, not on the basis of official approval and acceptance. There is as yet no canonised doctrinal formulation in the Church, no statement of orthodoxy. Much further analysis and debate will be required before this will be possible. One cannot say that there yet exists even a theological consensus, except in very broad terms. There are, however, already ominous signs that when this debate occurs, as occur it must, confusion and division will figure prominently in it.

Note

1. The writers and the works discussed here are: St Justin Martyr [d. c.167], *1 Apology, 2 Apology, Dialogue with Trypho the Jew*; Tatian the Syrian [d. c.180], *Address to the Greeks*; Athenagoras of Athens [d. c.185], *Supplication for the Christians*; Theophilus of Antioch [d. c.190], *To Autolycus*.

2. On the understanding of God in Greek philosophy and its influence on Christian thought over the patristic period, see now the study of Gerard Watson, published in this series, *Greek Philosophy and the Christian Notion of God*, Dublin, Columba Press, 1994.

3. Some scholars, however, question the authenticity of this text in Theophilus and suspect a later interpolation.

CHAPTER 4

The Great Controversy

The occurrence of a major debate in the Church concerning an understanding of God as Trinity was inevitable. The issue was too central and basic and too open to conflicting and contradictory positions to be avoided. But what would spark off this debate, that only the accident of history would decide. That accident was the viewpoint of one Arius, a priest in the church of Alexandria, as this came to be publicly aired in or around the year 318 AD.

The debate, which began innocently enough in Alexandria at this time, very quickly developed into a major controversy which eventually involved the whole Church of the time, arousing deep passions and causing deep divisions. It called forth the first General Council in the history of the Church, the Council of Nicaea in 325. It was resolved, in theory and principle at least, at the next General Council, the First Council of Constantinople in 381. This great controversy, which is still the subject of keen study, is complicated in terms of events, personalities and ideas. Its history cannot be treated here in any detail and, in any case, a number of excellent studies are readily available. I will attempt rather to concentrate on an outline of the movement of ideas which the affair presents, as this turns and twists its way, like a meandering river, through the various phases of the debate towards a final solution. But before proceeding with this programme, some general comments on basic aspects of this whole affair may be helpful.

There is first a question of nomenclature. The affair has traditionally been called the Arian Controversy and the Trinitarian Controversy. The accuracy of both descriptions, however, has been questioned. As the debate developed, Arius, in fact, ceased to play any central role in it and, in any case, he died in 335/336 when the real battle was only about to begin. Historically, his significance lies in first making the issue a public one, not for any influence he exercised on the course of the debate. It is somewhat odd, therefore, that he should give his name to a discussion which he accidentally initiated but which proceeded more or less in total independence of him. Actually, throughout the conflict no adher-

ent of this viewpoint in any of its forms ever described himself as
an Arian or a follower of Arius. Pope Julius I, writing to Eastern
bishops assembled in Antioch in 341, in effect accused them of being followers of Arius. In reply, the bishops angrily rejected the
accusation, as they saw it, stating: 'We are not followers of Arius.
How could we who are bishops follow a presbyter!' The issue
Arius raised was independent of him personally and he soon
ceased to play any central role in its discussion. The term 'Arian'
was an opprobious one only used by one side of its opponents –
Athanasius, for example, called them 'Arian-maniacs' – and dis-
owned by them. Historically, therefore, there is a certain distortion involved in describing the affair as the 'Arian' Controversy.
Yet, the description is traditional and it can claim some justification on the basis that the conflict was sparked off by the affair of
Arius himself.

The expression 'Trinitarian Controversy' has been questioned
on the ground that until late in the discussion the question of the
status of the Holy Spirit was not an explicit issue. For a long period
the sole issue was the status of the Son and the relation of the Son
to the Father. This was the issue Arius originally raised and which
for long remained the sole issue. For this reason, it has been maintained, the controversy was not originally or for a long period
properly trinitarian.

This point, however, is somewhat pedantic. As the response of
Nicaea and even Arius' own extant writings show, the context of
the dispute in and from its beginning was the Church's credal
confession of faith in God as Triad, Father, Son and Holy Spirit.
Even if the question of the Spirit remained in the background,
therefore, for a long period, it was involved implicitly in the context of the dispute from the beginning and inevitably it did eventually become an explicit issue. The controversy, taken as a whole,
has a coherent logic to it which the explicitly trinitarian character
of its final phase brings into the open. The traditional description
'Trinitarian Controversy', therefore, may be accepted as apt and
accurate.

A danger which the student needs especially to be alert to in
approaching the history of this controversy is one involved in all
historical study, but particularly perhaps where the history of
ideas is concerned. This is the danger of reading history back-
wards and succumbing to the insidious temptation of allowing
hindsight to colour and determine one's judgement of issues in an
earlier stage of development. In the present context this requires
not allowing the later orthodoxy which the Controversy eventual-

ly established to prejudice one's assessment of the conflicting viewpoints which characterised the earlier course of the debate. It is important to bear in mind that the Church entered this dispute possessing no established doctrinal consensus concerning the understanding of God as Triad. There was as yet no canonised formulation of orthodox doctrine. If there had been, no controversy could have taken place. The previous period, as we have seen, had produced various tentative efforts at developing such an understanding. These, however, were efforts of private theologians and, though influential in developing a climate of opinion, they had never received the official acknowledgement which would have given them the status of established doctrine. Moreover, this tentative, unfinished theology contained within itself unresolved tensions and was open to different and conflicting interpretations. In the absence of established doctrinal criteria, opposing viewpoints could claim some respectability on the basis of previous tradition. It is not surprising, therefore, that there was little black or white in the clash of viewpoints which marked the opening phases of the ensuing Controversy. Only conflict could resolve the tensions inherent in the theological tradition.

A new and often disconcerting factor in the situation as it developed was the intervention and role of the Emperor in Church affairs and theological discussion. Following the Edict of Toleration in 313, Constantine came more and more to espouse the cause of Christianity and even to patronise the Church, a sharp reversal of fortune for a body which had just emerged from the virulent persecution of Diocletian. When he became sole Emperor in 324, Constantine was already regarded as the Christian Emperor, even though he was not baptised until on his death bed in 337. His active interest in Church affairs seems to have been determined both by a genuine faith and political interest. It should be remembered that one of the functions and titles of the Roman Emperor was that of High Priest, Pontifex Maximus, of the Roman state religion, a position Constantine continued to hold throughout his life as Emperor. Constantine seems to have felt that a similar imperial responsibility extended also to his newly espoused religion, Christianity. In any case, he involved himself actively in Church disputes, sought earnestly to promote agreement and gave civil sanction to official Church decisions. Decrees of the Church now became also imperial policy and law. Those who refused to accept these decrees were liable as a result to have the sanction of the law invoked against them. Bishops, in these circumstances, might be deposed from their sees, exiled, even put to work in the imperial

mines. The most famous victim of this imperial displeasure was
Athanasius of Alexandria, deposed and banished five times from
his see.

This kind of imperial involvement in Church affairs inevitably
ensured that political intrigue became part of doctrinal discussion. The age of the court prelate had arrived. Some churchmen
were uncomfortable with this situation and opposed to it, some
gloried in it, the majority accepted it as in the nature of things. Ancient times were used to the idea of an official state religion and
even Christianity was prepared to allow some role to the Emperor
in matters of faith and doctrine. But this factor adds its own measure of complication to the history of the already complex discussion which is the Trinitarian Controversy.

A significant feature of the controversy as it developed was the
different approach to the central issue which emerged between
the Greek East and the Latin West. The controversy arose in the
East and it always remained a basically Eastern affair. In fact,
large parts of the West scarcely knew about it until it was over.
The Western response was largely dictated from Rome, though
there is little doubt that this was representative of Western senti-
ment generally. This response largely took the form of a reaction
to an Eastern process of thought which it regarded as moving too
far, too quickly and too speculatively. The difference can be
summed up, somewhat simplistically perhaps, yet not unfairly,
by observing that while the East wished to put the emphasis on
God as Three, Rome, suspicious of this approach, wished to keep
the emphasis on God as One. That a consensus agreeable to both
sides eventually emerged is a tribute to a small group of thinkers
who were able to transcend narrow loyalties and prejudices and
approach the issues in a broader and deeper manner. This difference between East and West, which runs throughout the Controversy, cannot be pursued here in any detail, but it needs to be kept
in mind as we proceed with our story.

The history of the Trinitarian Controversy may be approached
in different ways. The outline presented here will see the whole
affair as involving three periods or phases based on the determining influence of prevailing imperial policy. The first or opening
phase runs from the beginning of the trouble around 318 to the
death of Constantine in 337. This phase centres around the Council of Nicaea in 325 and reaction to it, but the role of Constantine is
crucial throughout. The second or middle phase is dominated
especially by the policy of Constantius, one of Constantine's sons
and successors, and runs from his accession in 337 to his death in

361. The final phase covers the period 361 to the Council of Constantinople in 381 and is much influenced by the opposing policies first of Valens and then later and finally of Theodosius.

In the account presented here the focus of attention will be on the theological issue and the conflict of ideas which this involved. This theological discussion, however, did not take place in a historical vacuum. It did not take the form of a polite academic seminar. It took place in the real world of events and personalities and was heavily influenced by this context at every stage. This setting and context needs to be borne in mind if the meandering development of the theological issue is to be understood. The account given here will therefore preface its outline of the theological issue in each phase with a summary outline of the events which determine that period and have a significant bearing on the theological discussion. It will adopt a structure, therefore, of an outline of the historical scene followed by a presentation of the theological issue.

The Opening Phase, c. 318-337

The Historical Scene

The Trinitarian Controversy began, apparently suddenly and rather innocently, in or around the year 318 in the great Christian centre of Alexandria. Arius, a priest in charge of the church in a part of the city known as Baucalis, gave public expression to views on the status of the Son of God and his relation to the Father. These views soon brought Arius into conflict with his bishop, Alexander, and eventually led to his excommunication and banishment from Egypt. Arius, however, did not accept his degradation easily. He already had, it seems, considerable support, lay and clerical, in Alexandria, but he now sought support also from farther afield and in more powerful quarters. He pleaded his cause to bishops in the Greek East outside of Egypt, including such powerful figures as Eusebius, bishop of Nicomedia, then the imperial residence, and the scholarly bishop of Caesarea, also named Eusebius. Though many of these bishops must have been very perplexed by the affair, Arius could not but have been gratified by the support he received, especially from the two Eusebiuses. Any hope Alexander had of confining the dispute within his own jurisdiction in Egypt had now vanished. He too was now obliged to circulate his episcopal colleagues in the East in order to discredit Arius and vindicate his own position. But the affair had now effectively passed outside his control and had become a public controversy involving and dividing the whole Church of the East.

Three parties are already discernible in the dispute: an anti-Arian party led by Alexander; a pro-Arian party led by Eusebius of Nicomedia; and a bemused middle party not at all sure what the whole affair was about. This was the confused situation which existed when the Emperor now decided to intervene.

Constantine's intervention took the radical form of calling an assembly of the bishops of the whole Church to meet in Nicaea in May, 325, to deliberate on and resolve the intractable issue which had arisen and was proving so divisive. This was the act of an administrator who felt that all that was needed was a decision to be sanctioned and imposed by imperial decree. Though Constantine was to get his decision and impose his decree, his hopes in the event were to be frustrated. He, and many of his successors after him, were to find that doctrinal questions were not amenable to resolution in this administrative manner. Meanwhile, however, he called his Council, paid the travelling expenses of the bishops and provided accommodation for all in Nicaea. The gathering must have proved something of a disconcerting experience for the attending bishops, many of whom, a few years previously, had been in prison and under torture by similar decree of the Roman Emperor. Something approaching three hundred bishops attended the Council. By the end of the century the number had become fixed at 318, the number of men in Abraham's household according to Genesis 14:14. The figure was probably not far out. The vast majority were from the East, only a handful were present from the West. The bishop of Rome, Sylvester, did not attend but was represented by two delegates, two priests of the church of Rome. The reason for Sylvester's non-attendance is not clear. It may have been for reasons of age, but more likely it reflected suspicion of interference by the Emperor in Church affairs and a desire to maintain some distance from and independance of such interference. Whatever the reason, this presence by proxy at the Council of Nicaea marked the beginning of the papal practice of not participating personally and directly in General Councils.

The Council was in session from May until July of the year 325. Though it took the opportunity of deliberating also on other matters, its main business was to adjudicate on the teaching of Arius. Arius himself was present as was his arch-opponent, Alexander of Alexandria. Indeed, from the point of view of personalities, the question for the Council to decide was which of these to support, Arius or Alexander. As events were to prove, in the run up to the Council Alexander had orchestrated his support more effectively than Arius.

Constantine himself attended the sessions of the Council and took a keen, in the end possibly even a decisive, interest in its deliberations. The assembly was presided over, however, by a Spanish bishop, Ossius, who belonged to Constantine's entourage and at this time was acting as what today might be called his Minister for Religious Affairs. Present also, in attendance on his bishop, was a young deacon from Alexandria named Athanasius, who here steps on to the stage of public history for the first time. Though accounts of the Council, ancient and modern, have often maintained that Athanasius exercised a decisive influence on the debate, this is certainly not true. He was young and only a deacon and, even if the fact that Alexander had chosen him to accompany him marked him as a young man with a future, any contribution he may have made to the discussion certainly did not take place in the public domain.

Though no minutes of the Council of Nicaea have survived, if indeed they ever existed, it is clear from the evidence of later ancient sources that the assembly quickly showed itself resolutely anti-Arian and that this attitude was shared by Constantine and Ossius. The Council eventually issued its final decision in the form of a Creed which, though it mentioned no names, condemned the teaching of Arius as heretical. This decision was endorsed and signed by all the bishops present with but two exceptions, Ossius signing first and the papal representatives in second place. The signatures included such erstwhile supporters of Arius as the bishops of Nicomedia and Caesarea. The two bishops who refused to sign were deposed by the Council and, together with Arius himself, were banished into exile by the Emperor. Constantine had got his decision and imposed it by imperial decree. The shortlived Arian crisis had, apparently, come to an end.

But only apparently. By the year 328 the banished Arians, including Arius himself, were back in Constantine's good graces by simply submitting an innocuous confession of faith of a pre-Nicene form which studiously avoided any mention of the Creed of Nicaea itself. In accepting this position Constantine showed himself prepared to accept a statement of faith which did not explicitly reject Nicaea – something it could do simply by ignoring it. In adopting this position he effectively removed the imperial decree sanctioning Nicaea.

This softening on Nicaea to the point of neutrality on the part of Constantine quickly led to a dramatic change of scene in the East and a reversal of fortune for those who supported the Council. In effect, it brought into existence two opposed parties and initiated the real controversy. These parties comprised the defenders of Nicaea, or Nicenes as we shall here call them, and the opponents of Nicaea or anti-Nicenes. This latter body was for the moment a heterogeneous group which included strict Arians, pro-Arians like Eusebius of Nicomedia and a large middle group which, while certainly not Arian, were very uncomfortable with the statement of Nicaea and especially its touchstone term, *homoousios*, at least in the form this was now being interpreted by such figures as Marcellus of Ancyra. The leader for the moment of this multifaceted anti-Nicene party was that strong personality, Eusebius of Nicomedia. This sudden change of attitude towards Nicaea suggests that the consensus reached at the Council was perhaps more cosmetic than real.

The policy of the anti-Nicene leaders at first was as much political as theological: they sought the rehabilitation of Arius and his supporters and the removal of his chief opponents, especially Athanasius, who had succeeded Alexander as Bishop of Alexandria in 328, Marcellus of Ancyra and Eustathius of Antioch. Soon after becoming bishop, Athanasius refused to obey the command of Constantine to receive Arius back again as a priest in Alexandria, thereby initiating a breach between himself and the Imperial Court which was to last throughout his long life. By the mid 330s all three had been removed from their sees and banished into exile. Marcellus and Eustathius were never restored. Athanasius was to undergo removal and restoration four more times until finally he established himself so strongly in Alexandria that even the Emperor was unable to touch him.

Then in 337 Constantine died. The First Phase of the Trinitarian Controversy had ended with, apparently, in the East a fragile Arianism in the ascendent.

The Theological Issue

An understanding of the theological issues which underlay and determined the series of dramatic events which we have just outlined depends upon the answers to three questions: What was the theological position of Arius? How did the Council of Nicaea counter this position? Why did this conciliar teaching so quickly prove so fragile and so unpopular? To these three questions we must now address ourselves.

The traditional view of the teaching of Arius saw it as a theology strictly so called, that is, an understanding of God simply as God without reference to creation or the economy of salvation. This God was the one God emphatically asserted in biblical and

Christian faith. Arius saw this God as a simple, indivisible Monad. Whatever came forth from this God and came to exist alongside God could not be, in any strict sense of the term, truly divine but had to be simply a creature of God. Since the Son of God had manifestly come forth from God, this Son was, just as manifestly, brought into existence by God and was a creature. The Son, therefore, and *a fortiori*, of course, the Holy Spirit, was not truly divine, not truly God. From this basic and simple concept of God, according to this view, and the denial of the divinity of the Son which it entailed, all the other tenets of Arianism logically followed.

This traditional view of the basis and origin of Arius' theology has been challenged in recent years. According to this more recent view, the starting-point of Arius' thought is not a strict theology or understanding of God as such, but rather a christology and indeed, more precisely, a soteriology, a particular view of redemption and the Redeemer-figure which this view entails. Arius saw redemption, according to this view, in moral terms, as a breaking out of the cycle of moral weakness and evil which envelops the human scene to union with God. Redemption was a moral achievement. The Redeemer was the one who achieved this union with God and in so doing made it possible for all to share this union with him. This Redeemer was the Word of God become incarnate as Jesus Christ. But since the Redeemer achieved this union with God, he could not have been one with God from the very beginning or in his essenial being. He had to be less than God, in fact, a creature, however otherwise exalted.[1]

A refinement of this view maintains that Arius' central problem was to develop a theology which could accommodate the notion of 'a crucified God'. Since the true God could not suffer or die, Jesus Christ, the Word Incarnate, who did suffer and die, could not be truly God, truly divine. He had to be less than God.[2]

This recent view has, I think, established the point that christology was much more central and prominent in the Arian system than the older understanding allowed for. But, if Arius' basic problem was how to accommodate the notion of 'a crucified God', this meant his problem really was how to accommodate the idea of a true Incarnation. For Arius, the true God could not be the subject of the limiting experiences which incarnate existence involved, and the apex of these was suffering and death. For him, therefore, the Incarnate had to be less than God. The concept of Incarnation was the crux of the issue.

Arius' christology, therefore, led him back to and reinforced his theology, his understanding of God as a strict, undifferentiated Monad. From this basic position, the whole Arian theological system followed with devasting logic. In this way, as it seems to this writer, the recent view, when fully analysed, leads one back to the older view, but now acknowledging the central role of christology in the Arian system.

The Creed issued by the Council of Nicaea was designed to directly counter the main points of the teaching of Arius and it can be understood only in the light of that teaching. It is necessary, therefore, to outline the basics of Arius' thought before examining the text of Nicaea. These may be summarised in a schematic way as follows:

a) God is a Monad, an indivisible One. To admit another to this status would mean dividing the indivisible and destroying the notion of God.

b) The Son has a beginning and is not eternal. He is a creature of God brought into existence from non-existence before creation. Since time, a dimension of creation, did not then exist, the Son 'was born outside time'. Hence Arius' slogan: 'There was when he was not'.

c) Being a creature, the Son is infinitely inferior to God. Like every creature, he is limited in his knowledge of God, knowing only what God wills to reveal to him. And in principle he is liable to change and even to sin, though Arius grants that, due to the prevenient grace of God, he was in fact sinless.

d) The Son is the first and totally pre-eminent of all God's creatures and the one through whom all else was made. This pre-eminence of the Son over all other creatures is recognised in the titles applied to him, which refer to his status in relation to creatures rather than to his relation with God. They are titles of honour reflecting his pre-eminent status. They include such high titles as 'Son of God' and even 'God' which are and may be used of him provided it is recognised that they are simply courtesy titles and do not have a real meaning. As Arius put it, the Son 'is called God not truly but in name only'.

It is easy to recognise that Arius' approach to the question of God belongs within and is determined by the general framework of the Economic Trinitarianism of the pre-Nicene period. This gave Arian theology at first sight a traditional, even a conservative, flavour and explains why so many at the time did not see any great novelty in it. But Arius brought the basic presuppositions of this approach to their logical conclusion and in so doing went far beyond what any of its earlier proponents would have allowed. Where others, approaching the precipice towards which their logic was leading them, suddenly and instinctively cried Halt, Arius, displaying here the logical and rationalist bent of his mind, had no hesitation in going straight over. Arius put his finger on the central problematic of the pre-Nicene theology, Origen apart, and boldly followed its implication. The Logos, eternally immanent in God as God's Mind or Thought, was at a particular moment expressed forth by God for the purpose of the Economy and this expression was the generation of the Son of God. The Son, therefore, had a beginning prior to which he did not exist, for the immanent Logos could not be considered a distinct existent alongside God. It followed very clearly that the Son was a creature.

Crucial to this display of logical reasoning is the way Arius equates origin from God and creation. Only God, the Monad, eternally exists; everything else has origin in and from God and is created. In the case of the Son, the terms origin, generation, creation are simply synonymes. But what perhaps emerges above all from Arius' rationalising theology is the way it focuses attention on the central issue which divides Christian thought from both Judaism and paganism, namely, the doctrine of Incarnation, that God has truly entered and become part of God's own creation. To both Judaism and paganism, with their stress on the utter transcendence and immutability of God, this suggestion was both absurd and blasphemous. From the time of the Apologists and their effort to engage pagan thought, Christianity had assimilated much of the way Hellenistic philosophy had thought about God, ideas which ultimately were irreconcilable with the tenets of Christian faith. Arius brought this tension to the surface and forced the whole Christian world to recognise it and confront it.

The answer of the Council of Nicaea to the teaching of Arius took the form of an existing baptismal Creed into which were inserted a number of anti-Arian phrases and to which were added some statements directly repudiating some well-known Arian slogans. It should be noted that the Creed usually known today as the Nicene Creed and used in the Mass is the version issued later by the Council of Constantinople in 381, not that issued by Nicaea itself. The full text of the statement of Nicaea is as follows:

> We believe in one God, the Father almighty, maker of all things, visible and invisible.
>
> And in one Lord Jesus Christ, the only-begotten generated from the Father, that is, from the being/substance/*ousia* of the Father, God from God, Light from Light, true God from true God, begotten, not made, one in being/substance/ *homoousios* with the Father, through whom all things were

made, those in heaven and those on earth. For us and for our salvation he came down, and became flesh, was made human, suffered, and rose again on the third day. He ascended to the heavens and shall come again to judge the living and the dead.

And in the Holy Spirit.

As for those who say: 'There was [a time] when he was not' and 'Before being begotten he was not', and who declare that he was made from nothing, or that the Son of God is from a different substance/*hypostasis* or being/*ousia*, that is, created or subject to change and alteration – [such persons] the Catholic Church condemns. (Neuner/Dupuis, *The Christian Faith in the Doctrinal Documents of the Catholic Church*, 6 – with minor alterations.)

Before commenting on the specific phrases which the Council inserted into or added to this credal statement, some more general comments will first be in place. The Council probably decided to issue its statement in the form of an adapted existing Creed partly because it recognised that this was the context of the dispute, but more so, perhaps, because it wished not to appear too innovative by speaking as far as possible in the terms of hallowed tradition. It is not known what particular Creed was chosen for this purpose. From its form it can be recognised as an Eastern type Creed and it probably belonged to some church in the general area of Syria or Palestine. The Fathers of Nicaea left the first and third sections of this Creed untouched, that concerning the Father and the bare reference to the Holy Spirit. Doctrine concerning God the Father was not in contention in the dispute and the question of the Holy Spirit had not yet become an explicit issue. The question at issue was the status of the Son and the relation of the Son to the Father. As a modern writer has put it: 'The question which it [Nicaea] had to settle was whether both the Father and the Son were God in exactly the same sense of the the word God.' (G.L. Prestige, *God in Patristic Thought*, 213) Accordingly it was the christological section which here was the focus of attention.

The statement opens with the traditional confession of faith in the one God: 'We believe in one God, the Father, maker of all things, visible and invisible ...' This statement immediately raises the crucial question of Arius: If all reality divides into two categories, the one God, the Father, and all created things, to which of these categories does the Son belong? The assertions concerning the Son which now follow are meant to answer this question. The subject of these statements is the 'one Lord Jesus Christ, the Son of

God'. The following are the crucial predications of the Son which the Council inserted into the Creed to identify and condemn the teaching of Arius:

a) 'begotten from the Father, only-begotten'. The Son comes from and derives his being from the Father who, therefore, is the origin and source of the Son. This derivation from the Father is described as a generation, a begetting, and the one so derived is called the Son. Being the 'only-begotten', he is the only Son. The Son, therefore, has an origin in and from the Father. The Father, however, has no origin; he is without origin, the Unoriginate. This statement of the Son's origin was, of course, emphatically endorsed by Arius. It represented common ground. It was an agreed basis, however, after which both sides now begin to diverge.

b) 'that is, from the substance/*ousia* of the Father'. This phrase is the first directly anti-Arian insertion into the original Creed. It was introduced to contradict Arius' assertion that the Son came into being from non-existence and was therefore a creature. The phrase suggests, though it does not say so explicitly, that in coming from the substance of the Father the Son receives that substance, the divinity of the Father. The phrase is probably also meant to exclude Arius' exploitation of the traditional statement that the Son came from the *will* of the Father. The pre-Nicenes in making this statement, which they all did, simply meant that the Father did not beget the Son from necessity. Arius understood the statement to mean that the Father *at some particular moment* decided to have a Son and the Son therefore was not eternal but had a beginning and so was a creature.

This phrase in the Creed of Nicaea does not reappear in the Creed of Constantinople and is not in the Creed we say today in the Mass.

c) '[So he is] God from God, Light from Light, true God from true God'. The image of light had been much appealed to in pre-Nicene theoloy to describe the origin of the Son from the Father. There as here, it was meant to illustrate how the divinity of the Father was communicated to the Son, just as the one light was passed from one torch to another. This is an assertion of the divinity of the Son who is, therefore, rightly called God and true God. It should be noted, however, that Arians, since they were prepared to accept such titles of the Son in a courtesy sense, could accept them here in that sense, however much they might have disliked the expressions.

d) 'begotten, not made'. The Council here introduces a crucial distinction which Arius had ignored and which would yet prove very important in unraveling the trinitarian problem. Arius had equated the notion of origin with that of beginning to be, coming into existence. Since it was indisputable that the Son originated from the Father, for Arius this could only mean that the Father brought the Son into existence and the Son therefore was a creature. The Council points out that having origin from the Father does not necessarily mean having a beginning, being made or created. It could, and here does mean *eternal* origin, *eternal* generation. This is made very plain in the statements added at the end, where the Arian theses 'there was when he was not' and 'before being begotten he was not' are rejected and condemned.

e) 'one in being/*homoousios* with the Father'. *Homoousios* was the term which came to typify Nicaea and which was to become the touchstone of Nicene orthodoxy. It was what was most distinctive and provocative about the statement. Some general remarks about the term are required before proceeding to its precise meaning and function here.

The term is a compound adjective formed from the noun *ousia*, meaning substance, and the adjective *homos*, meaning the same, and it means therefore 'of the same substance as'. In ordinary usage the term had a rather materialist sense, 'of the same stuff as'. But it was also used to express belonging to a particular class or category, more or less equivalent to the English word homogeneous. Though the term had not been prominent previously in theological discussion, there is evidence that it was coming into use in the latter part of the third century. Origen may have used it and Dionysius of Rome certainly seems to have insisted on it. Further, prior to the Council of Nicaea, Arius had explicitly rejected it as applicable to the Son's relationship with the Father. Already by the time of the Council, therefore, the term had something of an anti-Arian bite to it.

It would appear that one of the reasons why the Council introduced this term into its statement was a negative one: it effectively identified, isolated and excluded the Arians. They in their subtle way could accept most of the other expressions in the statement by putting their own interpretation on them. But the term *homoousios* was one which they could not accept in any sense whatsoever. This was a bridge too far, a definite dividing line and marker.

But as well as acting as an identifying, negative criterion, the term as used at Nicaea also had a positive content and meaning. It asserted that the substance, that is, the deity or Godness, of the Father and the Son is one and the same. As one modern commentator has put it, it asserts 'the full unbroken continuation of the Being of the Father in the Son'. (A Robertson, *NPNF*, 4 [St Athanasius], xxxii) It states, therefore, though of course it does not explain, that the Father is God and the Son is God in the same sense of the word 'God', and yet there is but one God because the divinity communicated from the Father to the Son is one and the same. Though some commentators have maintained that the term as understood and used at Nicaea had a generic sense, this seems to the present writer to be definitely not so. The biblical sense of the uniqueness of God was too deeply embedded in the Christian mind to allow the concept of Deity to be seen as a category which could be shared by a number of individuals. The Creed of Nicaea opens with the traditional confession that there is one God, the Father. The substance or Godness which makes the Father God is passed on to the Son who, therefore, is *homoousios*, one in substance with, the Father. This is a clear assertion of the divinity of the Son. It encapsulates in a single term what earlier writers had been trying, not perhaps very clearly or very successfully, to say.

The Creed of Nicaea ends very abruptly. It simply states: 'And [we believe] in the Holy Spirit.' The local creed which the Council adopted as foundation for its statement presumably ended in this abrupt manner. It was for this time a rather primitive, undeveloped credal statement. The early baptismal creed would have ended as simply as this, containing little more than the baptismal formula of Matthew 28:19. But the bare reference to the Holy Spirit here shows that this question was not an issue at Nicaea. This, however, would change later. Meanwhile, even this bare reference alerts us, as we noted earlier, to the fact that the outer context of the dispute was trinitarian from the beginning.

A word remains to be said about the statements which the Council added to the credal text at the end. These statements are obviously directed against a number of explicit theses which are regarded as constituting the basics of the teaching of Arius. They reject any suggestion that the Son is a creature, has had a beginning, is the subject of change or alteration. But they also include a statement which was to create great problems for the future. This statement rejects the idea that the Son is 'from a different substance/*hypostasis* or being/*ousia*' to the Father. The problem with this statement is the identification which it seems to envisage between the words *hypostasis* and *ousia* as synonymous terms signifying divinity or divine substance. The problem here was that as many in the East had by this time come to accept Origen's language of three Hypostases to describe the members of the Triad,

this use of language suggested to these that the Council was oblit-
erating all distinction between the Three and teaching a form of
Modalism. This confusion between what were now becoming important technical terms was not the least of the semantic problems
which the Controversy involved and which would have to be
unravelled before a solution would prove possible.[3]

We come now to the third of the questions we set ourselves, the
question why this firm doctrinal position asserted by the Council
of Nicaea and endorsed and sanctioned by decree of the Emperor
had, within ten years, collapsed, leaving the rival, condemned
position apparently in the ascendent. I have already suggested
that the consensus which Nicaea seemed to involve was more cosmetic than real. There is evidence that different people read different interpretations into the Council's statements. If so, this was
bound to emerge eventually, making the Council itself a bone of
contention. Also, there may well have been a certain amount of
arm-twisting at the Council, especially on the part of Alexander,
Constantine and Ossius. But a major factor in the reversal of fortune which took place certainly was the ambivalent attitude
which Constantine adopted towards the Council position so soon
after it. By showing himself prepared to accept a confession of
faith, even from Arius himself, which avoided all reference to the
Nicene Creed and its key terms, he effectively neutralised the
Council. The Arians and their supporters proved themselves
much more adept than their opponents at exploiting the vacuum
which this imperial attitude created.

But the most influential factor in casting doubt on the Council
teaching was undoubtedly the rather modalist interpretation of it
soon put forward by figures such as Marcellus of Ancyra. This
must have confirmed many 'neutrals' in their discomfort with
what they must have regarded as the novelty of the conciliar
teaching and its untraditional terminology. For to meet the crisis
which had suddenly arisen, the Council had had recourse to novel
expressions, whereas Arianism in large part was couched in the
language of tradition. This 'offence' of Nicaea was centred above
all in its use of the term *homoousios*. Many objections could and
were brought against this term: it conveyed a materialist view of
God; it was unbiblical and untraditional; it represented an in-
vasion from the language of the pagan, secular world of that of
the world of faith. But, above all, many were uncomfortable with
it because they felt that it could too easily be taken to mean that
the Son was to be identified with the Father without any distinction other than that of mere name, in other words, Modalism. The

interpretation of the term given by Marcellus of Ancyra did little to allay these fears. The Council's apparent identification of the terms *ousia* and *hypostasis* would have proved a further, confirming stumbling-block for those who accepted the language of three Hypostases to describe the Triad.

There was, therefore, at the time sufficient novelty about the statement of Nicaea to cause discomfort for many. Once Constantine's insistence on adherence to the statement softened, this discomfort could be given expression. Eusebius of Nicomedia now reverted to his old support for Arianism and, repudiating his signature at the Council, assumed direction of the growing disillusionment with its teaching and of the attack on its main defenders. Indeed, these latter were now calling Arianism 'the party around Eusebius'. This policy won the support of Constantine, who was now seeking compromise and conciliation. Then in 337 Constantine died.

The Middle Phase, 337-361

The Historical Scene

On the death of Constantine the Empire was divided between his three sons as follows: Constantine II – the Western Provinces (Spain, Gaul, Britain); Constans – Italy, Africa, Greece; Constantius – the East and Egypt. In 340 Constans defeated Constantine II to become Emperor of the whole West. He died in 350 and soon afterwards, 353, Constantius became the sole Emperor. Both Constans and Constantius took a keen interest in the doctrinal dispute which had now become very divisive and was beginning to involve the whole Church, East and West. But each Emperor adopted his own stance, Constans a pro-Western one, Constantius a pro-Eastern. Divergent imperial policies, therefore, only added to the deepening divisions and the growing confusion. For this is the period when the Controversy displays its maximum of confusion. It will be helpful, however, to note that this phase involves two parts, the two decades, 340-350 when both Emperors were pursuing divergent policies, and 350-360 when Constantius was able to attempt to impose his own. This difference should be borne in mind in reading the following summary of events which were significant for the course of the dispute.

A definite Western position on Nicaea, centred in Rome, had emerged by 340, in the wake of the apparent triumph of Arianism in the previous decade. This position was a stout defence of the Council and of its defenders, especially Athanasius and Marcel-

lus. Both of these had visited Rome during exile in 340 and given
the Pope, Julius I, their own version of events in the East. Julius acknowledged the orthodoxy of Athanasius and Marcellus, that is,
he approved their defence of the Council of Nicaea. He wrote to
the Eastern bishops assembled in Antioch in 341, demanding adherence to the teaching of Nicaea and in effect accusing the East-
eners of being Arians. This papal letter represents the first overt
intervention of Rome and the West since the Council in what had
been until now an almost exclusively Eastern affair. The Eastern
bishops replied to the Pope by letter repudiating the accusation of
being Arian and then proceeded to state their own position in a
Creed usually termed in the text-books the Second Creed of Antioch. This document is important both because it expressed the
views of a large body of Eastern bishops and because it was to become a basic statement of position in the Controversy as it now
developed, calling forth various expressions of agreement, modi-
fication and rejection. This position is anti-Arian but not fully
Nicene in that it rejects the term *homoousios* and what it regards
the term as here standing for. It obviously associates Nicaea with
Marcellus of Ancyra's defence of it and sees it as too close to Modalism for comfort. The bishops who issue this statement are obviously very anti-Marcellus and anti-Athanasius. But they are also
anxious to reach a rapprochment with Rome and the West and
they are conciliatory to western theological sensibilities, especially
the traditional western stress on the *one* God.

The bishops who issued this Creed of Antioch have here
framed a middle, mediating position between the extremes, as
they see it, of Arianism and the teaching of Nicaea. They are clearly
uncomfortable with what they regard as the novelty of Nicaea
and attempt to adopt a rather traditional pre-Nicene position
which has now simply become obsolete. In the circumstances,
they may justly be termed Conservatives. But this is the group
and the position which Constantius now pins his hopes on for a
general settlement and decides to support. Intended to be his instrument of peace, this body would yet break into two factions
and eventually dis-integrate. Events would yet show that there
was no middle, mediating ground; the issue was a straightfor-
ward one, *either* Arianism *or* Nicaea.

For the moment, however, there are three positions in the field:
Arianism, Nicaea, and the mediating position of the Conservatives. Constans now decides to intervene in the affair, adopting a
pro-Western, pro-Nicene stance. But all efforts to find a compromise formula agreeable to both East and West prove a failure.

They simply mean the holding of more synods or councils and the
issuing of more credal statements which change nothing and
achieve nothing. The end result is really the hardening of attitudes on both sides. Then in 350 Constans dies and in 353 Constantius becomes sole Emperor.

Constantius now increases his efforts to find a solution. His
policy, however, is simply to impose the Conservative position on
all. But now the Conservatives themselves split into two parties,
one veering somewhat towards Nicaea, the other away from it
and towards Arianism. Meanwhile, Arianism and Nicene theology have also been on the move. A new generation of Arian theologians develop a more radical, less compromising and indeed
more logical version of Arianism. And Athanasius in a succession
of works has taken up his pen in defence of Nicaea. Constantius,
who had found himself supporting now one, now the other, of the
Conservative parties, finally opts for the left-wing, pro-Arian faction and, in 360, after a series of councils enforcing his policy,
eventually imposes this position by imperial decree. A form of
Arianism was now the official 'faith' of the Empire. It is of this
series of events that St. Jerome later wrote: 'The whole world
groaned to find itself Arian.' Then in 361 Constantius died.

The Theological Issue
By the year 340 the theological scene in the East comprised three
groups: the Nicenes, the Arians, and the Conservatives. Throughout this phase, as indeed for long after, the Nicene position is on
the defensive, a defence, however, very ably promoted by, above
all, Athanasius. Strict Arianism, meanwhile, is now developed in
a radical way normally termed today Neo-Arianism. The Conservatives, who attempted to hold a middle, mediating position
between Nicenes to the right and Arians to the left, were not
themselves an united, homogeneous party. They included different factions who were united more by what they were against
than by what they stood for. Eventually, these tensions split the
party into two, a right-wing, anti-Arian faction, whose leading
figure was Basil of Ancyra, successor since 336 of the deposed
Marcellus, and a left-wing pro-Arian party. There are now four
theological positions – and a maximum of confusion!

The easiest way to understand and differentiate between these
four positions is to see them in terms of the formula which, to a
greater or lesser extent, they tended to rally around and which is
usually attached to them today. For the Nicenes this formula was
the *homoousios*. It took time, however, for even Athanasius to rec-

ognise that this term, which figures little in his early writings, held the key to the conflict and the controversy. The right-wing Conservatives, in their eventual effort to approach without fully adopting the Nicene position, settled on the rival term *homoiousios*, the Son is 'of similar substance' to the Father – a term perhaps better known from Gibbon's famous, caustic comment in *The Decline and Fall of the Roman Empire* to the effect that the Controversy was all about the use of an iota! The left-wing Conservatives, seeking a vaguer, more all-embracing term, opted for *homoios*, the Son was simply 'similar to' or 'like' the Father. The Neo-Arians, bringing the original position of Arius to its logical conclusion, described the Son as *anomoios*, 'unlike' the Father. The four theological positions can be accurately identified and differentiated by these convenient, if somewhat inelegant, terms: *Homoousians* – Nicenes; *Homoiousians* – right-wing Conservatives; *Homoians* – left-wing, rather Arian, Conservatives; *Anomoians* – the radical Neo-Arians.

For a period these four positions seemed so diametrically opposed, so deeply entrenched, and relationships so embittered, that no movement appeared possible. Two factors, however, one theoretical and the other historical, dictated otherwise. The theoretical factor was a matter of simple logic: only two of these positions could claim logical validity. Once Arius raised explicitly the fundamental question about the status of the Son, only two answers were logically possible: either the Son was truly divine, God in a true sense, or he was a creature. Logically, there was no middle ground here, no room for compromise or mediation. To think otherwise was to succumb to an illusion. This was the position of the Conservatives, whether of the right or left. Opposing and disliking the new theologies of Arius and Nicaea, they took refuge in the old tradition which, because it had not directly addressed the question Arius had raised, was unable to answer it. Like the ostrich, they buried their head in the sand hoping, when they raised it again, the problem might have gone away. But the only way to get rid of Arius' question was to face it and answer it, and this they refused to do. The structure they attempted to build lacked foundation and could not but collapse.

The historical factor which speeded this collapse was twofold. The rise of the Homoians, with their leanings towards Arianism and enjoying the powerful support of Constantius, frightened the Homoiousians and made them unsure of their position. At the same time and for the same reason, they now become more open and willing to listen to the arguments of Athanasius as he hammers out his attacks on Arianism and defends Nicaea and the *homoousios*. Athanasius himself, sensing their predicament and his own opportunity, becomes very conciliatory towards them. Writing c. 359, he describes them as 'brothers, who mean what we mean, and dispute only about the word [=*homoousios*]'. (*On the Synods*, 5) Among his converts were three young men from Caesarea in Cappadocia who, building on his foundations, would yet play a decisive role in the resolution of the Trinitarian Controversy.

The main thrust of Athanasius' argumentation in his defence of Nicaea lies in his explanation why the Council had to resort to a philosophical as distinct from a biblical form of discourse in issuing its teaching and in his effort to show that the meaning of the biblical revelation had been truly preserved and presented in this non-biblical language. In one way, the Controversy was about the true interpretation of a corpus of biblical texts bearing on the relation of the Son to the Father and drawn from both the Old and the New Testament. The Arians maintained that their teaching was either the plain meaning of these texts or a logical inference from them. *Facile princeps* among these texts, the one the Arians were ever throwing in the face of their opponents, was Proverbs 8:22, where Wisdom states: 'The Lord created me the beginning of his ways' (LXX). This text had been much appealed to by the pre-Nicenes from the Apologists on who understood it as referring to the generation of the Logos/Son. It was, therefore, accepted on all sides that here the Logos/Son spoke in the figure of Wisdom. The interest of the Arians in parading this text centred on the verb 'created': the Logos/Son here states as plain as plain can be that he is a creature. This text was a huge embarrassment to all opponents of Arianism but especially to strict Nicenes such as Athanasius. It has to be remembered that the ancients had no sense of what we take for granted today, the historical character and conditioning of the biblical revelation. Athanasius attempted to deflect the thrust of the text by understanding the reference to be to the created humanity of the Incarnate – a rather desperate exegesis! Oddly, no-one at the time seems to have noticed that Origen understood the text as referring to the eternal origin of the Son from the Father.

Athanasius was more successful, however, in countering the general Arian scriptural argument by showing that it was selective, disingenuous and tendentious. And he also helped to convince many that the only way to overcome this clever exploitation of Scripture was to adopt another, more precise form of discourse

– hence the rather philosophical language of Nicaea. The different language was necessary in the interest of defending biblical truth itself. The 'novelty' of Nicaea was a necessity in the circumstances for the vindication of true doctrine. In this enterprise Athanasius contributed significantly to the development of biblical and theological hermeneutics.

Athanasius' main interest in his discussion of this biblical material is to establish the divinity of the Son of God, the Word Incarnate, and so vindicate the doctrine of Nicaea. His basic argument here is soteriological: the Son is divine because he accomplishes what only God can do, the salvation of humankind. But further discussion of this topic would mean entering deeply into Athanasius' christology and cannot be pursued here.

Little of this developing trend of thought, however, was openly discernible as this middle phase of the Trinitarian Controversy draws to a close. It can be recognised in hindsight, but at the time it represented more an undercurrent beneath the surface whirlpool of passions and frayed tempers which characterise this period. The period ends with a form of Arianism, Homoian Arianism, in the ascendent by imperial decree. But if this position appealed to Constantius, it commanded little general support and offered little hope of an acceptable solution. If this is to emerge, new forces and new ideas will have to assert themselves and, by shifting discussion on to a new level, create a climate of mind capable of resolving existing tensions. Contrary to all appearances of the moment, this unexpected development is about to occur.

The Final Phase, 361-381

The Historical Scene

Following the death of Constantius in 361, and the brief interval of the reigns of Julian the Apostate and Jovian (361-364), the Empire was again divided and imperial rule was shared between the two brothers, Valens in the East, 364-378, and Valentinian in the West, 364-375. Valentinian sympathised with the Western, pro-Nicene position, but he avoided any direct involvement in the dispute. Valens, on the other hand, in his support for Homoian Arianism continued where Constantius had left off. Indeed, he was even more aggressive in promoting the cause. Eastern adherents of Nicaea now found themselves the subject of active persecution by imperial authority. But perhaps the most significant development in terms of new personalities was that the Western defence of Nicaea now receives a new leader in the forceful character of Pope Damasus (366-384). Damasus, contrasting here with his predecessor, Liberius, pursued an active, vigorous policy in defence of the Nicene cause. Under his leadership, the Latin Church was united in its adherence to the teaching of Nicaea.

Theologically, the most significant feature of this period is that in the East, which remains the crucial arena, Athanasius ceases to stand almost alone in public defence of Nicaea *–Athanasius contra mundum*. He is now joined by the group of bishop theologians from Caesarea in Cappadocia known as the Cappadocian Fathers: Basil of Caesarea (d. 379), Gregory of Nazianzus (d. 389), and Basil's younger brother, Gregory of Nyssa (d. c. 395). Building on the foundations which Athanasius had laid, these theologians supply the theoretical solution and clarification which the Nicene position required and had always been seeking but which even Athanasius himself had failed to provide. Their writings, especially from the 370s on, were widely read and made an immediate and lasting impression, winning many waverers to the Nicene cause and helping it win the intellectual and theological battle. For the first time, since Constantine softened his support for the Council, the cause of Nicaea began to be in the ascendent throughout the Church, both East and West. The crucial question now concerned the reaction of imperial policy to this situation.

Valens was killed fighting the Goths at Adrianople in 378. His young nephew, Gratian, who had succeeded his father, Valentinian, as Emperor of the West in 375, now called upon the able administrator, Theodosius, living peacefully on his estates in Spain, to share the imperial purple with him and appointed him Emperor in the East. Theodosius arrived in the East a convinced Nicene and immediately set about promoting the cause effectively and energetically, removing Arian bishops appointed by Valens and replacing them with staunch Nicenes. To finalise his reform programme and give it legal sanction, Theodosius now called a Council of Eastern bishops to meet at Constantinople in the summer of 381. Over the previous decade, through a series of synods or councils at Rome, Damasus had seen to it that the Nicene faith was now the official and established doctrine of the West. Theodosius now wished to ensure a similar consummation in the East.

The Council of Constantinople in 381 was not, according to the intent of Theodosius, meant to be a General Council of the Church. It only received this status *post factum*, through subsequent recognition from the whole Church. In origin and purpose, it was an assembly of bishops of the East called together to recognise and establish the faith of Nicaea as the official doctrine of the

Church in the East. Even Damasus had not been invited from the West and was deeply suspicious of it. But the Council fulfilled its, and Theodosius', purpose. It re-endorsed and re-issued the Creed of Nicaea, but expanded substantially Nicaea's bare reference to the Holy Spirit in order to assert the Spirit's divinity. Immediately following the Council's conclusion, Theodosius gave its decision civil sanction by means of an imperial Edict. Suddenly and unexpectedly, the Trinitarian Controversy had come to an end. The Council of Nicaea was finally vindicated and its teaching endorsed as the official doctrine of the Church, East and West.

The Theological Issue

It was only in this final phase that the Controversy became explicitly trinitarian in that only now did the question of the status of the Holy Spirit become an overt issue. The subordination of the Spirit to both the Father and the Son had always been a logical implication of Arianism but it was only in the late 350s that this position came to be openly asserted. The argument which ensued constitutes the first public airing of the topic of the Spirit in the Church. Something of the confused thinking on the subject which prevailed can be gauged from the following comment of Gregory of Nazianzus in his Fifth Theological Oration delivered in Constantinople in 381 on the eve of the Council: 'Some assume he [the Spirit] is a power, some a creature, some that he is God, some cannot decide which of these is true ...' Clearly, the 'advanced' pneumatologies of Irenaeus and Origen had not yet made any general impact on theological thought.

Many different names were given at the time to those who denied the divinity of the Holy Spirit. They were variously called: Pneumatomachians, 'Fighters against the Spirit'; Macedonians, from a Bishop Macedonius whose connection with this position is very unclear; Tropici, meaning those who gave a very metaphorical meaning to biblical texts; Semi-Arians, a term coined first by the very orthodox Epiphanius of Salamis to refer to those who affirmed the divinity of the Son but denied that of the Spirit – and too often applied inaccurately in textbooks to the Conservative Homoiousians in general.

Those who maintained the subordinate status of the Holy Spirit, whether Arians or Semi-Arians, based their argument on both Scripture and tradition. They pointed out that in the Bible the Spirit was never called God. They read a clear subordinationist implication into the mission language used of both the Word/Son and the Spirit in both Testaments: the fact that the Word/Son was said to be 'sent' by the Father implied subordination and the Spirit 'sent' by the Son still greater subordination. A subordinationist meaning was also seen in and argued from the doxology: 'Glory be to the Father through the Son in the Holy Spirit' – the most common form of short doxology in use over the early centuries and one presenting clearly and succinctly the structure of most other forms.

Those on the Nicene side who wished to rebut these arguments had to do so on the basis of the same sources, Scripture and tradition. The two most influential works which appeared from this side, affirming and defending the divinity of the Spirit, were the *Letters to Serapion* of Athanasius (c. 359) and Basil of Caesarea's *On the Holy Spirit* (375) – though perhaps it is too little noticed that Athanasius had already been preparing his position in some of his earlier Festal or Easter Letters.[4] In these works Athanasius and Basil argued that divine titles, attributes and functions were predicated of the Spirit in Scripture and that this same divine status continued to be acknowledged in the prayer and life of the Church. Basil wrote his *On the Holy Spirit* to defend the doxology he had introduced at Caesarea and which had been criticised as untraditional and illegitimate. This doxology read: 'Glory be to the Father with the Son together with the Holy Spirit' and emphasised the equality of all three Members of the Triad in the worship given to the Godhead. Basil forcefully defended his doxology as rooted in the Church's tradition but took the occasion also to write a comprehensive treatise on the Spirit which was to have a decisive influence a few years later on the statement of the Council of Constantinople.

A main plank in Basil's argument for the divinity of the Spirit was his appeal to the life-giving function of the Spirit. To give life, whether natural or supernatural, is a divine prerogative. This function is at times attributed to the Spirit of God in both the Old and the New Testament and this attribution is continued in the life and faith of the Church where the salvation of Christ is dispensed as new life from God communicated in the Spirit. Baptism, the sacramental source of this life and where the Spirit is associated with the Father and the Son on an equal basis, is a particular illustration of this status of the Spirit as a Member of the divine Triad acknowledged in Christian faith. The argument is well summed up in the comment of a modern writer: 'The Holy Spirit was God because he did what only God could do.' (Pelikan, *Christian Tradition* , 1, 215)

The emergence of the question of the Spirit ensured that the

issue under debate had now become properly and formally trinitarian. It was no longer a question simply of the status of the Son,
but of the Triad as a whole. The issue now was to find a coherent
language with which to speak of God as one and as three. Such an
issue could be resolved only on the basis of precise, well-defined
concepts together with a corresponding terminology. The problem was that at the time such a conceptual and linguistic system
did not exist. Central to the theological development which now
occurred was the understanding and use of the terms *ousia* and
hypostasis. Many Easterners by this time had come to accept Origen's language of three *hypostases* to describe the Members of the
Triad, however they might have understood the question of the
status of the Son and the Spirit. Many others, reinforced here by
the Council of Nicaea itself, identified the terms *ousia* and *hypostasis*, and so understood *hypostasis* to refer to divinity or the divine nature, and so appropriate to and confined to the reference
'the one God'. For those who followed this usage, to speak of the
Triad as three *hypostases* meant speaking of three Gods. Athanasius always adhered to this usage. But then in 362, at a synod of
Egyptian bishops presided over by Athanasius, this question of
the different usage of these terms was adverted to and discussed.
The synod forwarded the results of its deliberations to the church
of Antioch in a document known as the Tome to the Antiochenes.
This text was very probably penned by Athanasius himself and
certainly had his approval.

The significance of this document lies in the fact that it accepts
the language of one *ousia* and three *hypostases*, which it acknowledges some are in the habit of using, as capable of being orthodox
in speaking of the Triune God, provided all subordinationist implications are excluded, even though it prefers itself to adhere to
the language of Nicaea which speaks of God simply as one *hypostasis*. This means that the formula one *ousia* -three *hypostases* now
has the qualified approval of Athanasius, leader of the Nicene
party. The problem, however, concerns the meaning of this formula. The Tome gave the formula its guarded approval, but it
made no attempt to explain the meaning of the distinction between *ousia* and *hypostasis* which the formula involved. Athanasius had effectively defended the statement of Nicaea on the
ground that it expressed the meaning of the biblical revelation
concerning the Son. But no-one had as yet attempted a theoretical
solution to the trinitarian question as such, that is, how one could
justify speaking of God as both one and three. This is precisely the
task which the Cappadocian Fathers, taking over leadership of

the Nicene cause after Athanasius' death in 373, now undertake.

The Cappadocians work out their solution throughout a series of dogmatic works which issue from them. It will be more convenient here, however, to present their argument in a more systematic manner and to see it as consisting of two stages.

The Cappadocian Argument

The first step in the argument calls attention to the distinction between that which is generic or common [Gk *to koinon*], shared equally by all members of a class, and that which is particular or individual [Gk *to idion*], the distinctive possession of one member alone. Human beings, for example, all share the same common humanity, yet each is also a distinct individual. How is this so? Since Peter and John share the same common humanity, the same human nature, the distinction between them as individuals, that which makes one Peter and the other John, cannot arise at this level. It must be sought elsewhere. The distinction between Peter and John arises from a series of elements or factors peculiar and particular to each, such as origin, age, size, appearance, etc., etc. The same nature is individualised in these two beings by means of these distinguishing characteristics which give each his distinct identity over against all other members of the class. They are distinguishing, individuating characteristics, factors which make a common nature a distinct individual possessing that nature. Among other terms, the Cappadocians called these factors *idioma/idiomata* or *idiotes/idiotetes*. Reserving the term *ousia* for the nature (*to koinon*) and *hypostasis* for the particular or individual (*to idion*), they get the equation: *Ousia + Idioma/Idiotes = Hypostasis/* individual person

Having thus clarified the distinction between *ousia* and *hypostasis*, nature and person, the Cappadocians are now in a position to proceed to the second stage of their argument, namely, to apply this distinction to the question of the unity and distinctions in God, to the one and the three. They asked what are the individuating characteristics, the *idiomata*, which distinguish the three in the Triad from one another and give them distinct individuality. In simple language: What has the Father got which the Son and the Spirit have not got? What has the Son got which the Father and Spirit have not got? What has the Spirit got which the Father and the Son have not got? These distinguishing characteristics cannot arise from the divine *ousia* or nature itself, since this is the identical same in all three. There can be no distinction at this level. The only distinction which can be discovered between the three is to be found in their manner or mode of origin, what in Greek is called their *tropos hyparxeos*. The Father is distinguished from the Son and the Spirit by the fact that he is their origin or source without himself having any origin or source: he is the Unoriginate, the Origin without origin. The Son is distinguished by the fact that he has origin in and from the Father by a process of begetting or generation, for which reason he is in some proper sense called Son. The Spirit has origin in and from the Father by a process which is not a begetting or generation – and so the Spirit is not and cannot be called Son – but by another kind of process for which there is no analogy or name in human experience. The Gregories call the origin of the Spirit simply Procession or Mission.

It emerges from this analysis that the distinguishing characteristics, the *idiomata/idiotetes*, which establish three distinct existents within the Deity or Godhead are determined by the three distinct modes of origin which, according to Christian faith, the Godhead presents. Basil calls these characteristics Fatherhood, Sonship, Sanctification. The Gregories, applying a more rigorous and more abstract analysis, describe them as follows:

No origin – Unbegotteness (Gk *Agennesia*) = The Father.

Origin by Generation (*Gk Gennesia*) = The Son.

Origin by Procession/Mission (Gk *Ekporeusis/Ekpempsis*) = The Holy Spirit.

It now emerges that what the modes of origin establish, the three of the Triad, are a set of mutual relations, 'opposing' relations as theology will later call them and as the personal names given them in the tradition, Father-Son for example, show. These beings exist totally in and for relationship with one another. 'For "Father,"' writes Gregory of Nazianzus, 'is not a name of substance or of activity, but of relationship (*schesis*), and of how the Father is related to the Son, or the Son to the Father'. (*Theological Oration* 3)

The conclusion of the Cappadocian argument is that each member of the Triad possesses a distinguishing characteristic, an *idioma/idiotes*, which the others do not. Recalling the basic formula and equation which is being applied, this now yields, in very schematic form, the following solution.

Ousia/Nature + *Idioma* = *Hypostasis*/Person.

God = 1 *Ousia* + 3 *Idiomata* = 3 *Hypostases*/Persons.

= 1 *Ousia* existing in 3 *Hypostases*/Persons.

= 1 Nature and 3 Persons.

One may ask, however, how this very abstract analysis is related to and relevant to the biblical revelation and Christian understanding of God. The Cappadocian Fathers would, I think, summarise their answer to this question somewhat in the following manner. God reveals Godself as one and three, Unity and Trinity. According to revelation, both the one and the ohree are real –the three refer to real, existing distinctions. The one or unity means the one God, the Father, and the divine nature or Godness of the Father. No distinction can be allowed within the one divine nature; to do so would be to admit a plurality of Gods and negate the reference 'the one God'. In this context, to speak of God as three can only refer to individuating characteristics, *idiomata*, attaching to the one divine nature and individuating it in three particular ways, that is, as three *hypostases* or persons. According to revelation, the only *idiomata* which can be identified in the Godhead concern the mode of origin of the Father, the Son and the Spirit. Since the distinctions Father, Son and Spirit are real, these modes of origin are also real and acting as individuating characteristics individuate the divine nature as three *hypostases* or persons. These existing, real hypostatic or personal distinctions identify themselves as relations. The persons of the Godhead, therefore, are real, existing or subsistent relations. We have no experience of such an entity as a subsistent relation, a relation which exists or subsists independently on its own. We only know of beings who have a relation with others; we never experience a being who is simply and purely relation. But revelation forces us to acknowledge that the distinctions in God, the distinctions which form the Triad, are just such – subsistent, pure relations.

The basis of the Cappadocian argument was the distinction which it established between *ousia*/nature and *hypostasis*/person. This distinction enabled the Cappadocians to give a coherent meaning to the language of one *ousia*/nature and three *hypostases*/persons as used of God and the Triad. This in turn helped to clarify and vindicate the teaching of Nicaea by showing that the Council was mainly concerned to assert the one divine nature communicated from the Father to the Son, so justifying the term *homoousios* on the one hand while preserving the statement from any suggestion of Modalism on the other by means of the distinct concept of *hypostasis*.

By the time and occasion of the Council of Constantinople in 381, and the pro-Nicene climate then developing, this sophisticated argumentation supplied the theoretical, conceptual clarification which the statement of Nicaea had always required, but which even the pen of Athanasius had failed to provide. This helped convince many who still harboured doubts about Nicaea and ensured that when the Eastern bishops assembled at Constantinople the prevailing theological outlook had swung round decidedly in favour of the Nicene cause.

The Council of Constantinople, 381

Basically and simply, the Council of Constantinople endorsed and re-affirmed the Creed of Nicaea, but it expanded the bare third article on the Holy Spirit to ensure recognition of the divinity of the Spirit as well as that of the Son. Constantinople, therefore, completed the agenda begun at Nicaea, responding to the issue raised by Arius by seeing it and treating it as a question properly concerning God as Trinity. The theological perspective on which the Council relies and from which it speaks is that provided by the Cappadocian Fathers. Gregory of Nazianzus, in fact, for the moment Bishop of Constantinople, was president of the Council for a period, before departing in a fit of dudgeon and retiring to Nazianzus. Something of the atmosphere prevailing in the city, which had been the special object of Valens' Arianising policy, is captured in the following description of the occasion by Gregory of Nyssa:

> If you ask for change, the man launches into a theological discussion about begotten and unbegotten; if you enquire about the price of bread, the answer is given that the Father is greater and the Son subordinate; if you remark that the bath is nice, the man pronounces that the Son is from non-existence. (*Deity of the Son and Holy Spirit* – trans R Hanson, *The Search for the Christian Doctrine of God* , 806)

Constantinople endorsed Nicaea by simply re-issuing the Nicene Creed, with some minor and insignificant verbal variations, and expanding the third article. The reason for the variations seems to be that the version of the Nicene Creed which Constantinople used already contained these phrases. Ancient times were not as concerned as we today with minor verbal accuracy. The most noticeable of the variations is the non-appearance of the Nicene phrase describing the generation of the Son as 'from the being/*ousia* of the Father'. The non-appearance of the phrase was scarcely deliberate; Constantinople did not mean to reject the point Nicaea wished to make. The phrase may have been innocently ommitted in the version of the Creed used at Constantinople. But it must be remembered that Constantinople means to endorse everything Nicaea had said and the original phrase must be regarded as included in this endorsement.

Constantinople's statement on the Holy Spirit is a condensation especially of Basil of Caesarea's position in his work *On the Holy Spirit*. It follows his approach in avoiding all use of the technical philosophical terms which had proved such an obstacle to the reception of the Creed of Nicaea. It relies instead on the language of Scripture and the living faith, the *lex orandi*. The statement reads:

> [We believe] in the Holy Spirit, the Lord (*to Kurion*) and Giver of life (*Zoopoion*), who proceeds from the Father, who together with the Father and the Son is worshipped and glorified, who has spoken through the prophets. (Neuner/Dupuis, *Christian Faith*, 9)

A theological commentary on this statement requires it to be taken phrase by phrase.

'Lord' is the special title of God throughout Scripture and Basil had argued (*On the Holy Spirit*, 21 – though modern exegesis will scarcely support him) that in 2 Corinthians 3:17, St Paul had used this divine title of the Holy Spirit: 'The Lord is the Spirit, and where the Spirit of the Lord is, there is freedom.' The argument is that the Spirit is God because Scripture gives the Spirit God's special name and title.

To give life, whether natural life or, above all, the supernatural life of grace, is an exclusively divine function proper to God alone. This function is attributed to the Spirit in the New Testament – as also in some passages of the Old. In Romans 8:2, St Paul terms the Spirit 'the Spirit of life in Christ'; 2 Corinthians 3:6, and John 6:63, state that 'the Spirit gives life'. To attribute this function to the Spirit is again to assert the Spirit's divinity.

The clause 'who proceeds from the Father' – later the subject of the famous, controversial addition by the Latin West, 'and from the Son/*Filioque*' – is, at first sight, simply a reproduction of the text of John 15:26: 'the Spirit of truth, who proceeds from the Father'. But there is more to it than this. A classical Arian argument for denying equality of status with the Father to both the Son and the Spirit was based on the statement that the Son and the Spirit were both 'sent'. One sent, the argument claimed, was under the command of and inferior in status to the sender. By this criterion, the Son was inferior to the Father and the Spirit to the Son. The Council, again adopting here the perspective of Basil (*On the Holy Spirit*, 9 and, esp. 16), parallels the origin of the Spirit with that of the Son: both are 'from the Father', not from non-existence as is the case with creatures, and through this origin both receive the being or divinity of the Father. There is certainly an echo here, I think, of the phrase of Nicaea discussed earlier which describes

the generation of the Son as 'from the *ousia* of the Father'. The
Spirit's procession from the Father is here paralleled with the generation of the Son; both receive the same divinity from the same
source and are, therfore, equal in status. This statement concerning the origin of the Spirit, as introduced into the Creed at Constantinople, does not, therefore, envisage in any direct way the
subtle question of the double procession of the Spirit which was
later to become so divisive an issue doctrinally between East and
West and remains so still.

The Creed next refers to the Spirit as one 'who together with
the Father and the Son is worshipped and glorified'. Worship and
glory describe the reverence due to God alone by rational creatures. It expresses recognition of God's Godness and divinity. In
stating that the Spirit is the recipient of this divine worship 'together with' the Father and the Son, the Creed asserts the Spirit's
equal, divine status. The argument is derived from the Church's
living faith and especially its basic prayer statement, the doxology. It was a basic argument put forward for the divinity of the
Spirit by both Athanasius and Basil.

The Creed's final statement on the Spirit, 'who spoke through
the prophets', is an old, traditional one recalling the classic understanding of the Spirit in the early centuries and one which, because of its anti-Marcion, anti-Gnostic significance, had been incorporated into baptismal creeds from an early stage in their
history.

There is a sharp contrast here between this scriptural, pastoral
language used of the Spirit and the more abstract, philosophical
terminology used of the Son at Nicaea. This contrast has to be deliberate and, no doubt, reflects in some way the wounds and scars
of the Controversy. But the old thesis that this was a deliberately
conciliatory language, designed to accommodate and win over
the Macedonian or Semi-Arian bishops who attended the Council, cannot be upheld and is abandoned today by most scholars.
The thirty or so Macedonian bishops who attended the Council
packed their bags and went home rather than subscribe the statement which, this thesis maintained, was deliberately designed to
win their acceptance. Yet, the Council now proceeded to issue the
statement which had so conspicuously failed in its purpose! The
truth of the matter really is that by this time Nicene theology had
developed so far in wisdom and confidence that it was able to express its position on the Holy Spirit, following the lines already
laid down by Athanasius and Basil, in language simpler and more

pastoral than that adopted by Nicaea on the Son. The judgement of a modern commentator may be accepted with confidence: 'The Creed [of Constantinople] was intended to convey the conception of the divinity of the Holy Spirit, though in language which was guarded and calculated to give no more offence than was unavoidable'. (J N D Kelly, *Early Christian Creeds*, 341)

The Creed of Constantinople, 381, endorses that of Nicaea, 325. The total focus of Nicaea lay in its assertion of the divinity of the Son of God. Constantinople adds to this an equal assertion of the divinity of the Holy Spirit. The theological perspective which formed the basis of the teaching of Constantinople was that developed by the defenders of Nicaea, above all, by Athanasius and the Cappadocian Fathers. This theology had eventually solved the problem of the Triune God on the basis of the distinction between *ousia*/nature and *hypostasis*/person worked out by the Cappadocians. God, in the full reference of the term in Christian faith, was now seen to consist of one nature possessed equally by three persons, Father, Son and Holy Spirit. This position ensured that any suggestion of an essential subordination of the Son and the Spirit was to be deemed heretical. This theology, hammered out in the heat of controversy by the Greek theologians of the East, was now the common mind and possession of both East and West. The Greek theology, with all its subtlety, had been introduced to the West by such figures as Hilary of Poitiers, Ambrose of Milan, and even the obscure writings of the Neo-Platonist philosopher turned Christian, Marius Victorinus. This introduction to Greek theological thought was sufficient to enable Latin theology to move out of its conservative, pre-Nicene mould and to overcome its deep suspicion of the language of three persons as used of God. Shortly before the Council of Constantinople, probably in 378, a synod at Rome, presided over by Damasus, issued a statement, known to history as the Tome of Damasus, which reproduced in all its essentials the theology of the Cappadocians. A synod at Constantinople in 382 officially informed Rome and other Western centres of the teaching of the Council the previous year. As regards matters of trinitarian doctrine, at least, an orthodox consensus had finally been achieved throughout the Church. Theologically and officially, the Trinitarian Controversy had come to an end.

Notes

1. This view has been proposed and forcefully argued by R. Gregg and D. Groh, *Early Arianism: A View of Salvation*, Philadelphia, Fortress, 1981.

2. This qualified acceptance and refinement of the Gregg/Groh thesis is proposed by the late R.P.C. Hanson in his extensive study, *The Search for the Christian Doctrine of God: The Arian Controversy 318-381*, Edinburgh, T & T Clark, 1988: see chapter 4, 'The Rationale of Arianism', 99-128.

3. A good, clear and comprehensive study of the Council of Nicaea may be found in C. Luibhéid, *The Council of Nicaea*, Galway, Galway University Press, 1982.

4. On this point see C. Kannengiesser, 'Athanasius of Alexandria and the Holy Spirit between Nicea and Constantinople 1', *ITQ*, 48 [1981], 166-180.

CHAPTER 5

The Latin Tradition and Scholastic Theology

The Christian doctrine of God as Trinity was hammered out in the heat of the Trinitarian Controversy. The theologians engaged in this task, most of them bishops busy with many pastoral cares, had little leisure in the troubled times which prevailed to reflect on the ideas, and the interconnection of ideas, which they were formulating. Such effort at systematisation was a later development. It achieved its final form in Latin theology at the hands of the great medieval Scholastics of the twelfth and thirteenth centuries. As in practically all other areas of medieval theology, its finest and most influential presentation is to be found in the *Summa Theologica* of St Thomas Aquinas.

Aquinas' great work, however, was the culmination and fruit of a long period of effort, spanning a number of centuries, to systematise the theology of the Trinity. Indeed, this effort may be said to have begun very soon after the Council of Constantinople itself. But before attempting to outline some major stages in this systematic development, it is first necessary to look back and reflect on the understanding of God which the Controversy produced and made standard. For the systematisation which now gradually gets under way, and which Aquinas completes, largely consists of working out and interconnecting the implications of basic positions which the Controversy established.

The understanding of God which emerged from the Trinitarian Controversy and became standard doctrine spoke of God as consisting of one divine nature and three divine persons. As a language to describe God as one and three, this formula could easily be taken to mean that God was one in terms of the unity of the divine nature and three in terms of the distinct persons. But, apart from what we have already noted with the similar formula of Tertullian, this understanding meant giving a new meaning to the expression 'the *one* God' and a departure from the meaning which the phrase had in the New Testament and all previous tradition, where it meant simply the Father. In other words, the expression

'the one God' now had two different meanings: the Father or the
one divine nature. Though it was the Cappadocians who theologically vindicated the language of one nature and three persons, the
traditional understanding is preserved and still strong in their
writings, though the new is also beginning to appear. The point
may be illustrated by quoting a few sentences from Basil's *On the
Holy Spirit*. Basil can write here: 'We do not lose the true doctrine
of the one God in confessing the persons'. (18,47) What does 'the
one God' mean here? Two further statements provide the answer.
'There is one God and Father, one only-begotten Son, and one
Holy Spirit' (18,44): 'As unique persons, they are one and one; as
sharing a common nature, both (Father and Son) are one'. (18, 45 –
Basil could easily have included the Holy Spirit here and spoken
of the three persons) With these two statements Basil has given
two different explanations to the reference 'the one God'. This can
now mean either the Father, the traditional concept of the divine
monarchy, or the one divine nature. The approach of later theology
to the question of God will be determined by which of these two
answers it will choose to emphasise and make basic.

Closely allied to this question of the meaning of the reference
'the one God' is the way the action of God in the economy of salvation now begins to be conceived. The pre-Nicene tradition, going back to and rooted in the New Testament itself, had described
this activity as that of the Father coming to us through the Son in
the Spirit. The Son and the Spirit were, in Irenaeus' terms, 'the
two hands' of the Father. Within this perspective, it will be recalled, Irenaeus and Origen had attempted to discern a differentiation between the economic activity of the three. Here again, however, a subtle shift of position now begins to occur which will
have repercussions on later theology. The pre-Nicene tradition is
still evident in the Nicene writers of the fourth century and appears, for example, in the following statements of Basil: 'He (the
Father) creates through the Son and perfects through the Spirit'
(*H Sp* 16, 38); 'The way to divine knowledge ascends from the one
Spirit through the one Son to the one Father'. (ibid 18, 47) But
these writers, in defending and attempting to vindicate Nicene orthodoxy against Arians and Semi-Arians, base their argument
that the Son and the Spirit share the divinity of the Father on the
ground that according to Scripture and tradition the Son and the
Spirit accomplish the same saving work, redemption and sanctification, as the Father. Because the Father, the Son and the Spirit
perform the same distinctive divine action, they possess equally
the same divinity, the same divine nature. This argument back

from saving action in the economy to divine status within the immanent Godhead now reinforces the emerging understanding of 'the one God' as meaning the one divine nature. A tendency is beginning to appear here which, if not corrected, could all too easily lead to a virtual obliteration of the significance of the distinction of Persons in favour of an emphasis on the unity of nature. As we shall soon see, later trinitarian theology quickly and readily succumbed to this tempting tendency.

The Legacy of St Augustine

Coincident with and immediately following the Council of Constantinople, Rome was issuing its own statements of trinitarian doctrine, such as the Tome of Damasus, couched in the succinct phraseology characteristic of the Latin language. These statements and phrases will be re-echoed over the following centuries in Latin liturgical, credal and theological texts. But the document which above all others determined the thought of Western Christendom on the meaning of God as Trinity was St Augustine's great work of that name, his *De Trinitate/On the Trinity*. Augustine began this work about 400 AD and completed it twenty years later. A document of impressive length, comprising fifteen Books, and written intermittently over the years, the work nevertheless displays a coherent structure and is a product of Augustine's mature thought. A detailed study of this great work would not be in place here. Our interest lies in the subsequent, dominating influence which this work exercised on later Latin theology of the Trinity. Concentration here, therefore, will be on outlining the major emphases of Augustine's thought and approach and the implications of these emphases. For this is what constitutes the foundation and determines the shape of the later Latin theological tradition right through to St Thomas Aquinas and later.

The main concerns of St Augustine in the *De Trinitate* may be summarily described as follows: to state and explain the basic doctrine of God as Trinity as now established in the Church; to show that this is the understanding of God which is revealed and taught in Scripture; to work out the peculiar rules of human language and logic which must be observed if God as so understood is to be spoken of correctly; to attempt to discover in the highest form of creation immediately known to us, the human mind or spirit, vestiges or traces of the Triune God who is its Origin and Creator. In pursuing this daunting programme, Augustine shows himself a true heir of the Latin tradition which he has thoroughly read and absorbed down to his own time. But he also has a knowledge, whether direct or indirect, of Greek theology, especially the work of the Cappadocians. His own approach, however, will remain distinctly Latin and Western and the decisive direction which he gives to trinitarian theology will consist of his own very personal development of features long characteristic of that tradition.

Augustine's starting-point in approaching an understanding of God as Trinity is all-important. From the very beginning of his work he leaves the reader in no doubt what this starting-point is. 'We shall undertake,' he writes in Book 1,4, 'to the best of our ability ... to account for the one and only and true God being a Trinity, and for the rightness of saying, believing, understanding that the Father and the Son and the Holy Spirit are of one and the same substance or essence.' (tr Hill; so throughout) A little later he states that the teaching of the Catholic tradition before him has been that 'according to the Scriptures Father and Son and Holy Spirit in the inseparable equality of one substance present a divine unity; and therefore there are not three gods but one God.' (Bk 1,7) Augustine's starting-point is the unity of the one divine substance. In this, at one level, he simply continues a traditional emphasis of Latin theology going back to Tertullian. But where that tradition would have maintained a strong sense of the divine monarchy – the one God is first and foremost the Father – Augustine abandons this position and understands the one God to mean the one divine substance or nature which *then* is verified in Father, Son and Holy Spirit. The two meanings of the reference 'the one God' still discernible in the Cappadocians has here disappeared. To speak of the one God for Augustine is to speak of the one divine nature. In giving primacy here to the concept of substance or nature as against that of person, Augustine has removed the concept of *taxis* or order from its central place in the traditional understanding of the Triad. In doing so, he has separated the concepts of substance and person and in giving primacy to the former he has, unwittingly to be sure, introduced an *impersonal* concept of God. This shift of meaning and emphasis at so basic a level now has serious implications for the way Augustine is forced to conceive the way God relates with humanity, that is, the understanding of salvation hist-ory and grace. It also faces him with the problem how to conceive the distinctions in God, what, in other words, the concept of person means here.

The problem which Augustine sees very clearly with the notion of distinctions in the Godhead called persons is how to understand these without thereby multiplying or diversifying the one divine substance. He finds his answer to this question by following the direction already indicated by the Cappadocians. They, it will be recalled, had identified the distinction here in question as subsistent, pure relationship (*schesis*). Augustine probes and clarifies in a very thorough way what this concept means and involves. This analysis is probably his greatest contribution to trinitarian theology. The terms 'Father', 'Son' and 'Holy Spirit' are the names which Scripture and the Christian tradition give to these distinct, subsistent Relations within the Godhead. Greek theology is now referring to them as three *hypostases* and Tertullian's term person is becoming established as the equivalent term in Latin. There is, however, still a certain coolness and resistance towards this term on the part of Latin writers. Augustine's contemporary, St Jerome, is a case in point. (*Ep* 15,4) Augustine too has problems with the term as applied to the distinctions in the Triad. The main difficulty he sees in describing the three in God as persons is that this suggests that they belong to a particular species or class called person and so severally possess the common features or characteristics which distinguish that class. But the three in God, understood as subsistent, pure relations, are each of them unique and cannot form a member of a species or class. But language lacks a term for the pure unique and so, Augustine concludes, we have to make do in this context with the inadequate term person. His concluding words on this issue are perhaps the most quoted of the whole work: 'When you ask "Three what?" human speech labours under a great dearth of words. So we say three persons, not in order to say that precisely, but in order not to be reduced to silence'. (Bk 5,2,10) This discomfort of Augustine with the term 'person' in trinitarian theology will be re-echoed in the later Latin tradition, which in any case is heavily dependent upon him. St Anselm of Canterbury, for example, will describe the three in God as 'Three I know not what' / *tres nescio quid*. (*Monologion* 79) As we shall see again, this discomfort is still reflected in contemporary theology.

Having clarified the meaning of God as one and three in terms of one substance and three relations/persons, Augustine turns his attention to the question of the peculiar demands this understanding makes on human language and logic when it attempts to speak of God as so understood. Once the formula one and three is understood in terms of substance and person, then a distinction is immediately imposed between what one may say of God as substance and what one may say exclusively of a particular person.

Since here one and the same substance is verified in all three persons, then whatever is predicated of the substance is common to all three persons without distinction. Such predicates are used of God *absolutely* and apply equally to all three persons. On the other hand, the only terms one may apply exclusively to a particular person are terms referring to the distinct relation which that person is, that is, relational terms such as 'Father', 'Son', 'Only-Begotten'. Such predicates are used of God *relatively* and are proper or exclusive to the particular person in question. It is this Augustinian teaching which the Council of Florence (1442 AD) will later sum up in the statement: 'everything [in God] is one where there is no opposition of relationship.'

On the basis of this principle, it follows that all divine attributes are predicated of God absolutely, not relatively, and therefore belong to all three persons equally. As a later Creed was to put it: 'Theirs is an undivided and equal Godhead, majesty and power, which is neither diminished in the single persons nor increased in the three ... For they are inseparable both in what they are and in what they do'. (IX Co Toledo, 675 AD) Similarly, all divine activity outside of the Godhead itself, that is, all the operations of God in Creation and the history of salvation, what Latin theology will later call *opera divina ad extra*, these too must be predicated absolutely of God and not relatively of particular persons. Because all such activity is an exercise and expression of the one divine substance, it is common to all three persons and produced by them without distinction: 'just as Father, Son and Holy Spirit are inseparable, so do they work inseparably'. (*On Trin* 1,7) There is therefore no act of God relating to us humans of which it can be said: That is the Father or Son or Holy Spirit *alone* acting. To quote the Creed of Toledo again: 'They [the persons] are inseparable both in what they are and in what they do'.

But this position now confronts Augustine with a major problem. For if the actions of God relating to humanity in salvation history are common to all three persons without distinction, how is it that Scripture and Christian faith speak a different language, attributing plainly and confidently some actions to the Father alone, some to the Son, some to the Holy Spirit? Or, since the way God relates to us determines the way we relate to God, how could the Lord himself have instructed us in prayer to address the Father alone, saying 'Our Father ...'? Augustine's answer to this quest-ion is to propose a linguistic fiction which trinitarian theology will later term the principle of appropriation. Augustine maintains that Scripture and the language of faith simply adopt a type of linguistic shorthand whereby they often attribute to one person what is really common to all three. He sees a basis for this attribution in some affinity between the action in question and the distinctive characteristic or *proprium* of that Person. Thus, the Father alone may be described, as in the Creed, as the Creator of all, since he is the Origin of all within the Godhead; the love with which God graces us may be and is (e.g. Rom 5:5) attributed to the Holy Spirit, since, in Augustine's understanding, the Spirit is the gift of love of the Father and Son.

A major flaw in Augustine's great enterprise emerges clearly here. This, very simply, is that he has made the language of Scripture and Christian faith conform to his conceptual analysis of the doctrine of the Trinity rather than approaching matters the other way round. In matters theological, Scripture and the historical, living tradition must always be the dictating starting-point, the basic position calling for exegesis and elucidation, the irreplaceable first or major premiss in syllogistic argument. Augustine has reduced this position to the level of the minor premiss, giving his own theological construction the role of the major. The unfortunate effect of this inversion of right theological method may be seen most clearly, I think, in the area of pneumatology. The theology of the Holy Spirit was a topic close to Augustine's heart and his contribution to the development of this theology is surely the richest in the whole Christian tradition. In particular, his writing on the theme of the Spirit in the Church, his concept of the Spirit as the soul of the Church, is profound and significant. Yet, this rich theology now becomes a victim of Augustine's own theological construction. As a comment on this odd situation, the writer may, perhaps, be permitted to quote himself.

> The controversial Spirit-theology of the fourth century incurred the danger of confining pneumatology within the area of the immanent Trinity, to questions of procession and relation, and of ignoring the economic Trinity, the role of the Spirit in the history of salvation and in the experience of the Church. By and large Greek theology succeeded in avoiding this danger and developed a living theology of the Spirit giving a prominent pneumatological dimension to its ecclesiology. Western theology, on the other hand, largely succumbed to the danger, mainly through the greater emphasis which it gave to Augustine's doctrine of appropriation. Applying this concept strictly meant seeing the Spirit as such operative only within the Trinity and the life of the Church was thus removed from his personal influence. To speak of

the Spirit in the Church could only be a manner of speaking. As Augustine's pneumatology was the most comprehensive of the whole patristic period, especially in dynamically relating the themes Spirit and Church, it was ironical that he should unwittingly take with the left hand what he had so generously given with the right. (T. Marsh, 'The Holy Spirit in Early Christian Teaching', *ITQ*, 45 [1978], 113)

Augustine devotes most of the second half of the *De Trinitate* to investigating whether the human being may contain within itself some reflection of its Creator, the Triune God. This is his famous effort to discover some traces or analogies of the Trinity within the human psyche. Though his probing search in this elusive area is never conclusive but remains throughout tentative, nevertheless this discussion had an enormous influence on later Latin theology. It therefore requires here a brief word of explanation.

The basis to which Augustine appeals to legitimise this investigation is the text of Genesis 1:26, 'Let us make man in our image …'. If the human being is made in the image of God, and this God is the Trinity, then, even despite the ravages of the Fall, one must surely expect some traces of this image to remain in the fallen but redeemable human. If this is so, one may hope that careful reflection on the processes of the human psyche may bring to light these traces and so assist the mind to understand, however feebly, this great mystery. With this justification and in this hope, Augustine undertakes his psychological trinitarian exploration.

Augustine here is seeking triads within the rational or spiritual processes of the human being which will reflect accurately, however inadequately, the Triad which God is. He considers first the phenomenon of human love and the triad which it involves: the Lover, the Loved, and the Love. Looked at from the centre-point of the person who loves, there does seem to be some form of a three-in-one phenomenon here. Augustine, however, abandons consideration of this avenue of exploration because of its inadequacy, as he sees it, to properly parallel the divine Triad. But some later theologians will be more impressed with this model and find merits in it which Augustine himself did not suspect.

Augustine's preferred avenue of investigation, in his effort to find an image of the Trinity in the human, lies in the rational processes of the human mind, the triad which he describes as mind or memory, understanding, will. Though he is often said to be totally original here, it should not be forgotten that both Irenaeus and Origen had already pointed thought in this direction. By memory here Augustine means, not what the word normally means with us today, but rather the mind itself as present to itself, self-consciousness. When it is so activated, the mind through its faculty of intellect or understanding produces knowledge, both of itself and of other things and then through its faculty of will chooses or loves what it now knows. This mental process seems to involve a true three-in-one triad: the mind, its knowledge, its love. Further, this triad seems to parallel neatly the divine Triad. The mind, the originating source of the whole process, reflects the Father; the production of knowledge by the understanding reflects the Father's generation of his Image, the Word; the love which terminates the process reflects the mutual love of Father and Word/Son which is, according to Augustine, the Holy Spirit. According to this model, therefore, the Word proceeds from the Father by an act of the divine intellect: the Father in knowing himself expresses himself and this expression is his Image, his Word. And since we naturally speak of the mind as conceiving and giving birth to its thought, this procession of the Word from the Father is more specifically a generation and so the Word which so proceeds is in some true sense rightly called the Son of God. Augustine had earlier in this work identified the Holy Spirit as the gift of love which results from the Father and the Son knowing one another. Since love is an activity of the will, the Holy Spirit is therefore said to proceed by way of the divine will. Augustine thus identifies the two divine processions, that of the Word/Son from the Father and that of the Holy Spirit from the Father and the Son, as coming about by way of the divine intellect and the divine will respectively. This understanding of the divine processions will become part of Augustine's legacy to the later Latin tradition. That tradition, however, will tend to distinguish and separate the two forms of procession more sharply than Augustine intended and, indeed, give a priority to the intellectual procession of the Son which he would scarcely have endorsed.

One further point in this summary review of St Augustine's trinitarian theology requires mention. Augustine understands the personal characteristic of the Holy Spirit to be gift, the gift of love between the Father and the Son. Logically, therefore, he maintains that the Spirit proceeds from *both* the Father *and* the Son, though, he constantly insists, from the Father principally, *principaliter*, a rare recognition in Augustine of the traditional trinitarian *taxis*. This is the source of the later Latin insistence on the double procession of the Holy Spirit and of the dogmatic difference on this point between the Latin and Greek traditions.

The Latin Tradition

St Augustine's work *On the Trinity* was being disseminated, even pirated, as he was writing it over the first decades of the fifth century. A product itself of the Latin tradition, it quickly came to exercise a dominating influence on the way the doctrine of the Trinity was understood and stated in the Latin Church. From the fifth century on every Latin statement of this doctrine, whatever the genre of the text, liturgical, credal, catechetical, theological, reflects and re-presents Augustine's understanding and even his verbal formulations. If this means that the Latin tradition inherited the many great strengths of Augustine's trinitarian theology, it also means that it inherited as well its weaknesses. And since the authority of the great Bishop of Hippo always stood above question in this tradition, this meant that this theology, at least until very recent times, was never subjected to the kind of critical scrutiny which would detect and expose these inadequacies. It is one of the main tasks of theological study of this doctrine today, as it seeks to clarify for our time the Christian understanding of God, to perform this function of critical reflection on the inherited tradition. And the first step here is to note well the dominating influence of Augustine's presentation.

The influence of St Augustine on Western theological thought, even in Rome itself, was already widespread and strong even in his own life-time. Thereafter, as the corpus of his works were collected and disseminated, and despite the disagreement which his theology of grace aroused, this influence grew in force until Augustine became the theological authority *par excellence* for Latin writers. This authoritative status applied above all to his theology of the Trinity. The result was that the doctrine established in the fourth century Controversy, to the satisfaction of both East and West, came to be understood in the West in terms of the personal interpretation given to it by St Augustine.

It was not purely theological interest which gave Augustine's approach in this area its quasi canonical status. Dramatic political developments in the West were now creating a totally new context which faced orthodox Latin Christianity with its greatest challenge since the Age of Persecutions. As St Augustine lay dying in Hippo Regis in the year 430 AD, the city was already being besieged by the Vandals. These Vandals were Arians. So too were most of the other Germanic peoples who now were beginning their conquest of the Western Mediterranean and encircling Rome from North Italy through Gaul and Spain as far as Carthage in North Africa. These tribes had been converted to an Arian Christianity in the middle of the fourth century by the half Goth Ulfilas who had been consecrated a bishop by Eusebius of Nicomedia with a view to this mission. Arriving in the lands of the West as conquerors, these peoples sought to impose their own Arianism upon the mainly Catholic population they had taken over. This was, in effect, for most of the West its first practical experience of Arianism. It was an experience which challenged and threatened the very existence of Western Catholicism.

Over the course of two disturbed centuries Roman and Germanic peoples fused together politically and culturally. The result was the birth of Medieval Europe. But above and apart from the many and complicated political manoeuvres which marked the road towards this fusion, the fundamental question which faced the process was what form of Christian faith, Arianism or Catholicism, would prevail and predominate in the new, emerging Western Europe. Here no fusion, no compromise, was possible. The answer had to be simply either one or the other. In the event, it was Catholicism. But the struggle to achieve this goal was long and difficult and challenged deeply the resources of Latin Catholicism. In meeting this challenge, it sharpened the Catholic doctrine of God as Trinity in a markedly anti-Arian manner. In a formal manner, the response certainly involved asserting strongly the orthodox doctrine of one divine substance and three divine persons. This, however, was simply a formal statement of abstract principle. The really significant and important development was at the more experiential level. Here the concentration and emphasis was on asserting the true divinity of Jesus Christ over against the Arian denial of that doctrine. This emphasis became so strong and pervasive that it practically obliterated consciousness of the Father and the Holy Spirit as active participants in the work of salvation and the human predicament. It was as if Christ sufficed to exemplify the one God, the one divine substance, and to motivate the faithful in prayer and in Christian living. As J A Jungmann has remarked of our period: 'Frequently we feel that "Christ" is used synonymously with "God".' (*Pastoral Liturgy*, 41)

The theological background and basis of this perspective and developmemt is to be found in the previous Latin tradition generally but above all in the theology of St Augustine. His particular emphases – such as on the divine unity understood as the one divine substance, the attribution of divine attributes equally and indifferently to the three Persons, the unity of divine operations *ad extra* – these and others are easily recognisable in this approach and have obviously been used in its formation. His influence, not merely as regards theological content but even in the rhythmic verbal formulations, is obvious in the important credal texts, the Pseudo-Athanasian Creed at the end of the fifth century and the late seventh century Creed of Toledo. Yet Augustine has also been used selectively here and his emphases sharpened in a way he would scarcely have fully approved. But the practical trend and concentration of this perspective remain clear: there is one God and as far as we are concerned in this life this one God is Jesus Christ.

This understanding of God and God's way with humankind formed the main thrust of Christian preaching and instruction in the early Middle Ages. It was an outlook which represented a sharp change from the way God's relation with humans had been understood and felt in the pre-Nicene period. There God was seen as an ordered Triad and the members of that Triad, in accordance with that order or *taxis*, were understood to play distinctive roles in the work of human salvation. Irenaeus' image of the Son and the Spirit as 'the two hands of the Father' is a striking illustration of this outlook. This outlook was able to highlight the mediatorial or high priestly role of Christ in giving us access to the Father. This explained and illuminated the structure of Christian prayer which was based on and exemplified this role. To see this one need look no farther than the words which usually concluded such prayer: '... through Jesus Christ, our Lord'. Theological outlook and Christian piety were here in harmony and alignment.

In the change of perspective which has now occurred this mediatorial role of Christ has been lost to view. Instead, Christ has now practically taken over the total reference and meaning of God. Though the doctrine of God as Trinity continues to be stated and acknowledged in principle, this statement and acknowlege-ment is abstract and formal. In practice, a trinitarian understanding of God has disappeared. This tendency to collapse the Three in God into One shows itself even in the statement of doctrine itself. One may illustrate this from the Preface for the Mass in honour of the Trinity which, though obviously older, first appears in the Gelasian Sacramentary of around 750 AD.

> It is truly meet and just, right and for our salvation, that we should at all times and in all places, give thanks unto You, holy Lord, Father almighty, everlasting God; who, together with your only-begotten Son and the Holy Spirit, are one God, one Lord: not in the oneness of a single person, but in the Trinity of one substance. For what we believe by your revelation of your glory, the same do we believe of your Son,

> the same of the Holy Spirit, without difference or separation. So that in confessing the true and everlasting Deity, distinctions in persons, unity in essence, and equality in majesty may be adored ....

We find here, without any doubt, an orthodox statement of trinitarian doctrine. Yet, neither can there be any doubt where the emphasis lies: one God, one Lord, one substance, the same ..., the true Deity, unity in essence, equality in majesty. The rhythmic formulas roll out hammering home the message that God is One. This emphasis, indeed, is even clearer in the opening of this Mass, the Introit.

> Blessed be the holy Trinity and undivided Unity: we will give glory to him (*ei*), because he has shown us his mercy (*fecit nobiscum misericordiam suam*).

It was perhaps inevitable that, granted the strong stress on the divinity of Christ in the anti-Arian polemic, that this consciousness of the one God should have been construed in terms of the divine Christ. It was a perspective which was to leave a deep mark upon the medieval mind and on all its forms of expression – literature, art, architecture. That it perdured throughout the Middle Ages into modern times may be illustrated from the opening of the popular play *Everyman*, a late fifteenth century text which has been described as 'a product of Catholic Europe'. The play opens with God speaking:

> *God:*
> I perceive, here in my majesty,
> How that all creatures be to me unkind,
> Living without dread in worldly prosperity:
> Of ghostly sight the people be so blind,
> Drowned in sin, they know me not for their God;
> In worldly riches is all their mind,
> They fear not my righteousness, the sharp rod.
> My law that I showed, when I for them died,
> They forget clean, and shedding of my blood red;
> I hanged between two, it cannot be denied;
> To get them life I suffered to be dead;
> I healed their feet, with thorns hurt was my head.
> ...
> Where art thou, Death, thou mighty messenger?
> *Death:*
> Almighty God, I am here at your will,
> Your commandment to fulfil.

The identification of God with Christ *tout court* could scarcely be clearer or more explicit than in this passage from this popular text.

In spite of the formal, notional acknowledgement of the doctrine, a real understanding of God as Trinity practically disappeared from the Christian consciousness of the Middle Ages. Modern times, down indeed to our own day, has inherited this mentality. This is the situation which has justly merited Karl Rahner's much-quoted judgement: 'despite their orthodox confession of the Trinity, Christians are, in their practical life, almost mere "monotheists".' (*The Trinity*, 10)

Scholastic Theology

Meanwhile, the theological effort to understand and formulate the doctrine of God as Trinity continued throughout the period of the Middle Ages. This was an effort towards systematisation, towards producing a systematic tract of trinitarian theology. It attained its finest and final achievement in St Thomas Aquinas' tract on God as Trinity in his *Summa Theologica*, 1, qq 27-43. Since then this exposition of Aquinas has determined the structure and content of textbook theology on this subject down to the recently deceased manuals of our own century. I wish to emphasise immediately that the concentration here will be on this later textbook theology and not on the particular exposition of Aquinas. This latter is a subject of the highest significance. But it is a specialised study beyond the scope of this book. The later Latin Tract *De Deo Trino/On the Triune God* was meant to be a faithful summary of St Thomas' position. That it was fully such, however, is open to serious question. St Thomas' exposition is full of subtle nuances which passed unnoticed in the summary version of his theology offered by the manual tradition. The contention may well be true, therefore, that the Angelic Doctor would not have recognised his theological position in that offered in his name by these later textbooks. Certainly, the inadequacies nowadays generally recognised in these latter may not be automatically attributed to St Thomas.

In formulating his theology of the Trinity, St Thomas had at his disposal a rich mine of sources from the Latin tradition which he obviously had carefully studied. Some prominent milestones here deserve mention. *Facile princeps* among them is undoubtedly St Augustine. But Boethius (d. 524) has a particular importance. Described, with much truth, as the 'last of the Romans, first of the Scholastics', he set himself as a life-task to translate into Latin the works of Plato and Aristotle and provide an explanatory commentary on them. Though by the time of his untimely death not much of this mammoth undertaking had been accomplished, he had provided Latin translations of Aristotle's works on Logic and even had demonstrated, in separate works, how this basic tool of philosophic thought could be applied to the doctrines of the Trinity and Christology. Here he invented and demonstrated the dialectical method of argumentation in theology, becoming indeed the 'first of the Scholastics'. St Thomas later will pay close attention to Boethius' work *On the Trinity/De Trinitate* and write his own (unfinished) study of it. Another who will come under the influence of Boethius and his dialectical method and become in turn an important theological source for the Scholastics of the great medieval period is St Anselm of Bec and Canterbury (d 1109). The burgeoning of scholasticism in the twelfth century will produce many studies which will have formed a significant part of Aquinas' own theological training, for example, the works of Abelard, Peter Lombard, Richard of St Victor. To these must be added the writings of his own contemporaries such as Albert the Great and Bonaventure.

All these scholars belong to and continue the Latin theological tradition of which they are the products. They do not, however, all speak with the one voice. Though belonging to the one tradition, they represent different approaches within that tradition and severally highlight and give priority to different emphases. Richard of St Victor (d. 1173), for example, will opt to develop a different side of St Augustine to that which St Thomas will make his central focus. St Augustine explained the Trinity in terms of the activities of the divine intellect and the divine will. Whereas Aquinas will opt to give priority here to the activity of the divine intellect, Richard develops his understanding of the Trinity from an analysis of the divine will and its act of love. Taking as his scriptural basis the text of 1 John 4:16: 'God is love', Richard points out that love demands Another whom it can address and to whom it can devote itself. In God this Other can only be Another in God, since anything less could not totally absorb God's love. If God is love, therefore, God must consist at least of two persons. But pure love, given its altruistic, social character, goes beyond two and issues in a third, the shared gift in which lovers express their mutual love. In God this process terminates in this Third, the shared gift of the Father and the Son which is the Holy Spirit. Richard's approach will be followed later by St Bonaventure and Duns Scotus and the Franciscan or Scotist School. It is an approach which is showing signs today of taking on a new life. Aquinas' more intellectual, less affective emphasis will determine the approach of the Thomistic tradition.

The existence of such different approaches within the scholastic system would have been sufficient to force a critical awareness and a critical discrimination on St Thomas as he develops his own theology in the middle of the thirteenth century. The *Summa Theologica* is the record of his achievement in this enterprise. What claims our interest and attention here is how Aquinas in this great work situates and approaches the question of God. We are concerned, therefore, primarily and centrally with the question of the structure of the *Summa* and within that of the structure of the discussion of God .

It is the generally accepted view that the structure of the *Summa Theologica* is based on the *Exitus-Reditus* model, that is, on Creation as coming forth from God and then, through God's redemptive providence, returning again to God. Naturally and logically, the first issue requiring discussion and elucidation in this vast perspective is that of God simply as God, the One who is the transcendent Origin of the whole process here coming under consideration. This, accordingly, is where Aquinas begins. The opening section of the *Summa*, Book 1, Questions 2-43, is devoted to a discussion of God simply as God, that is, without for the moment envisaging Creation (introduced next, Questions 44-49) or God's relation with Creation. The fundamental character of this opening discussion is obvious; the perspectives adopted here will run like a determining thread throughout the whole work. What interests us, however, is how this discussion of God is itself structured.

The opening section of the *Summa*, devoted to a discussion of God simply as God, itself consists of two parts. The first part, Questions 2-26, discusses the existence, nature and attributes of the one God. The second part, Questions 27-43, then introduces God as Trinity and discusses the three persons, Father, Son, Holy Spirit, and their relations to one another. The significance of this method of approach needs to be noted. However closely related the two discussions involved here may be, there are two discussions, one devoted to God as one, the other to God as three. Further, the discussion of God as one here is essentially a discussion of the one divine nature or substance. This is what the reference 'the one God' means here. This is the question Aquinas chooses as the starting-point of his whole work and of the discussion of God which opens the work. In effect, a separation, more explicit than anything heretofore, has here been introduced into the theological discussion of God between the one divine nature and the three divine persons. This separation is further reinforced by the assertion of the principles concerning God's external activity in creation and salvation history and appropriation (1: q 39, aa 7-8; q 45, a 6; 3: q 23, a 2).

The question has been asked, though actually only in recent years, why Aquinas decided to adopt this procedure. He certainly was not here following any previous or existing model. The immediate answer to this question lies in the grand design of the *Summa*, the way Aquinas conceived the structure of the work. Opting for the *Exitus-Reditus* structure, St Thomas was committed to beginning with, not God as God relates to us in the economy of creation and history, but with God in Godself, the immanent Deity. Then, since all external divine action is an exercise of the divine nature, it was totally logical for him to make this his starting-point and only later introduce discussion of the distinctions which Christian faith acknowledges within this one God, the persons of the Trinity. (It might be noted that Origen had adopted a very similar structure in his great work, *On First Principles*, though, significantly, his starting-point is not the one divine substance, for which he has no term, but God the Father.) But it is obvious also that in the background here is the strong influence of St Augustine who also began his discussion of God with a consideration of the divine unity understood as the one divine nature. But whatever the reasons, Aquinas' procedure imposes upon the mind a virtual separation between the concepts of nature and persons in God which formal statements to the contrary will scarcely effectively negate. This distinction, however procedural in origin and conception, will then inevitably have an overflow effect in that it will effectively confine the understanding of God as three persons within the immanent Deity and see God as relating to humankind as simply one, meaning the divine nature.

The unhappy legacy of this method of procedure displayed by the *Summa Theologica* becomes evident in the later scholastic manual system where, not only are dogmatic and moral theology divided into distinct disciplines, but even within dogmatic theology different areas are separated into independent Tracts with little effort to interconnect their content. St Thomas is in no way to blame for this carve-up of dogmatic theology. His *Summa* is a unified, harmonious whole and its particular sections have to be understood and assessed, not as isolated, independent units, but as parts of the whole. Inconsistencies which are more apparent when a section is treated on its own are often redeemed when the section is situated in the context of the whole work. The *Summa* loses this harmonious balance when it is carved up into independent, isolated units, as in the later scholastic tract system. Conflicting tendencies which the original work was able to hold together in admirable tension here lose this tensive relationship and now often emerge as independent and conflicting positions.

Aquinas' discussion of God at the beginning of the *Summa* is a particular, indeed perhaps the most notorious, victim of this later system. Here St Thomas' two discussions concerning God as one and as three are separated into two independent Tracts, *On the One God/De Deo Uno* and *On the Triune God/De Deo Trino*. In this presentaton the one God clearly means the one divine nature and constitutes a separate, independent subject from consideration of God as three, a Trinity of persons. When in this latter Tract, the activity of the divine persons in their very personhood is confined within God simply as God, the immanent Deity, whereas God relates to us in the economy simply as one, the impression is inevitably conveyed that our relationship is really with the divine nature, not the persons as such. This understanding will be strongly reinforced by the Tract which specifically discusses our relationship with God, the Tract on (created) Grace. This Tract will give unusual prominence to a late and rather isolated text of the New Testament, 2 Peter 1:4, simply because it speaks of our calling as being to 'become sharers of the divine nature'. Conversely, it will have great difficulty finding any real meaning for the concept, so prominent in the New Testament and the patristic tradition, of the Indwelling of the Trinity. The theologian reported as saying: 'we are sons of the divine essence' had understood his scholastic theology well.

Aquinas' introduction of a procedural separation between the one divine nature and the three divine persons was thus developed in later scholastic theology into a real separation. The effect of this development was to confine the reality of God as Trinity within the immanent Godhead and thereby de-personalise the understanding of God's relationship with us. The net result was to reduce the theology of the Trinity to a matter of abstract and purely academic interest, somewhat like a problem in pure mathematics. The role of St Thomas here represents but one stage in this historical development. The tendency in this direction was built deep into the Latin tradition in particular, going back indeed to the beginning of that tradition in Tertullian. A similar tendency, rooted in the fourth century Controversy, is discernible also in Greek theology. This will eventually lead to a development analogous to that in the Latin tradition which, from the fourteenth century on, will take concrete form in Palamite theology and have its basis in the distinction between the divine essence and the divine energies. The dominating and determining force in the later Western development, however, is unquestionably the trinitarian theology of St Augustine.

The structure which St Thomas devised and gave his grand design, the *Summa Theologica*, involved an endorsement of this tendency in the Latin tradition, though as a procedural arrangement or method. But this was far from being his only contribution to the systematic theology of the Trinity as this now developed. He also determined the basic structure of this treatise. The later scholastic Tract *De Deo Trino* is but a summary of St Thomas' discussion of the Trinity in the *Summa*, Book 1, Questions 23-43. This Tract presents the same structure, the same central concepts, the same arguments as Aquinas' treatise. This is certainly theology *ad mentem Sancti Thomae*. Nor need there be in general any regret about this. St Thomas identified the basic concepts which the doctrine of the Trinity involves, arranged them in logical order, and explained their meaning and implications. These concepts were, in the following order: the divine Processions, the divine Relations, the divine Persons, the divine Missions. This constitutes the basic structure of the treatise in the *Summa* which the later Tract represents in a summary manner. This was a fine achievement of structure, clarity and precision typical of Aquinas' theological approach. It is but another example of his great contribution to rigorous but clear theological thought. We now turn our attention to this classic presentation of the theology of the Trinity as this appears in the later scholastic Tract.

The Tract On the Triune God

This Tract, modelled on Aquinas' discussion of the topic in the *Summa*, follows closely the structure of that discussion. Its centre and core consists therefore of an exposition of the concepts which the history of the theology of the Trinity had shown to be basic to an understanding of the doctrine. These are the concepts of Procession, Relation, Person, Mission. To this material were added certain principles which scholastic theology saw arising as implications of these concepts. This section will provide a summary exposition of this well-structured corpus of theology.

The Divine Processions

The term 'procession' means the origin or coming forth of one thing from another. The term came into theology originally, espe-

cially Greek theology, from the Bible, where the Word of God and
the Spirit of God were described as 'coming forth' from God and a
text such as John 15:26 spoke of 'the Spirit of truth, who proceeds
from (*ekporeuetai*) the Father'. Procession thus became the technical term in theology to describe how the Son and the Spirit originated within the Godhead. For what is being spoken of here is the
immanent being of God, God in Godself. The inference is – and it
should be well noted – that God in Godself, the immanent Deity,
is as God is revealed in the economy of salvation, that is, as Father
who is the origin from whom proceeds the Son and the Spirit but
who himself does not proceed, who is without origin, the Unoriginate, and the Son and the Spirit who each in their own distinctive
way proceed from the Father. There are accordingly two divine
processions, that of the Son from the Father and that of the Holy
Spirit from, in the Latin tradition, both the Father and the Son.
Since we are talking here of the immanent being of God, these are
eternal processions.

At this point some further analysis of the meaning of procession is necessary. Procession involves a real distinction between
the principle, the origin or source from which something proceeds, and the term, that which proceeds from the source, originates. Further, a procession is described as immanent or transient
according as its term, that which proceeds or originates, comes to
exist within or without its principle or source. For example, an
idea is developed by the mind, proceeds from the mind, yet remains within it – immanent procession; creation proceeds from
God but exists outside God – transient procession. Applying this
analysis to the divine processions, we have to say that each procession involves two distinct, opposing factors, the principle and
the term of the procession. The processions in question here are
immanent processions – their terms, the Son and the Spirit, remain
within the Godhead. The reason for this is that the one divinity,
the one divine substance, is fully communicated to the Son and
the Spirit in their proceeding. Thus the divine processions are
eternal events within the Godhead itself from which emerge the
divine Triad, all three Members of which are truly, fully and
equally divine, God.

Like all human concepts, the concept of procession is applied
to God analogously. In applying it to God, therefore, one must re-
move from it those aspects which attach to it in human experience
but which do not apply to God. In accordance with this principle
two particular features of procession as we experience it must be
excluded when we use this concept of God. First, there can be no

question of causality proper or causal dependence in the divine processions. For example, the Father does not cause the Son in any proper sense of the term 'cause', that is, giving existence to something which did not previously exist, referring to a transition from non-being to being. Secondly, in the created order processions involve the passage of time, a temporal sequence, a before and an after. This is not so in the divine processions. They belong to the eternal Deity where time, a feature of creation, does not apply. The divine processions are eternal, they do not involve any before or after. There never was when they were not.

Following these general, explanatory remarks on the divine processions, we may now move on to a consideration of each of these processions in particular.

Processions may be of different kinds. Theology asserts that the first procession is by way of generation; here the originating principle generates or gives birth to the proceeding term. The foundation for this understanding is simply the fact that the New Testament describes the principle and term of this procession as Father and Son. Generation is defined as the origin of a living being from a living being by transmission of a likeness of nature. The first divine procession, it is maintained, fulfills this definition, though here it is an identity of nature which is transmitted, not just a likeness. This procession, therefore, is a procession of generation. Scholastic theology, following the lead of St Augustine, explains this procession as occurring through an exercise of the divine intellect, an act of divine knowing. The Father, contemplating and knowing himself, produces in the divine mind a perfect expression or image of himself. In God this mental expression, because it is the perfect expression of God, subsists as a distinct Other with the Father, the full expression of the Father's being in the Other: 'He reflects the glory of God and bears the very stamp of his nature'. (Heb 1:3) The Bible accordingly describes this Other as the Word, the Wisdom, the Image, the Son of God. It must be noted again, however, that all these descriptions are employed here analogically, that is, not all the features associated with these terms in human experience apply when these terms are used of God. This comment has particular significance when applied to the term 'Son', since generation in God does not have the sexual character of human generation. The New Testament reflects this difference when it uses other terms also to describe this Other. But bearing in mind this limitation of human language as used of God, the first divine procession is understood as a procession by generation.

According to the teaching of the Latin Church, the Holy Spirit proceeds from both the Father and the Son as from one principle. This formulation comes from the Council of Lyons in 1274 AD, but its immediate source is St Anselm of Canterbury. He, however, was here simply formulating the teaching of St Augustine. This double procession of the Holy Spirit, as it is often called, represents today the main dogmatic difference between the Church of Rome and other Churches of the West and the Eastern Orthodox Church. This is not the place to enter into the complex and sad history of this dispute. But it may be helpful to recall that the Creed of Constantinople had simply stated that the Spirit 'proceeds from the Father'. The Council here was paralleling the procession of the Spirit with that of the Son and thereby asserting the equal divinity of the Spirit. Then, beginning in Spain in the fifth century, Churches in the Western Provinces gradually began to add the words 'and from the Son/*Filioque*' to the statement of the Creed. The main reason for the addition was the fear that an Arian denial of the divinity of the Son could be read into the text of the Creed as it stood. Rome, however, though it accepted the teaching as correct, for many centuries never endorsed the addition to the text. Over this period the Creed was not in fact recited in the Mass at Rome, though this practice had become common in the Provinces since the sixth century. Finally, Benedict VIII in 1014 AD, bowing to imperial pressure, sanctioned the recitation of the Creed in the Mass at Rome with the *Filioque* included. This change of attitude and policy now made the differnce between West and East on this issue, which until then had been basically theological, official and dogmatic.

The procession of the·Holy Spirit is not a generation – and therefore the Spirit is not and may not be called another Son of God. Theology, however, has not been able to identify any corresponding procession within human experience to which this procession might be related, even by analogy. 'The manner of that procession' writes Boethius, 'we are no more able to declare clearly than the human mind is able to understand the generation of the Son from the substance of the Father'. (*On the Faith*, 25-28) Greek theology simply calls it by the general name, Procession/ *Ekporeusis*. Scholastic theology, to distinguish this procession clearly from the generation of the Son, invented a new term from the word *Spiritus* and called it Spiration.

The Latin tradition, following here again the lead of St Augustine, explains the procession of the Holy Spirit as coming from an act of the divine will, an act of divine loving, just as it explained

the generation of the Son as coming from an act of divine knowing. It is on this basis that it distinguishes and differentiates the
two processions. Loving is an act or exercise of the faculty of will.
In God, the Father, contemplating his Image, the Son, loves the
Son and the Son returns this love of the Father. This mutual love
of the Father and Son, this bond of love which unites them, subsists as a third Other in God, the Holy Spirit, the fruit of the
Father-Son relationship. For Augustine the characteristic proper
to the Spirit, the *idioma* or *proprium* distinguishing the Spirit from
the Father and the Son, is gift/*donum*. The Holy Spirit is the gift of
the Father to the Son and of the Son to the Father, their mutual
love. This property, gift of love, characterises and distinguishes
the Holy Spirit in the Godhead and represents also the role of the
Holy Spirit in the economy of salvation. The text of Romans 5:5,
one of Augustine's favourite texts, comes readily to mind here:
'God's love has been poured into our hearts through the Holy
Spirit which has been given to us.'

Scholastic theology exercised all its great capacity for subtle
thought in an effort to explain precisely why the procession of the
Holy Spirit was not also a generation like the first procession. At
first sight the definition of generation would seem to fit perfectly
here also. Scholastic theologians, however, denied this and called
attention to the difference between acts of knowing and acts of
willing. Only the former, they maintained, could properly be
called generative, the latter were not. Hence, the second procession, which came about through an act of divine willing, was not
an example of generation. Without attempting to enter any further into this subtle analysis, one might try to illustrate the point
by calling attention to our natural use of ordinary language. We
naturally enough speak of the mind in its process of knowing as
generating a thought or idea, conceiving, bringing forth or giving
birth to a thought; we can describe a thought as the child of the
mind. We would not use such language, however, of acts of the
will such as loving. Love is not something we possess of ourselves
or produce of ourselves. Love is a gift to us which attracts us out
of ourselves towards its object. It is not therefore a process under
our control like our intellectual acts of knowing. It is a different
kind of mental activity which does not display in itself the generative features characteristic of intellectual activity. It is on the basis
of this distinction in kind between the activity of knowing and the
activity of willing that scholastic theology explains the difference
between the two divine processions and justifies the assertion that
the procession of the Spirit is not another generation.

The Thomist tradition in its understanding of rational being gave a priority to the faculty of intellect and its activity over that of the will and its voluntary activity. This basic option now influenced also the understanding of the divine Processions in that it entailed giving a certain priority here to the first procession, the generation of the Son. This emphasis had an unfortunate consequence in that it led to and entailed a diminished interest in the second procession, the procession of the Holy Spirit. The figure of Christ the Son dominated this theological perspective. The Christocentrism which now came to characterise scholastic theology had at least one of its sources here. The double procession of the Spirit, as it came to be understood and presented in this system, further reinforced this attitude. A proper theology of the Spirit could scarcely develop in this theological environment. The contrasting option of Richard of St Victor, giving priority to the faculty of will and its act of love, presented a different approach here which avoided this onesidedness and allowed scope for a more balanced and more comprehensive theological development. This is one reason why this Scotist approach is arousing new interest today.

The Divine Relations

The two divine processions show the Godhead as consisting of a Triad, the members of which can now be identified as relations. The processions, in other words, are the basis for the recognition in God of three, distinct relations. But before we proceed to show this, it is first necessary to explain what the notion of relation means and involves.

Relationship is, happily, one of the familiar aspects of our lives, indeed the very stuff of our lives. Yet, for all its familiarity, relation also remains one of the deeply mysterious aspects of our being. When we begin to analyse what relation means, we find that it involves three factors. First, there are the two terms which are related. Second, there is the ground or basis of the relationship, the reason why the terms are related. There are different kinds of relation according as these grounds of relationship differ in kind. A parent and child, for example, are related on the ground that the child has origin from the parent; this is a relation of origin. A husband and wife, on the other hand, are related on a different basis, the matrimonial consent. But, third, relationship in itself, the essence of relationship, does not consist in these two factors, the two related terms and the ground of their relationship. These factors are but the prior conditions for the relationship to exist, the foundation upon which the relationship stands. They do not constitute the relationship as such. To develop an understanding of this, we need to probe further and deeper.

Relation describes a mode of presence of terms to each other, an ordering, directing, facing of beings towards each other. Towardsness is the essence of relation. This towardsness implies a capacity of each for the other, an opening of each to the other. Relationship signifies the activation of this capacity, the enriching and fulfilling of this openess. Relationship, therefore, is something dynamic, creative. It means achievement of greater being. Relation in God signifies the achievement of greatest being, divine Being.

Returning now to the divine processions, we find that each procession sets up two terms which are related to each other on the basis of origin: the principle from which proceeds and that which proceeds. These two terms are related to each other on the basis of the origin of the one from the other. They are relations of origin. Theology describes them as 'opposing relations' meaning that they are set over against one another, face one another, in this relationship of origin. Since each procession establishes two relations, two related terms, there are in God four real relations. But only three of these four are distinct or opposing relations, since the principle of the second procession, the Father and Son, simply reproduces the two terms of the first and so does not constitute a new, additional opposing or distinct relation. Therefore, while there are in God four relations, only three of these are distinct or opposing relations, the Father, the Son and the Holy Spirit.

The divine relations are not distinct from the divine nature, except in a virtual or logical sense, that is, as so considered by the mind. In reality, they are each of them identical with the divine nature though distinct among themselves. Each relation is the divine nature existing in a distinct relative way, as a distinct relation. Thus: the divine nature in the relation of paternity is the Father; the divine nature in the relation of sonship is the Son; the divine nature in the relation of gift of love is the Spirit. There is no distinction between the relations as regards nature; this they all possess equally. The relations are distinct from one another purely as relations.

It results from this analysis that the relations in God are subsistent relations, that is, relations which exist in themselves and not simply as an aspect of something else. We have no experience of subsistent relations, since with us relation is always an aspect of that which is related. We only know beings who have relation; we have no experience of a being who simply is relation. But since in

God the one divine nature exists in three distinct relative ways, relations in God are subsistent relations.

This understanding of the one nature existing as three relations now leads us back again to a consideration of the essence of relation, the notion of pure relation. This, we noted, is simply a facing towards, a towardsness, what Latin theology called *esse ad*. It is not, therefore, a constituent element of a nature, one element among others making up what a nature in total is. Relation in its essential meaning is simply the way a complete nature faces, its towardsness. Pure relation, one might say, is the face which a nature wears.

Revelation forces us to recognise that in God the one nature exists in three distinct, relative ways, as three subsistent, pure relations. But because pure relation, relation in its essence, does not form part of the nature, this existence of the nature as three pure relations does not diversify or multiply the nature. This is the reason the doctrine of the Trinity is not a contradiction. The three relative ways in which the one divine nature exists do not interfere with the unity of that nature.

The Divine Persons

We saw earlier that in the third century Tertullian had described the distinctions in God as three persons. Latin theology later adopted this term as a translation for the equivalent Greek word *hypostasis*. Theology then presented the relations which the divine processions establish as three persons. To explain this use of terminology, it was necessary to show that the concept of divine relation fulfilled the definition of person. A problem here, however, was that neither biblical thought nor that of Hellenistic philosophy could supply theology with such a definition. The approach to anthropology, where one might expect this definition to emerge, in both these sources seemed too vague and imprecise to serve the needs of theology here. Theology here, therefore, was thrown back on its own resources. Its achievement in elaborating a coherent concept of person was to make a major contribution to the history of ideas and the political implementation of such ideas, for example, in the area of human rights.

It was Boethius early in the sixth century who provided theology with its basic and classic statement of the meaning of person. He defined person as 'an individual substance of a rational nature' /*naturae rationalis individua substantia*. (*Against Eutyches and Nestorius*, 3) Boethius constructed this definition on the basis of the logic of Aristotle, using the concepts of genus, species, individual.

His interest and his purpose was to develop an understanding of person which would clarify and vindicate the Church's christological and trinitarian doctrines. Medieval theology gratefully accepted this definition and put it to service with the same interest and purpose. It also discovered, however, a certain incompleteness in it. To remedy this it added to it the further note of autonomy and incommunicability. Person now meant an individual substance of a rational nature existing in an autonomous, incommunicable way. In this form the definition applied quite neatly to the divine relations who thereby could be shown to be and be described as persons.

The application of this definition to the concept of divine subsistent relation can perhaps be most easily seen by observing that the definition consists of four notes which this concept fulfills perfectly. These notes are: substantiality, rationality, individuality, autonomous, incommunicable existence. Recalling that divine relation means the one divine nature existing in and as a distinct relation, it can be seen that all four are verified in this concept. Here there is: substantiality – the divine substance or nature; rationality – this is a *rational* substance; individuality – the divine substance is *one*, individual; autonomous, incommunicable existence – each divine relation is the one divine nature existing in a distinct, autonomous, incommunicable way. The three divine relations are, therefore, three divine persons.

Following the application of this definition of person to the divine relations, Latin scholastic theology maintained that the divine relations constitute the divine persons, the relations are the persons. A subtle difference emerges again at this point between the Latin approach and the Greek. Greek theology does not see the relations as *constituting* the persons, but prefers to say that they *manifest* the persons. This subtle difference leads to some further differences of approach and emphasis in the understanding of trinitarian theology in the two traditions. This question, however, cannot be pursued further here. But this identification of relation and person does, at least, alert us to the fact that the divine relations are not for us cold abstractions, such as the terms sometimes used for them in theology might suggest, for example, Unbegotteness, Begotteness. They are personal Beings whom we can approach and address and whom we call by personal names, Father, Son, Holy Spirit.

The concepts of procession, relation, person, led theology to identify and highlight another significant aspect of God as Trinity. The divine persons do not live in isolation from one another.

They are not isolated, cut-off islands. As relations their life totally consists in relating to each other. They live in and for one another, flow into one another. This co-inherence of the persons is indicated in the New Testament in such texts as John 10:38; 14:11. St Augustine expressed this notion with characteristic clarity: 'They (the Triad) are each in each and all in each, and each in all and all in all, and all are one.' (*On Trin* 6,12) A sixth century writer, Fulgentius of Ruspe in North Africa, a devoted follower of St Augustine, summed up the idea admirably and simply: 'The Father is fully in the Son and the Spirit; the Son is fully in the Father and the Spirit; the Spirit is fully in the Father and the Son'. (*On the Faith*, 4) The Council of Florence, in its Decree for the Jacobites in 1442 AD, will repeat this statement of Fulgentius almost verbatim. St John Damascene (d. c. 749), the last of the Greek Fathers, coined a term for this dynamic interrelationship of the Persons, *perichoresis*, literally 'moving around in' each other. This term was later translated into Latin by its equivalent Latin word, circumcession/*circum-incessio*, but more usually by the more static term circumsession/*circuminsessio*, 'sitting around in' one another, an expression which illustrates the tendency of Latin theology to think of God in more static terms than the Greek. Though scholastic theology did little to develop the potentiality of this idea, it is a concept which today is receiving prominent and significant attention in trinitarian theology, as we shall have occasion to notice later.

The Divine Missions
The explanation of the concepts of procession, relation, person, constitute the basic presentation of the theology of the Trinity in the Tract *On the Triune God*. The Tract, however, completes its discussion with a consideration of the divine Missions. Mission here means the sending of a proceeding person in the economy of salvation. Since there are two proceeding persons, the Son and the Spirit, there are two divine missions, the visible mission of the Son, the Incarnation, and the invisible mission of the Holy Spirit, the event of Pentecost in the Acts of the Apostles. The mission of the Son is called visible because its term or result, Jesus Christ, the Word made flesh, was visible. The mission of the Holy Spirit, on the other hand, is an interior, supernatural event, a presence in the souls of the just, and therefore is invisible to human eyesight. The original manifestation of this sending or mission at Pentecost by means of the rushing wind and tongues of fire was a matter of merely outward signs, not a visible manifestation of the mission itself.

The Tract here for the first time relates its discussion of God as Trinity to the way God relates with us humans in the economy of salvation. In thus summarily introducing the topics of the Incarnation and the outpouring of the Spirit, it also establishes a link, however tenuous, with other areas of theology, especially Christology and the theology of grace. But the Tract's method of procedure has become obvious at this point. It began its discussion of the Trinity from the perspective of God in Godself, the immanent Deity, and effectively confined its discussion within that context. Here it is following faithfully, as we noted earlier, Aquinas' order of procedure. It has often been pointed out that this procedure follows the order of being, God's being, not the order of knowledge, how we come to know about God's being. For theology this knowledge is derived from the revelation of God in the economy, God as God relates to us. Since the way we know always conditions what we know, it would seem obvious that the God of the economy must be the starting-point and conditioning context for all discourse of God in Godself. We will return later to a consideration of the implications of this methodology.

Another important topic of trinitarian interest also arises in this context. This is the question of the Divine Indwelling, sometimes referred to as the Indwelling of the Trinity, sometimes the Indwelling of the Holy Spirit. This is an explicit and important theme in the New Testament. (Jn 14:16-17; 23; Rom 5:5; 8: 9-11; 2 Cor 6:16) It is a theme which receives great emphasis in the patristic tradition, especially in the Greek Fathers. Scholastic theology encountered great difficulty in understanding and situating this concept. A variety of nuances in the efforts at explanation reflect this difficulty. General agreement, however, emerged on some basic aspects. The Indwelling, being an external work of God, referred to a presence of the Trinity, of all three persons, in the souls of the just, those in the state of sanctifying grace. Reference to the Indwelling of the Holy Spirit was simply an example of appropriation. But how was this presence to be conceived? The scholastics attempted to explain what was in question by trying to identify how it came about, using Aristotle's categories of causality. The generally accepted view saw the Indwelling as the supernatural knowledge and love of God which sanctifying grace and the infused virtues produced in the soul, a kind of special intuition of and feeling for the God who had drawn so near. This was the result and consequence of the presence of grace, a kind of adorning of the soul as a result of grace. As such, the Indwelling was an example of the presence of the known object to and in the knower, of the loved object to and in the lover.

As so defined, the Indwelling could now be situated within and explained by the category of efficient causality. It represented an aspect of the impact of the efficient cause upon its object, who in this case is a rational being. The problem which arises here, however, is that the efficient cause is an extrinsic agency which acts on its object from outside and can only be said to be present to its object in terms of the effects it produces. By definition it is and remains a presence outside, not a presence within. This understanding of the Divine Indwelling, therefore, seems quite inadequate to explain the presence of God *within us* which the New Testament asserts and which the patristic tradition so strongly emphasises. Modern theology has been especially critical of scholastic theology on this issue.

Trinitarian Principles

The Tract on the Trinity incorporated with its presentation of the core concepts of this theology a statement of some basic principles which had emerged in the tradition as implications of the doctrine. These are the related principles concerning external divine works/*opera divina ad extra* and appropriation and a statement which attempts to sum up succinctly the whole understanding of the Triune God as scholastic theology has perceived it.

We have already seen how the question of God's external activity, God's action in creation and the economy, had emerged and was addressed by, for example, the Cappadocian Fathers and St Augustine. The medieval scholastics attempted no re-thinking here, but simply formulated Augustine's clear position in their own characteristic way. External divine works referred to the acts of God outside God's own immanent being and life, in other words, to God's acts in creation and the economy of salvation. Acts are always acts of a nature, that is, of what makes a being to be the kind of being it is. A being acts in accordance with its nature. Its action is simply its nature expressing itself. Scholasticism summed up this point in a simple axiom: action follows being or nature /*actio sequitur esse*. Since there is in God only the one divine nature, external divine acts are performed by all three persons in virtue of the one nature which they indifferently possess. In other words, these acts are performed by all three persons acting as one principle. This means that no one of the three persons relates to us apart from the other two; all three relate to us simply as one. Fulgentius had summed up this teaching very clearly: 'The holy Trinity operates inseparably, nor is there a work that the Father does and the Son does not; or that the Son does and the

Holy Spirit does not.' (*Against Fastidius*, 2,5,6) This position also has a corollary: the way God relates to us determines also the way we relate to God. Accordingly, if God relates to us as one, we too can only relate to God as one. We cannot address or relate to one particular divine person. When we pray 'Our Father', we are addressing not the First Person but the Trinity as one God, as St Thomas explicity maintains. (*Sum T* 3: 23, 2 con)

This principle, however, seems to be in direct conflict with the language of the New Testament and of the living faith which speaks very confidently of particular divine persons alone performing certain actions in creation and salvation history. And it sounds very odd to discover that when we address our prayer to the Father or to Christ the Son or to the Holy Spirit, we are addressing the Trinity as one God. Theology's answer to this problem was the principle known as appropriation. This principle states that a particular external divine action, though its execution is really common to all three persons acting as one, may nevertheless legitimately be attributed to one person, as a manner of speaking, on the basis of some perceived affinity between this action and the personal characteristic (*proprium*) of this person. For example, one may speak of the Father as the Creator, thereby attributing to the Father the work of creation, because in the Trinity the Father is the one who is source of all, the Origin without origin. Similarily, the Holy Spirit is traditionally called the Sanctifier because sanctification is the power of God's love active in us and in the Trinity the Spirit is personally the gift of love.

By this principle of appropriation theology attempts to accommodate its teaching concerning *opera divina ad extra* with the language of the New Testament and the living faith. It is scarcely necessary to add that the adequacy of this explanation remains open to question.

The Decree for the Jacobites, issued by the Council of Florence in 1442 AD, contained a statement that the later Tract rightly saw and paraded as summing up the scholastic theology of the Trinity. This statement reads: 'everything [in God] is one where there is no opposition of relation'/*omnia [in Deo] sunt unum, ubi non obviat relationis oppositio.* (N/P 325; D/S 1330) This statement emphasises that the only distinctions in the one God are the three distinct relations; everything else is one because everything else belongs to, indeed is, the divine nature. The distinction of persons does not in any way diversify or multiply the one nature. Divine attributes, being attributes of the nature, belong equally and without difference to all three persons. Accordingly, there is in God but one mind, one consciousness, one will, one power, one action. One might sum up the import of this statement as follows: subtract the one nature and all belonging to it from God and what remains is simply the three distinct, pure relations. The Tract was correct in seeing in this statement a compendium of scholastic trinitarian theology. But it can hardly escape notice that the statement also reflects the strong emphasis on the divine unity, the one God, characteristic of the Latin tradition.[1]

Conclusion

The presentation of the doctrine of the Trinity in scholastic theology is the subject today of critical assessment and evaluation. This question will be a central concern of the next and final chapter of this work. But whatever the verdict of that evaluation, it is only just to acknowledge the achievement which the scholastic effort represents. Elaborated in its basic framework over the centuries of the High Middle Ages, it organised the central concepts and principles which the fourth century Controversy had identified into a logical, coherent structure and presented this subtle material in a manner characterised by clarity of concept and precision of language. This is no small achievement.

The scholastic treatise on the Trinity is structured around the key concepts of procession, relation, person, mission. An understanding of the divine processions is here the starting-point and the basis for all that follows: the processions reveal the distinctions in God as relations; the relations are identified as persons; the two proceeding persons are the subjects of the divine missions. Despite all its subtlety of thought, the treatise has about it a clarity and even simplicity which is truly admirable.

Latin scholastic theology was the product and the flowering of a tradition which, despite the ravages of history, went back to the beginning of Latin theological literature. Its trinitarian theology continues the basic direction and emphases of that tradition. But from within that tradition it has also been able to incorporate and appropriate the central contribution of Greek theology. In garnering together this rich inheritance and giving it clear, systematic form, scholastic theology has done the history of theology great and lasting service. If the history of the theology of the Trinity, and especially its scholastic presentation, requires re-assessment today, it will at least be clear what it is which needs assessment. Part of the achievement of scholastic theology has been to provide the measure whereby it may itself be measured. In so doing, it also invites critical evaluation. This task of evaluating the scholastic system is one of the central concerns of trinitarian theology today. The significance of this assessment will be the subject of the next and final chapter of this work.

Note
1. The Tract usually spoke also of the three *personal properties* and the *five notions*. Personal properties refer to the characteristics which constitute and distinguish the Persons: Paternity, Filiation, Passive Spiration, that is, the being spirated of the Holy Spirit. (*Sum T* 1, q 40, a 4) Notions are notes which manifest the distinction of the persons. There are five such notions or notes: Innascibility and Paternity proper to the Father; Filiation proper to the Son; Passive Spiration proper to the Holy Spirit; Active Spiration proper to the Father and the Son as the principle of the Holy Spirit. (*Sum T* 1, q 32, aa 2-4) These refinements, however, add little to the teaching of the Tract and usually simply add to the confusion of the student.

CHAPTER 6

Theology of the Trinity Today

The subject of the Trinity has been a prominent topic of discussion in theology in recent decades. Many of the books which have attracted particular attention over that period have been devoted to this subject. This is a new and rather surprising development. Prior to Vatican II there was little evidence of it nor was the doctrine of the Trinity a prominent theme on the conciliar agenda. Though in the light of hindsight one can trace a gradual growth of critical interest slowly developing over a long period, beginning perhaps as far back as the seventeenth century with the studies of Petavius, 'the Father of the History of Dogma', there can be little doubt that the real catalyst catapulting the theology of the Trinity towards the centre of attention was the short study of Karl Rahner, *The Trinity*, first published in 1967. Rahner here demonstrated not only the need for a renewal of trinitarian theology, he also identified the key issues which such a renewal would have to address. Most of the studies which have since appeared have accepted the general agenda as outlined by Rahner and have attempted to develop the implications of his position.

The wide acceptance accorded Rahner's critical assessment of trinitarian theology as it then stood, and the readiness with which his invitation to a renewal of that theology was taken up, show that the need for this renewal was widely recognised and deeply felt. There was a general dissatisfaction with the scholastic theology of the Trinity which had prevailed for so long. To understand how trinitarian theology is developing today, it is first necessary to identify the basic cause of this dissatisfaction, to diagnose the problem. Then it will be possible to appreciate and evaluate the efforts which are being made to resolve this problem and the general approach which is emerging. Once this context is clarified, particular issues within the field of trinitarian theology topical today can be considered. The following discussion therefore will be concerned with outlining the basic revision of the scholastic theology of the Trinity which is now under way and then, finally, with a brief consideration of some particular issues which have become prominent in the light of this new approach.

The Basic Revision

The Problem

The basic problem with the doctrine of the Trinity as this is presented in scholastic theology, medieval and modern, is that as so
presented it seems to be totally isolated within the general body
of Christian doctrine, unconnected with other areas and practically
irrelevant to living Christian faith. Karl Rahner's remarks summing up this odd situation have been much quoted, but it will be
in place to quote them once again here.

> Despite their orthodox confession of the Trinity, Christians
> are, in their practical life, almost mere 'monotheists'. We
> must be willing to admit that, should the doctrine of the
> Trinity have to be dropped as false, the major part of relig-
> ious literature could well remain virtually unchanged. ...
> The treatise on the Trinity occupies a rather isolated position
> in the total dogmatic system. To put it crassly, and not with-
> out exaggeration, when the treatise is concluded, its subject
> is never brought up again. ... It is as though this mystery has
> been revealed for its own sake, and that even after it has
> been made known to us, it remains, *as a reality*, locked up
> within itself. We make statements about it, but as a reality it
> has nothing to do with us at all. (*The Trinity*, 10-11, 14 –
> slightly adapted; emphasis original)

The isolation and practical irrelevance of the doctrine of the
Trinity which Rahner so forcefully documents at the beginning of
his short study has since been widely acknowledged and re-
echoed in theological writing on this subject. But granting the validity of this critical assessment presents us with a very odd situation indeed. How God, the Absolute to whom everything else is
relative, is understood is the most fundamental and all-
determining notion of the human mind. For this will determine
how everything else is seen and understood, even how particular
societies and cultures are shaped. The notion of God as Trinity
represents the specifically Christian understanding of God. This
understanding should, therefore, determine the Christian vision
of life in all its forms, down to the simple practicalities. We are
concerned here with the very bedrock of Christian faith. It cannot
be a matter of indifference, then, how this understanding is in
practice perceived and presented. It is a vital issue. If over the
centuries, as Rahner and many after him have maintained, the
trinitarian understanding of God has become almost purely
theoretic and practically inoperative, then a situation has devel-

oped which requires serious re-consideration. This is the programme which has fueled interest in trinitarian theology in recent
years and which has determined the task upon which it is now engaged.

Rahner's criticism of trinitarian theology was directed against
the presentation of the doctrine in scholastic theology. This is
what had created the problem. If this is so, the first step towards
redressing the problem must be to identify it, diagnose it, and especially to identify the source of it, how it has come about, what
precisely has caused it. The basic problem can, in fact, be easily
enough identified: it is the separation which the scholastic
approach introduces between God in Godself and God as God
relates to us. Here God in Godself is a threefold God, a Triad:
Father, Son, Holy Spirit. But God relating to us humans is simply
one, a Monad. A separation has occurred here between what Rahner calls the immanent Trinity, God in Godself, and the economic
Trinity, God as God relates to us in the economy of salvation, the
God whom we experience and relate to. The God of this economy,
the God who is concerned for us and whom we are concerned
with, seems to be devoid of trinitarian character. This God effectively appears here as a Monad, not a Triad. When one recalls that
the most basic assertion of the early tradition, both pre-Nicene
and Nicene, was that the triadic experience of God in the economy represented and revealed God as God simply and truly is, this
understanding seems very peculiar indeed and at deep odds with
the tradition which it purports faithfully to interpret. The end result of the separation which this theological understanding has introduced is that in actual reality Christian faith reverts to a practical simple monotheism, a practical unitarianism. One has but to
notice how incapable this theology is of giving any real meaning
to the triadic language and structure of Christian prayer, which in
principle it should elucidate, to see that something here is serious-
ly out of joint. But we must turn now to see how scholastic theology manifests this understanding and attempt to trace therein the
source and root of the problem.

The clearest manifestation in scholastic trinitarian theology of
the separation between the immanent Deity and the economic
Deity is to be seen in the related principles of *opera divina ad extra*
and appropriation as these are here presented and applied. The
external acts of God refer here to the activity of God in the economy, that is, the ways God relates to us. All these acts, we are informed, are performed by all three persons acting as one principle. The distinctive personalities of the divine persons, therefore,

do not enter into, affect or contribute anything to the performance of these acts. The sole agency operative here, the one principle, is and can only be the one divine substance or nature which all three indifferently possess. The God acting here is a pure Monad. The principle of appropriation is now invented and invoked to explain away the problem posed by the language of Scripture and the faith which attributes certain external divine acts to particular persons or assigns specific roles to individual persons in such acts. Such language, it is maintained, simply attributes to one what is common to all; it is merely a manner of speaking, a figurative, not a real, reference. As here understood, these principles effectively reduce the three who constitute God in Godself to one in God as relating with us humans. The separation of the immanent and the economic Trinity is here clearly manifest.

These considerations, however, only reveal the problem; they show us its symptoms, they do not show us its cause. To discover this, we have to dig deeper. The root of the problem lies in the distinction which gradually, in the course of the fourth century Controversy, came to be recognised between the divine substance/ nature and the divine persons and which was encapsulated in the formula of the Cappadocians: God consists of one nature and three persons. The emergence of this distinction and its implications have already been commented on more than once in the course of this study. Beginning with the *homoousios* of Nicaea, Nicene orthodoxy insisted that the divinity of the Son and the Spirit was the same as that of the Father. The Son and the Spirit were God in the same sense the Father was God, though Father, Son and Spirit were nevertheless distinct. Essential to an appreciation of this sophisticated position was a logical distinction between divinity or divine substance and divine personhood. Problems begin to arise, however, when this logical distinction begins to take on real meaning, begins to operate as a real distinction. This, no doubt, was an unconscious development, but it was all the more powerful for that. The point can, perhaps, be best appreciated if one notices the change of meaning which occurs in the expression 'the one God' between the pre-Nicene period and the post-Nicene. In the earlier period, going back indeed to the New Testament itself, this expression always meant the Father. In the later period, it will usually mean the divine substance, divinity. St Augustine, making the divine substance the starting-point and central emphasis in his theology of the the Trinity, pushed the Latin tradition very effectively down this road. The Preface of the Trinity will now describe Father, Son and Holy Spirit as 'one God'

because they are a 'Trinity of one substance' and on this basis con-
fess 'the same' of all three 'without difference or separation'. 'The
one God' now means the divinity, the one divine substance, acting indifferently, 'as one principle', in and through all three persons. This direction of thought now issues very logically in the
principles concerning *opera ad extra* and appropriation.

It is certainly true that scholastic theology will insist that there
is not a real distinction between the divine nature and the persons; the persons are the divine nature. What is important to note,
however, is that the *distinction* of the persons leaves the operation
ad extra of the divine substance totally untouched; here there is
but one principle acting. The personal distinctions in God are operative only within and as regards God in Godself, the immanent
Trinity, not as regards God relating to us, the economic Trinity.
The God of the economy is one God unaffected by the triadic distinctions Christian faith recognises in this one God. On the basis
of this understanding, Rahner's judgement cannot be gainsaid:
'Christians are, in their practical life, almost mere "monotheists".'

Little purpose would be served here in subjecting this understanding of the Trinity to further, more detailed criticism. The
matter will, in any case, be under review, directly or indirectly, as
we proceed. But at least one very obvious exception to the *opera ad
extra* principle should be noted. This is the Incarnation. Here the
second divine person, and only the second person, assumes a
humanity and thereby becomes the sole ultimate subject of all the
activity of this human nature. Clearly there is question here of
opus ad extra, of God's very direct involvement in the economy.
Yet this involvement, and all the activity which it comprises, is
predicated of one divine person alone, the Word made flesh. This
is a clear exception and violation of the *opera ad extra* principle. A
general principle, like a chain, is as strong as its weakest link. This
general principle collapses here in the face of the doctrine of the
Incarnation. This collapse now calls into serious question the theological construction upon which this principle is based and of
which it is the logical fruit.

Redressing the Problem

The problem which the history of trinitarian theology produced
consists in the separation which this theology established between the immanent Trinity, God in Godself, and the economic
Trinity, God as God relates to us. The source of the problem lay in
the way God's external activity was conceived as flowing from
the one divine substance unaffected by the triadic distinctions in

God. This approach imposes a distinction and a separation between the immanent Trinity and the economic. One might counter this position by simply cancelling this separation and asserting with Karl Rahner the identity of the economic and the immanent Trinity: 'The "economic" Trinity is the "immanent" Trinity and the "immanent" Trinity is the "economic" Trinity.' (*The Trinity*, 22) This axiom, which is the basic thesis of Rahner's study, has won general, though not quite universal, acceptance from theologians, at least in so far as it asserts that God relates to us as God is in Godself, a Triune God.[1] Mere counter-assertion, however, is not sufficient. The new thesis requires explanation and substantiation. In particular, it needs to be shown, first, that the concept and assertion of the one God should not be taken to mean simply the divine substance conceived in a quasi independent manner of the distinction of the persons and, second and consequently, that the principles of *opera ad extra* and appropriation stand in need of radical revision.

Scholastic theology itself insisted, theorectically and in principle, that the divine substance did not exist separately from the divine persons: the substance is and only exists in the persons. God is a Trinity, not a Quarternity. But Latin theology, mainly due to the precedence which St Augustine accorded the concept of divine substance over against that of divine person, in practice conceived this substance or nature as acting in the economy in a manner unaffected by the distinction of the persons. When one remembers that the inter-relationship of the opposing relations/persons, the divine circuminsession/perichoresis, is confined within the immanent Deity, God in Godself, and is not a feature of God as acting in the economy, the summary statement of the Council of Florence tells its own tale: 'Everything [in God] is one [=divine substance] where there is no opposition of relation.' The issue briefly surfaced explicitly around the end of the twelfth century in Joachim of Fiore's accusation of Peter Lombard for conceiving God as a Quarternity, not a Trinity. But the rejection of Joachim's criticism by the IV Lateran Council in 1215 AD, and its rather vague vindication of the Lombard, shows that Joachim was swimming against the tide and that his perceptive point had fallen on deaf ears. Meanwhile, this impersonal understanding of the God of the economy now logically influenced all other areas of theology. Prime and significant examples of this follow through can be seen in the impersonal theology of grace, 'created grace', and of the sacraments as means of this grace which scholastic theology presents.

Against this position, it is necessary to return to the older tradition and understanding of the Triune God before the logical, abstract distinction of substance and person, the crucial development of the Trinitarian Controversy, came to be understood and applied in too realistic a way. This older approach, which is that of the New Testament and the pre-Nicene tradition and which is still strong in the fourth century, saw the one God as the Father who eternally and immanently originates the Son and the Spirit who then inter-relate intimately with the Father to form the divine communion which is the divine perichoresis, the Triune God. Here, God, divine Being, is the Father who, as it were, eternally and immanently explodes in triadic relationship. God's communication of this God-self *ad extra*, to creatures, is and can only be the opening of this triadic, relational Being to creatures with a view to their entry into and sharing in it in a creaturely manner. In this opening of God in and to creation, the immanent divine processions become the temporal divine missions, the mission of the Logos/Son and the mission of the Holy Spirit, the 'two hands of the Father'. But just as the outflowing of divine life within the immanent Godhead, from the Father to the Son and the Spirit, returns to its source, the Father, in eternal communion, so also this outreach of God in the economy through the Son in the Spirit gives us, God's creatures, access in the Spirit through the Son to the Father. This is the relation of God and humanity which is asserted and celebrated in Christian prayer. But now this threefold God of the economy, the basis and starting-point of all our knowledge and acknowledgement of God, is the threefold God of the immanent Trinity, God as God is in Godself. The separation of economic and immanent Trinity which scholastic theology had introduced is hereby cancelled.

But if the matter is as simple as this, and as traditional as this, how did it come about that theology took a different direction, ending in a separation of the economic and the immanent Trinity? To answer this question, it is necessary to return to the Trinitarian Controversy and to reflect for a moment on the basic problem which here confronted the Church and the solution to this problem which the Church eventually developed. The problem was to formulate an understanding of the God of Christian faith which steered a middle way between Modalism, such as many saw represented in Marcellus of Ancyra and even in Nicaea itself, and Subordinationism as represented by Arianism. This *via media* was found through the distinction of substance/nature and person, thus providing the formula: one substance – three persons.

This formula enabled orthodoxy to affirm, against Modalism, the real distinction of the Members of the Triad and, against Arianism, their equality in terms of the one divinity, the one divine substance. This solution, however, was the product of an abstract, logical analysis of concepts and terms applied to thinking about God as revealed in Christian faith. This analysis supplied the grammar whereby to write a correct statement about this God. It did not do more than this, nor was it meant to. What happened all too soon, however, was that the grammar with its rules came to be taken for and to replace the sentence. In this way an abstract analysis came to have an independent existence of its own and instead of the role of a servant took on that of the master. Sorcerer's apprentice once again!

The substitution of this logical grammar for the sentence itself led to the abandonment of what was true in the economic trinitarianism of the pre-Nicene period and the introduction of a new way of seeing how God was involved in the economy of salvation. The basis of the pre-Nicene approach had been the credal confession in the one God, the Father, who in a definitive manner had entered into a saving relationship with humanity through Jesus Christ, the Son, in the Holy Spirit. Whatever inadequacies may attach to the theological efforts of this period to explain this position, they rested on the conviction that here one met true God of true God, God in Godself. Indeed, it was this very conviction which now fueled such speculative efforts as there were as to how to conceive God in Godself. In other words, the conviction involved the position that the economic Trinity was the immanent Trinity and that one could in principle infer, however feebly and speculatively, the one from the other. The new formula, however, changed this perspective. On the basis of the distinction between nature and person, God in Godself was now seen as a Triad of persons, but God relating to humans was 'one principle', in other words , the one divine substance common to all three members of the Triad 'without difference or separation'. The distinction between the immanent and economic Trinity becomes operative here. As the pseudo-Athanasian Creed put it, in a statement re-echoed in many later Latin texts: 'the Godhead (*divinitas*) of Father, Son and Holy Spirit is one, their glory equal, their majesty equally eternal'. This text asserts the undifferentiated existence of the one divine nature in each of the three persons. The principle of external divine activity common to all three acting as 'one principle' follows very logically from this position.

But what is ignored in this application of the abstract analysis to the God of the economy is that divinity exists in each member of the Triad *in a distinct relative way*. This indeed is the very basis of the acknowledgement of the one God as a Trinity. But if so, it must surely follow that external activity of this divinity, the one divine substance, retains a triadic character. Such activity may be common to all three, but each one will make a distinctive contribution in accordance with their hypostatic or personal character, in their distinct relative way. One might well speak of the triadic activity of the one God. Recognition of this point now enables the important concept of order or *taxis* in the Trinity, a concept almost totally lost to view in later theology, because it had become otiose and meaningless, to resume its role. God's relation with us proceeds from the Father through the Son in the Spirit, ours with God in the Spirit through the Son to the Father. This taxic structure of the God-human relationship is basic to the understanding of God in the New Testament. It features prominently in the writers of the pre-Nicene period. It is still common in the fourth century, as the following quotations show:

> The Father through the Son with the Spirit gives every gift. (St Cyril of Jerusalem, *Catechetical Instructions*, 16,24)
>
> The Father does all things through the Son in the Spirit; and thus the unity of the Trinity is preserved. (St Athanasius, *Letters to Serapion*, 1, 28)
>
> He (the Father) creates through the Son and perfects through the Spirit. … The way to divine knowledge ascends from the one Spirit through the one Son to the one Father. (St Basil, *On H Spirit*, 16, 38; 18, 47)

This understanding of the involvement of God in the economy, while it sees such action as an action of all three persons in virtue of the one divinity which they possess equally, yet attributes a distinctive role here to each person in accordance with their personal characteristic and their place in the *taxis* which is the Trinity. Here, very clearly, the economic Trinity is the immanent Trinity, the God who relates to us is God as God is in Godself. This understanding has disappeared in later theology because of the unhappy separation it has introduced between the concepts of nature and person.

Because of the way later theology came to apply the distinction between the concepts of nature and person, giving precedence to that of nature in a way in which, in practice, a distinction became a separation, it ended by seeing God relating to us as a Monad, while still acknowledging that God in Godself is a Triad, a Trinity. To quote Rahner again: 'It is as though this mystery [the Trinity] has been revealed for its own sake, and that even after it has been made known to us, it remains, as a reality, locked up within itself. We make statements about it, but as a reality it has nothing to do with us at all.' (*The Trinity*, 14) On this basis and as an application of this understanding, later theology presented a view of God's external activity, *opera divina ad extra*, which now also stands in need of serious revision and correction.

The foundation of the principle concerning God's external activity was established by orthodox theologians in the course of the fourth century Controversy. Athanasius and the Cappadocians, for example, insisted that the Son and the Holy Spirit shared the one divinity of the Father because the activity attributed to them, namely, redemption and sanctification, was activity which only God could do. The IV Lateran Council (1215 AD), followed later by the Council of Florence (1442 AD), expressed this teaching by describing the Father, Son and Holy Spirit as constituting the 'one principle' of all divine activity *ad extra: unum universorum principuum*. [D/S 800; cf Co Florence D/S 1331] Invoking these authorities and basing itself on this formulation, later scholastic theology formulated its teaching on this issue in the proposition: *opera divina ad extra* are common to all three Persons acting as one principle/ *opera divina ad extra communia sunt tribus personis tamquam uno principio*. Medieval scholasticism explained and justified this principle by invoking the Aristotelian concept of efficient causality, the only form of causality it could envisage here. An efficient cause is one which, acting as an external agent, an outside force, produces an effect in something else. In divine external activity, God acts as an efficient cause. Such action is an exercise and expression of the nature in question: it simply signifies the nature in action. As there is but the one divine nature here and this one nature is common to all three Persons, the principle follows: such actions are performed by all three persons acting as one principle.

The problem with this interpretation of divine external activity is that it ignores another level of God's relationship with us which cannot be explained by the category of efficient causality. For God is not simply an agency acting on us from outside, God is also a presence within us transforming us. Applying the categories of Aristotelian causality, this transforming presence of God cannot be totally explained by efficient causality, but would seem to involve also some type of formal causality. Formal causality refers to an intrinsic principle which makes something the kind of being it is, gives it its specific 'form'. One might illustrate the distinction in question here by pointing to two different answers to the ques-

tion: Why is the wall white? One answer to this question might be:
Because the painter painted it white. This answers the question in
terms of the external agency, the efficient cause. But another answer might be: Because of whiteness in the wall. This answers the
question in terms of the intrinsic principle, whiteness, in the wall,
the formal cause.

As well as being an agency outside us acting on us as an efficient cause, God is also a sanctifying presence within us transforming us into God's image and likeness. Though this presence
cannot be a pure form in the Aristotelian sense, since this would
mean that we literally become God, it has something of the character of this type of causality. Theologians who adopt this approach describe this divine agency in different ways. Karl Rahner
termed it quasi-formal causality. The important point is that the
agency envisaged here does not act after the manner of an efficient cause and so the principles of divine external activity and
appropriation do not apply to it. In this presence of God within us
God now can, and indeed must, be seen as relating to us simply as
God is, as a Trinity of Father, Son and Spirit. Each person as such
here enters into relationship with us and we to them. God here is
the Triad which God is and not simply the Monad which the
divine nature is. But the Triune God is present in us and to us in
accordance with the *taxis* which structures the Triad in itself. This
presence is an opening to us of the Father through the Son in the
Spirit inviting from us a response in the Spirit through the Son to
the Father. This understanding of the way God relates with us
now gives real meaning to the structure and language of Christian
prayer. This need no longer be explained away by invoking the
principle of appropriation. The principles of *opera ad extra* and appropriation are now confined to God acting as an efficient cause,
though even here, as has been pointed out, the triadic manner in
which the divine nature exists must leave some, relative, trace.

On the basis of this critical evaluation, the problem which the
scholastic theology of the Trinity created can be identified and re-
dressed. The problem with this presentation was that God did not
relate to us as God is in Godself; the God of the economy is not the
Triune God. The root cause of this understanding can be traced to
the separation which in practice was allowed to operate between
the one divine substance and divine personhood, what I have
termed here the quasi independence attributed to the external activity of the divine substance. One can appeal to the principles of
scholastic theology itself to show that this position is not correct.
This theology correctly maintains that the divine substance exists

in and is identical with the three divine persons. Even when acting externally, this substance cannot lose this triadic character; such activity also is activity of the Father through the Son in the Spirit. This triadic character of God's being is discernible especially in God's sanctifying presence within us which, because it unites us with God as God truly is, relates us to the Father, the Son and the Holy Spirit. In this understanding separation of the economic Trinity and the immanent Trinity is cancelled; the God of the economy, God relating to us, is God as God is in Godself, the Triune God.

It follows that this trinitarian understanding of God applies to all aspects of God's relationship with us and to all aspects of our response to God. Christian life in all its forms and aspects bears a trinitarian character. This, obviously, should be true also of every area of theology. In this perspective, the isolation of the treatise on the Trinity within the whole field of theology is also overcome. All theology, whatever the area of discussion, systematic or moral, simply because it is a theo-logy, a discourse about God and the God-human relationship, should display a trinitarian character. This is an agenda which theology as yet can scarcely be said to have perceived, much less to have applied.

This recognition that the God who approaches us and relates with us in salvation history is God as God is in Godself, the Triune God who is the Father, the Son and the Holy Spirit, this recognition gives a whole new look to the theology of the Trinity. The approach of God to us determines the way of our approach to God, our response to God. This involves us in proper relationships with the Spirit, the Son and the Father, in accordance with the order or structure of the Trinity itself. Language expressing such relationships can no longer be described as 'mere appropriation'. This understanding now enables the language of Christian prayer and the living faith to take on real meaning and actuality. Trinitarian theology is now no longer the purely theoretic, academic exercise it had become. This theology is again in direct relationship with the primary language of faith and there is hope that it can elucidate, deepen and reinforce this experience. This new turn, or rather re-turn, in the theology of the Trinity has many implications and applications for the understanding of Christian life and for theology as a whole. Everything now begins to be seen from a somewhat different angle and takes on a new appearance. In this sense, this theology is also a fundamental theology, a determining centre for the whole field of theological discussion. It is not possible here, however, to travel further down this interesting road of

implication and application. But some special issues which have
become prominent in theological writing today in the light of the
new approach do merit some consideration here. This study will
therefore conclude with a brief consideration of some of these topics.

Particular Issues

A major and distinctive feature of theology in this century has
been the pluralism of method and approach which it displays.
Here it contrasts sharply with the unified method of scholastic
theology. This pluralism of theology reflects the pluralism of
knowledge generally in our time, the ever increasing number of
disciplines and specialisations with which the human mind is
now engaged. Theology has adopted and adapted, as it has
deemed appropriate, methodologies from these disciplines, and
especially from the human sciences, and has used these new ave-
nues of approach in an effort to understand and present its own
subject in a way relevant to the age. The theology of the Trinity is
no exception here. It too displays today a pluralism of approach.
Even a summary review of these various influences cannot be attempted here. But some reflection of their impact may be discerned as we turn our attention now to some particular issues
which feature prominently in contemporary trinitarian theology.
The list of topics chosen for discussion here is far from exhaustive.
But they do represent issues which are of particular importance
and concern in trinitarian theology today.

Nature and Person

The distinction between nature and person, in Greek *ousia* and *hypostasis*, was the crucial development of the Trinitarian Controversy which enabled orthodox Christian faith to identify and formulate its understanding of God over against Modalism and
Arianism. From then on this distinction, as expressed in the formula, one nature – three persons, became the basis for the understanding of God as Trinity. Yet, as we noted earlier and more than
once in this study, the Latin tradition has always displayed a certain reserve with regard to the adoption of the term 'person' in
this context. This coolness towards the term continues to be
echoed today. It is evident, therefore, that we are not dealing here
with a simple formula, one which can be readily understood and
easily applied. A warning light seems to be flashing here alerting
us to possible danger. This is an invitation to look more closely
and critically at this formula and to assess its adequacy to express
the Christian doctrine of God.

The distinction between nature and person, though purely as a formula anticipated by Tertullian in the early third century, was really the creation of Greek theology, and especially of the Cappadocian Fathers, in the course of the fourth century Controversy. It represented the adoption by orthodoxy of rather philosophical terms to express as precisely as possible what it wished to say of the Triune God in the context of the times. What it wished to say was that the Father, the Son and the Holy Spirit were distinct, yet all three were equally and truly God. Clearly emerging here was some distinction between being God and being Father, Son, Spirit. The Cappadocians adopted the terms *ousia* and *hypostasis*, current until then in a rather looser and more confused sense, to express this distinction. Here *ousia* meant 'being God', Godness, divinity, and *hypostasis* meant the distinct existence of the Father, Son and Spirit. Latin theology very quickly took over the formula, translating *ousia* as substance or nature and *hypostasis* as person.

The distinction between nature and person is not an arbitrary or artificial one. It is one which the human mind is instinctively aware of and constantly applies. Nature means that which makes something the kind of being it is. It answers the question: What (is something)? When used of God it refers to that which makes God God, Godness, divinity. The term 'person', however, confronts us with a much more subtle concept. The reality in question is readily ackowledged in ordinary language, since it is the answer to the question: Who (is someone)? But further effort to probe what person means and involves proves surprisingly difficult. Our interest here lies in the understanding of the concept in the Latin theological tradition and in the history of western thought and the impact of this understanding on trinitarian theology.

We noted earlier the reserve and indeed suspicion with which Latin theology received the introduction by Tertullian of the term 'person' as a description of the members of the divine Triad. This reserve is reflected again later by St Augustine who has problems with the term 'person' when used of the Trinity. His basic problem is an interesting one. Person is a common noun which refers to a category or class of beings who all possess the essential characteristics which the term connotes. But each member of the Triad is in itself unique and therefore a common term is not applicable to them. Augustine in the end grudgingly accepts use of the term on the ground that, since language has no word for the unique, some term has to be used and it may as well be 'person' as anything else. The validity of his sharp insight, however, should not be forgotten. Medieval theology, therefore, seeking a definition of person, found little assistance here in this, its great source and authority. This was provided, as we saw, by Boethius. His definition of person as an individual substance of a rational nature determined the meaning of the term in scholastic theology, medieval and modern.

It is necessary to observe that by this stage we have travelled some distance from the introduction of the trinitarian formula by the Cappadocian Fathers, and that not only in time but also in thought. As used by the Cappadocians, the Greek term *hypostasis* basically meant distinct individual. In applying the term to the members of the Triad they explained that here it signified distinct, subsistent relation. In this sense the Greek term had no equivalent in Latin. The choice of *persona* to translate it was, therefore, somewhat arbitrary. Part of Augustine's discomfort with the term has its source here. Boethius, living in the sixth century long after the trinitarian debates had subsided, constructed his definition of *persona*, not from the theological discussions where the concept had originated, but from the logic of Aristotle. The central emphasis and thrust of his definition highlights the distinctiveness and independence, indeed the isolation, of the individual subject over against all others. Contradicting John Donne's dictum: 'No man is an island,' that precisely is what person here means, an island. One is a person because one is distinct from and independent of all other persons. The notes of autonomy and incommunicability which many medievals added to the Boethian definition reinforced further this emphasis. The note of relationship, so basic to the Cappadocian understanding, is here lost sight of and has to be added on as an extraneous consideration. To speak of God as three persons now does not in itself convey quite the same meaning the expression had when first introduced.[2]

From the sixteenth century on a new aspect of human personhood gradually began to receive emphasis and achieve central prominence. This was a development of political theory and philosophy and its chief concern was to define the status of the human being as a member of political society. Theologians such as Francesco de Vitoria (d. 1546) and philosophers such as John Locke (d. 1704) made important contributions to this development. Person was defined here especially in terms of moral responsibility. Person meant an individual rational being capable of arriving at its own decisions and who was, and could be held to be, responsible for these decisions. Person means a centre of responsible willing and acting, a responsible decision-maker. The understanding of person which emerges here is that of one who is a subject of rights and duties, a moral, legal subject – the point which this approach especially wished to underscore.

Clarification of this aspect of personhood drew attention to something of fundamental importance and made a permanent contribution to human thought in highlighting the human person as a being of absolute, inalienable value which all human law must respect. The modern concept of inalienable human rights stems from this development. But as a definition of person this understanding emphasised still further the distinctive independence of the rational subject over against all others. Person is here regarded as an autonomous centre of thinking, willing and acting. All these faculties, however, are functions and expressions of the nature here in question. To speak of three distinct persons in this sense means speaking of three distinct natures. The thrust of the Boethian definition has now reached the point where as so developed the meaning of person stands in contradiction to what the term meant when it was first introduced to elucidate the theology of the Trinity. As this modern understanding of person gained common currency, use of the term in ordinary language could not escape reference to these implications. A distance had now opened up between the meaning of the term 'person' in common usage and its meaning in theology.

This difference in the meaning of person has not escaped the notice of contemporary theology. Both the Protestant theologian, Karl Barth, and the Catholic theologian, Karl Rahner, addressed the issue explicitly. Both pointed to the danger of misunderstanding which the word 'person' as used today involved for the doctrine of God as Trinity. Though neither theologian advocated dropping the term, so deeply entrenched in the dogmatic tradition, both counselled explaining it in a particular way in the context of preaching and doctrinal instruction. Barth advocated calling the Three three 'distinct modes of being', Rahner three 'distinct modes of subsistence'. Neither of these suggestions received much acceptance. Commentators were quick to point out that both these great figures of twentieth century theology had, very oddly, totally ignored a new trend and emphasis in recent philosophical consideration of the meaning of person.[3] This emphasis was highlighting the relational character of personhood which the Boethian definition had ignored and which had long been forgotten in the classical tradition. Being a person, these studies pointed out, meant to exist in relationship. Person means being-in-relation; personality means inter-personality. The 'I' of my thought and sentences and being has meaning only in terms of your 'Thou' whom it addresses and is addressed by. I need you to be me. A great, profound truth is coming to light here. As a being in and for relationship I am by that very fact already in relation with all human beings alive at this moment. Whether we realise it or not, we are all brothers and sisters. This is our Cosmopolis. But how has this horizontal line of present relationship come into being and where is it ultimately grounded? This horizontal line requires a vertical to uphold it and ground it. This vertical line is Absolute Being, God. But then God must be Absolute Being-in-Relation. We exist because we are addressed by this essentially relational God: 'In the beginning was the Word ...'

This philosophical analysis has reminded theology that the notion of person, which theology had introduced to human thought, meant, when first introduced, relation. This was precisely the achievement of the Cappadocians. This basic dimension of the term, however, was lost sight of in the Aristotelian determined understanding of Boethius and the scholastic tradition which continued that understanding. It can now be effectively retrieved. God can now be understood and presented as Absolute Being-in-Relation, a Being-in-Relation which involves a threefoldness which Christian faith names as Father, Son and Holy Spirit. '"Father",' wrote Gregory of Nazianzus, 'is the name of a relationship (*schesis*), of how the Father is related to the Son and the Son to the Father' (*Theol Orat*, 3); 'The determinations "Father" and "Son",' writes Augustine, 'have to do not with substances but with relations'. (*On Trin*, 5, 6) The relation between God and humans which salvation history accomplishes can now be understood as the opening of the relations which God is to us humans and our participation in this threefold relational Being of God. This fundamental perspective can and should now colour all aspects of Christian faith and have a determining application in all aspects of Christian living. Here again we glimpse the new agenda which trinitarian theology today is proposing for itself and for theology as a whole.

Here, therefore, theology has been led back to itself as the original source of a rich insight which later, unfortunately, it had itself lost sight of. It always needs to be remembered, however, that the formula based on the distinction between nature and person was introduced into theology as a tool to ensure correct statement about God. It was not meant to replace that statement. It is simply a grammar. This abstract language and logical analysis must always yield to the primary biblical statement of God as Father, Son, Holy Spirit. Language about God in the Bible is heavily influenced by biblical anthropology, by the Semitic understanding of the human being. In the Old Testament this has a tripartite structure: the human being consists of *basar*, the flesh, *nephesh*, very inadequately translated as the soul, and *ruah*, a dimension which indicates the human's capacity for and openness to God, an openness which admits of degrees. This loose, many-faceted understanding is certainly trying to conceive and describe the human as a relational being, above all one capable of relation with God, and therefore it sees God as absolute relational Being. Though by the time of the New Testament Jewish thinking here has come under many other influences, this way of understanding still persists. Addressing the Thessalonians, St Paul can refer to 'your spirit (*pneuma*) and soul (*psyche*) and body (*soma*).' (1 Thess 5, 23) It is intriguing to note that theology has never seen a source of insight here for its understanding of the distinctions in the one God. One is certainly dealing here with a very primitive form of thought. Primitive, however, does not necessarily mean obsolete. On the contrary, this very primitiveness ensures that the vision of thought is concrete, instinctive, very down to earth. It has a range and flexibility which the concepts derived from a more sophisticated but more abstract analysis are unable to match. Now that the relational dimension of personhood has again come into prominence, theology may well find here, on its very own doorstep, a promising source for reflection.

The Holy Spirit

For many years one could practically predict that any book devoted to the topic of the Holy Spirit would begin by referring to the Spirit as 'the forgotten God', or some equivalent expression. Further, most of these writers would then express surprise that this should be so. There should have been no surprise. What point could there be writing about the Holy Spirit when everything one wrote came under the ban of the textbook describing all such effort as 'mere appropriation'? With this principle scholastic theology had effectively removed the Spirit of God from the theological agenda. The revision of the theology of the Trinity in place today has now, thankfully, removed this stumbling block. A real pneumatology has now become in principle possible. Theology, however, is now faced with the daunting task of attempting to repair the neglect of centuries in this area. One has but to think for a moment of the vast contrast between the quantity of writing on, say, christology and on pneumatology to appreciate this point. In any particular field, systematic theology depends heavily on sound literary and historical study of texts of the past, both biblical and later. In the field of pneumatology the systematic theologian is not well served here, at least in comparison with most other areas. Something of the situation confronting the young Augustine is still true: 'The subject of the Holy Spirit, however, has not yet been sufficiently or so diligently treated by the great and learned commentators on the Sacred Scriptures, that we can easily understand what is proper to him …' (*Faith and the Creed*, 9, 19)

The new interest and the new direction developing in the theology of the Trinity today is certainly causing a welcome change here. Significant writing in the area of pneumatology is now very much part of this scene. No attempt can be made here to review this literature. Rather, this brief comment will concentrate on the fundamental character of the gift of the Spirit and the scope of this gift, which is to be identified with the Giver, as indicated in the New Testament and from that perspective seek to envisage how some old themes begin to take on new vitality in the theology of the Trinity now developing.

The outpouring or gift of the Spirit of God as presented in the New Testament (John 20:19-23; Acts 2:1-4) is the climax of the narrative of salvation history which the New Testament recounts. The significance of this simple statement must not be lost on us. It means that now, and only now, has God fully and definitively communicated Godself within the context of human history. The outpouring of the Holy Spirit is the final outpouring of God. As such this event is of the utmost importance for our understanding of God and of our relationship with God. We are not dealing here with an after event, an event subsequent to the accomplishment of salvation history, a coda to salvation history. This event *is* the climax and crowning of salvation history.

The gift of the Spirit is the fruit of the Easter victory of Jesus Christ; it is this Easter event bearing fruit, reaching conclusion. The event of the Spirit is therefore intimately linked with the event of Christ. The resurrection of Jesus means the exaltation of Jesus 'to God's right hand', his breakthrough to the world of God. But this event also means the opening of God's world to this world of ours, that 'opening of the heavens' briefly anticipated and rehearsed in the narrative of the baptism of Jesus. This 'opening of the heavens' is the outpouring of the Spirit of God, 'the promise of the Father'. (Acts 1:4) Here is definitively reversed that alienation of God and this world which occurred at the Fall. God's Sabbath celebration, disrupted by the Fall, can now be resumed. (Gen 2:1-3) God's world and this world are now in union once more – through the gift of God's Spirit.

These two events, the event of Christ and the event of the Spirit, now coalesce to bring into existence and establish the Church, the Spirit-filled community of the disciples of Jesus Christ. The Church is established and ever maintained in its identity by these two events. They are its foundation events and give it its charter. It can only explain itself and be explained by reference to both. It constantly demonstrates this in its ceremonies of Christian initiation. Here, in renewing itself with new members, it re-presents sacramentally these events of its foundation in its sacraments of baptism and confirmation. It needs to be emphasised that the gift of the Spirit is, first and foremost, an endowment of the Church itself, the community of believers in its corporate existence. This is the Indwelling of the Holy Spirit which theology will later speak of, but will have such difficulty giving real meaning to. St Paul had no such difficulty:

> Do you not know that you are God's temple, and that God's Spirit dwells in you? If any one destroys God's temple, God will destroy him. For God's temple is holy, and that temple you are. (1 Cor 3: 16-17)

On this text, George T. Montague correctly notes: '"The temple" refers here not to the individual body of the Christian but to the Christian community as such'. (*The Holy Spirit*, 138) This is very real ecclesiology. But endowment of the community also means endowment of its individual members. St Paul goes on to underscore this point also:

> Do you not know that your body is a temple of the Holy Spirit within you, which you have from God? You are not your own; you were bought with a price. So glorify God in your body. (1 Cor 6: 19-20)

As a member of the community, the Spirit indwells the individual Christian also. From this basis St Paul is able to develop a profound, vital and actual pneumatology. A simple outline of his thinking must suffice here.

St Paul sees the gift of the Spirit as the presence of the Spirit in the community and in the Christian. It is for this reason that he declares: 'you are not your own'. He is a witness to the understanding of the Spirit in early Christianity as 'power from on high'. (Lk 24,49) The presence of the Spirit within us is the enabling source of our Christian living. It is the Spirit of God in us which prays and enables us to pray.

> Because you are sons, God has sent the Spirit of his Son into our hearts, crying: 'Abba! Father!'. (Gal 4:6)
> For all who are led by the Spirit of God are sons of God. For

> you did not receive the spirit of slavery to fall back into fear,
> but you have received the spirit of sonship. When we cry:
> 'Abba! Father!', it is the Spirit himself bearing witness with
> our spirit that we are children of God. (Rom 8:14-16)

It is this same Spirit which is the source of the extraordinary gifts
with which the early Christian communities are so liberally en-
dowed. But the divisiveness which these gifts led to in the Corin-
thian community forces St Paul to think out much more deeply
the meaning and implication of this presence of the Spirit. He
records the fruit of his thinking in 1 Corinthians 12-14. These gifts
are not meant to be the private possession of, or for the private
benefit of, the individual. They all have the one source, the one
Spirit of God, and they are given not to a select few but to all for
the common purpose of building up the community.

> There are varieties of gifts, but the same Spirit; ... To each is
> given the manifestation of the Spirit for the common good.
> (1 Cor 12: 4,7)

But Paul now proceeds to emphasise that these spectacular manifestations are all rooted in and are themselves expressions of the
primary effect of the presence of the Spirit in Christians. This is
simply Christian love, 'the greatest of these'. This theme now issues in the lyrical anthem which is 1 Corinthians 13. But this love,
seeking expression in our lives, has its source in the presence
within us of God's Spirit; in fact, it is the presence of the Spirit.

> God's love has been poured into our hearts through the
> Holy Spirit who has been given to us. (Rom 5:5)

Paul is now able to outline clearly his programme for Christian
living. This is a life where we are 'led by the Spirit of God'. (Rom
8:14) For this Spirit is life-giving and liberates us from slavery to
the law and to fear into the freedom of the children of God: 'For
the law of the Spirit of life in Christ Jesus has set me free from the
law of sin and death'. (Rom 8:2) This is a theme which always ex-
cites St Paul and forces him into lyricism. At the end of his Letter
to the Galatians he gives expression to it again with force, clarity
and beauty:

> The fruit of the Spirit is love, joy, peace, patience, kindness,
> goodness, faithfulness, gentleness, self-control; against such
> there is no law ... If we live by the Spirit, let us also walk by
> the Spirit. (Gal 5:22-23, 25)

It is, I think, clear from even this summary outline of St Paul's
thought that for him and the Christians of his time the phrase 'in
the Spirit' had real and very actual meaning. It expressed a real
and deeply felt experience. Being 'in the Spirit' is here a vivid de-

scription of what being a Christian means. The Christian is in relation with God because the Spirit of God is an activating presence
in the Christian. Something of the old meaning of the Hebrew
term *ruah* can still be seen here: openness to God, space for God
which God enters and fills through the gift of the Spirit of God. It
is important to note that in the expression 'the gift *of* the Spirit', in
any of the forms in which it occurs in the New Testament, the gen-
itive here is subjective: the gift is the Spirit. This gift does not refer
simply to some effect brought about in us by external divine
agency acting on us, a form of 'created grace', whether sanctifying
grace (*gratia gratum faciens*) or charism (*gratia gratis data*). This was
the only interpretation of the phrase which scholastic theology, on
the basis of its understanding of the *opera divina ad extra* principle,
could envisage. Once theology has freed itself from this straitjacket, this New Testament language can again be understood in a
realistic way. The concept of the Indwelling of the Holy Spirit
need no longer now be explained away as 'mere appropriation'.
Because the Spirit has been given to us, the Spirit dwells in us. Being 'in the Spirit', we are united to Christ and can now share in his
relationship with the Father: through him in the Spirit we have
access to the Father. The Indwelling of the Spirit means also the
Indwelling of the Trinity. The language of Christian prayer now
no longer sounds so unreal and so forced. It expresses simply and
vividly our situation and our experience.

The new approach to the theology of the Trinity opens the way
to a new theology of the Holy Spirit. This in turn now helps to illu-
minate and deepen the theology of the Trinity. Indwelt by the
Holy Spirit, we are given entry to and become participants in the
cicumincession of the persons, the co-inherence of Father, Son
and Spirit which constitutes the life of God. In the new approach
the divine perichoresis is no longer confined within the immanent
being of the very distant God. God has drawn near. With 'the
opening of the heavens' in the outpouring of the Spirit, we enter
and become part of this divine movement. The celebration of
God's Sabbath, interupted at the Fall, is here resumed.[4]

We believe in the Holy Spirit, the Lord and Giver of life ...

The Trinity and Society

Theology today does not envisage the God it seeks to talk about as
a distant, unconcerned God inhabiting another world, 'the next
world'. The God theology talks about is certainly the transcendent
God, the coming God, the God of the future. But this transcendent
God of the future has now drawn near. The kingdom of this God

is now 'at hand'. The concern of this God now embraces this world and its concerns. Theology today is much engaged in attempting to develop the implications of this concern of God for our actual world. This dimension of theology today is strongly reflected in contemporary trinitarian theology. Understanding God as Trinity, it is maintained, has profound implications for the way we understand and shape our society. This 'social doctrine of the Trinity', as it is often called, has now become a prominent feature of theological writing on this subject. This was not a task even remotely contemplated by scholastic theology or even possible within its terms. It is a totally new development made possible by the renewal of trinitarian theology now under way. The following comment will simply seek to introduce this new issue, explain the basic thesis which is being proposed and indicate the general reaction to it.

As was stated earlier in our study, the way we see and understand God, the Absolute to which everything else is relative, is the most fundamental notion in the human mind. Whether we are conscious of it or not, this will determine how we see and understand ourselves and everything around us, how we understand our world and how we shape our world. According as one finds a different notion of God, one finds a different form of society and a different kind of culture. In any particular age, therefore, the prevailing Christian understanding of God will attempt to shape the society of its time in accordance with this understanding. The age will reflect the understanding of God which it professes.

Those theologians who propound a social doctrine of the Trinity simply apply this principle to the history of Christianity and attempt to develop the social implications of a genuine trinitarian understanding of God for our world today. They maintain that while theology conceived and presented the God who relates to us and with whom we are concerned as, in effect, a Monad, this understanding of God engendered and fostered an authoritarian, hierarchical form of political society. The 'practical monotheism' of theology issued in an absolutist political structure of society. From the early Middle Ages on, rulers such as Justinian and Charlemagne saw themselves as viceregents of Christ who now, as Jungmann has pointed out, for most people functioned as the one God. The notion of the divine right of kings now very naturally developed from this outlook. The result was a very hierarchical, absolutist system of political society which now reproduced itself at every level of the social scale down to the home itself. Authority here claimed direct sanction from God. To protest against this authority was to protest against the rule of God. A monadic, non-trinitarian understanding of God, according to this view, has here naturally engendered an oppressive, authoritarian social system.

Advocates of the social doctrine of the Trinity maintain that a properly trinitarian understanding of God is incompatible with the existence of authoritarian political regimes. If Christianity sheds its monadic view of God, therefore, and adopts an effective triadic understanding, it will deprive such regimes, which are still with us, of their traditional justification and help achieve their eradication. But how would even a genuine trinitarianism have such far-reaching effect? This is not at all evident at first sight. In fact, the opposite would seem to be true. Does not the doctrine of the Trinity itself, in its own way, present a hierarchical under-standing of God – the Son and the Spirit proceeding from the Father, the one Source of all? Is this not a picture of the hierarchy of all hierarchies? Not so, reply these theologians. The members of the Triad do not represent a descending chain of being. The origin of the second and third persons from the Father does not involve any substantial subordination of these persons to the Father. All such subordination is in principle excluded as hereti-cal. In the divine processions the Father communicates to the Son and the Spirit everything that the Father is, except Fatherhood. As regards divine substance, all three persons are equal. The divine processions are eternal processions of origin which conclude in the divine perichoresis where all three are united in the closest relationship. There is here no greater and less, no place for domin-ation. All three are bound together in absolute equality, harmony, relationship. This is a picture of a harmonious society founded on equality, respect, harmony. If this was our understanding of the Absolute, God, it is maintained, the social structures of our own world would eventually but inevitably reflect this understanding and produce this harmonious structure. A right doctrine of the Trinity has these deep social implications – and this profound social mission.

The advocates of this interesting thesis have certainly presented and argued their case with great cogency. They have not, how-ever, succeeded in convincing everyone. The thesis has also had its critics. The reservations which have been expressed take many forms. But they can perhaps be summed up in the overall criti-cism that the argument is too selective and too simplistic. It is too simplistic, the criticism runs, in its reading of political history and it is too selective in the aspects of trinitarian doctrine which it chooses to emphasise and highlight. More particularly, some critics have accused advocates of this thesis of allowing their own notion of an ideal human society to influence their understanding of the doctrine of the Trinity. They have read, it is suggested, their own hopes and dreams of a just society into their understanding of the Triune God. This is not right theological method and cannot but result in some degree of theological distortion. Perhaps there is a suggestion here also that in this kind of approach too much is being asked of and hoped from the discipline which is theology.

Despite these criticisms, the presentation of a social doctrine of the Trinity continues to impress many. It certainly represents one of the main ways in which theology today is generating an actual social comment. Perhaps something of the force of the argument may be glimpsed if one recalls the theology of the Holy Spirit outlined earlier. The Holy Spirit leads us out of slavery into the freedom of God's children. If the human being was genuinely regarded and respected as a temple of this Spirit, would not this understanding have definite social implications? Discussion of this thesis and its method of argument will no doubt continue. Whatever refinement or nuancing of position may emerge as a result of this debate, the evidence of the moment suggests that advocacy of this perspective will continue to be a prominent feature of contemporary trinitarian theology.

The Trinity and Sexist Language
The issue of sexist language concerning God is another topic prominently featured in theological writing over recent decades. A review of this discussion is not required here. A general familiarity with the issue and the perspectives it has generated can, I think, now be presupposed. The literature where the general issue has been canvassed is extensive and widely available. But this study would be incomplete without acknowledgement of the importance of the issue and some comment on it. For trinitarian language raises this question in a very direct way. Beginning with the New Testament itself, this language speaks of God in explicitly masculine terms as 'Father" and 'Son'. Those, and today they are very many, who find exclusively masculine language for God offensive and oppressive see here the apex of the problem. Christianity in and from its very origins expressed its understanding of God in these terms. This is simple fact. But how are we today to interpret and understand this fact? Are we simply committed to blind acceptance of this language of the origins or are there other options open to us here? Some feel so deeply about this issue that they substitute other terms for the traditional ones. Is this an

acceptable option? This is the kind of question this issue raises. Clearly, we are faced here with an issue which is important, wide and deep: how are we to evaluate our inherited ways of describing and imaging God? The following comments will not attempt any comprehensive review of the wide-ranging discussion of this topic in contemporary theology. They simply offer some reflections on the particular problem traditional trinitarian language presents here.

Christianity inherited its language for God from Israel. This language was here the product of, and strongly reflects, a patriarchal and very male-dominated culture. The predominant images and names for God here are masculine. Christianity, at its origins and throughout its subsequent history, continues this way of thinking and speaking about God. It too has developed within and has had its history within a patriarchal culture. Yet, this is not the whole story. Jesus' 'Abba/Father' language for God is obviously masculine expression born of a traditional patriarchal culture. Jesus here speaks the language of his time and place. Yet, as in so many other aspects of his ministry, here also Jesus inverts traditional values and attitudes. When one takes into account the whole character and context of the ministry, paying attention especially to the freedom which Jesus' revolutionary attitude towards women involves and the implications of the parables for his understanding of God – for example, the parable of the Prodigal Son – it begins to become clear that, while Jesus does use patriarchal language for God, he does so in a non-patriarchal way. His Abba/Father concept is not derived from the status of the father in the family culture of Judaism nor from that of the *pater familias* in the Roman tradition. Though using the patriarchal language of his time, Jesus speaks of a non-patriarchal, non-dominating God, a God of love who confers freedom and equality on all. The implications of this freedom of the Founder of Christianity regarding language for God must be appreciated and respected throughout all subsequent Christian history.

Further, it is important to remember that the Bible, both the Old Testament and the New, does not restrict itself to one title or one image for God. It uses a multiplicity of titles and images. It is estimated, for example, that the New Testament uses over fifty titles for Christ. Moreover, some of these biblical expressions and images for God are feminine in character. Nor is this usage confined to the Bible. It continues to be a feature, however minor, of Christian God-language through the centuries. The Creed of Toledo in 675 AD describes the generation of the Son as follows: 'We must believe that the Son is begotten or born not from nothing or from any other substance, but from the womb of the Father, that is from his substance'. (N/D 309; D/S 525f) The Council of Toledo is not being original here. This odd expression and inversion of language already had a venerable history. It is borrowed here directly from Tertullian who describes the Son as begotten 'from the womb of his [the Father's] own heart'. (*Ag Prax* 7,1) And Tertullian has derived this idea from the writings of Apologists such as Theophilus of Antioch. Julian of Norwich (d. 1416 AD) will speak confidently of God as 'our Mother in nature and grace' and even describe Jesus as 'Mother Jesus'. One of her modern editors explains simply: 'Julian believes in God's motherhood because she believes in God's love.' (C. Wolters, ed., *Julian of Norwich: Revelations of Divine Love*, 34]

This multiplicity and range of language for God in biblical and Christian history reveals language's awareness of its own inadequacy to describe the Absolute. No one word or expression is adequate to this task, many have to be pressed into service. The multiplicity is an inherent necessity. But now this multiplicity relativises all particular language. Every particular term and expression needs to be complemented by others if some justice is to be seen to be done to the rich and deep meaning which is God. No particular expression here is absolute. From basic principle our language for God has to be an inclusive language. History and principle speak here with one voice.

It follows from all this that even consecrated terms such as 'Father' and 'Son', whatever their prominence in Christian literature and in the Christian mind, cannot claim absolute status. The history of Christian language will not allow this, since it insists also on so many other ways of speaking of God. And behind this history and justifying it at its foundation stands the freedom of vision of the Founder himself. If all these other ways were to be abandoned and these terms, Father/Son, alone held the field, they would atrophy and die.

This relative character of all our efforts to name and describe God and the consequent need for an inclusive range of expression can be demonstrated also if we return once more to the implications of God's reply to Moses at the incident of the Burning Bush. We noted then that God here does not disclose God's name. Instead, God makes a statement: 'I am the One who will be there with you – in the way I will be there'. 'This,' God then declares, 'is my name forever and thus I am to be remembered throughout all generations'. (Ex 3:15) We are here faced with a refusal by God to disclose God's name. We are simply told that this God is a God of saving concern and that this divine saving concern will be given expression and brought to final conclusion in salvation history. This is the only 'name' we have for God on God's own authority. As regards human history this position is final: 'This is my name forever ... throughout all generations'. God is and will remain for us the Anonymous One.

This understanding has not been lost sight of in the Christian tradition. The ultimate incomprehensibility of God and the apophatic character of our knowledge of God and language about God is constantly emphasised down the centuries in Christian thought. An early witness who merits quotation in this context is St Justin Martyr. In his *Second Apology*, in a passage which refers also to the 'inexpressible God', Justin makes the following statement.

> To the Father of all, no name is given; for anyone who has been given a name has received the name from someone older than himself. Father and God and Creator and Lord and Master are not names but appellations derived from his beneficences and works. (2 *Apol*, 6)

Justin points out to us here that we have no name for God; all the names we do have are names for what God has done for us.

This general principle applies to the terms 'Father' and 'Son' as well as to all our other terms. All our expressions for God are metaphors drawn from our own experience to express what God means to us. They all have a valid but limited application, and therefore we need many of them. The terms 'Father' and 'Son' are metaphors which attempt to express the relationship between these members of the Triad and the saving concern and love which this relationship means for us when it is communicated to us in the Spirit. Like all human language when used of God, this is a limited and vulnerable language.[5] Further, it must always be remembered that there is always a certain subjectivity and selectivity attaching to our language for God, both at its origin and also in the way it will strike a particular listener today. Everyone tends to interpret language in terms of their own particular experience. As this experience may vary widely from one individual to another, so also may particular interpretations. (What does the statement: 'In the beginning was the Word ...' mean to a deaf person?) The Father/Son terminology, therefore, is not and cannot in principle be absolute. Individuals who find other expressions more helpful and meaningful are fully entitled to their personal option in their own discourse and in their own prayer. Public prayer,

however, and public, official language are a different story. These
terms have a hallowed origin in Christian history and a hallowed
place in Christian tradition. It is not conceivable that the Church
will forget this origin and abandon this tradition in its official
language. But it is not committed in principle, nor has it ever been
in fact, to this language as the *only* language for God. Alternative
languages already exist and must not be forgotten. Moreover, a
new language for God is always in principle possible and may
well merit public sanction and approval. But all such new pro-
posals also require testing and critical assessment of their own
limitations. For example, one might observe of one suggested
Triad, Creator/Redeemer/Sustainer, that it lacks something of
the intimate personal note that the Father/Son terminology conveys. But it must also be acknowledged that the discussion of
God-language which this issue has generated has already made a
great positive contribution to the theology of God and the theology of the Trinity. One might mention in particular the new perspectives on the doctrine of the Trinity which the retrieval of the
biblical concept of Wisdom/Sophia is now opening up.[6]

Today a conscious sensitivity to personal perspectives should
always accompany use of the traditional terminology. And especially it is necessary today to explain the historical background and
origin of these terms and to make the public of the Church aware
of their metaphorical character and their limited and vulnerable
range of reference. Our understanding of the Triune God can only
be enhanced by this effort at a deepening awareness.

Conclusion

The theology of the Trinity today has a new appearance to it. This
is a theology which has undergone and is still undergoing an in-
tense renewal. It has today a vibrancy and vitality to it unknown
in this field since the stormy days of the fourth century. This new
interest and renewal grew out of a gradual awakening to and real-
isation of the serious limitations which scholastic trinitarian theology involved. This critical evaluation of the scholastic presentation, however, has not remained purely negative. It has led to a
positive renewal of this theology and a basic re-thinking and re-
shaping of the treatise. The basic insight which has grounded and
fueled the new development has been the thesis that the God who
relates to us is the Triune God of Godself: the economic Trinity is
the immanent Trinity. This insight has led to a comprehensive review of trinitarian theology and to the development of a range of

new interests and new possibilities. The theology of the Trinity emerging from this programme of renewal is now claiming a central place within the whole enterprise of theological discussion. It is claiming that the understanding of God as Trinity is the basis, criterion and driving axis of *all* theology and of all its applications. A wide agenda is being proposed here. This theology is envisaging many new tasks and confronting many new areas and issues.[7] How it will cope with these ventures remains to be seen. But the vibrancy and vitality of trinitarian theology is, I think, here to stay.

Notes

1. While Rahner's thesis concerning the unity of the immanent and the economic Trinity has won general acceptance, some reservations have also been expressed concerning possible misinterpretation of it. Some commentators have seen a danger that the thesis could be understood to mean that God's being in itself, the immanent Trinity, is determined by and exhausted in God's being with the world, the economic Trinity. In other words, the thesis could be read in a way which does not adequately recognise and protect the transcendence of God.

2. See the discussion of this issue in G.L. Prestige, *God in Patristic Thought*, London, SPCK, 1952, 235-241.

3. For discussion of this issue, see especially: J. Moltmann, *The Trinity and the Kingdom of God*, London, SCM, 1981 139-148, 171-174; W. Kasper, *The God of Jesus Christ*, London, SCM, 1984, 285-290; C. LaCugna, *God for Us: The Trinity and Christian Life*, San Francisco, Harper, 1991, 243-266.

4. The question of the double procession of the Holy Spirit, the *Filioque* issue, has over recent decades been the subject of much discussion and ecumenical dialogue between theologians representing the Eastern and Western traditions. It has not been possible to incorporate a review of this discussion here. Greater mutual understanding of positions is emerging here and, interestingly, some new perspectives on the theology of the Holy Spirit also. The theological reflection emerging from this discussion is now becoming an important source in the development of a real pneumatology and is helping to modify the Christocentrism so long characteristic of the Latin tradition. Anyone interested in reading further on these developments might consult: L. Vischer, ed., *Spirit of God, Spirit of Christ: Ecumenical Reflections on the Filioque Contro-*

versy, London/Geneva, SPCK, 1981; and, for a more recent comment: J. Moltmann, *The Spirit of Life: A Universal Affirmation*, London, SCM, 1992, 306-310; F-X. Durrwell, *The Spirit of the Father and the Son*, London, St Paul Publications, 1989; C. LaCugna, 'Towards Ecumenical Agreement on the *Filioque* Clause in the Creed' in F.S. Fiorenza and J. Galvin, eds., *Systematic Theology: Roman Catholic Perspectives*, Dublin, Gill & MacMillan, 1992, 184-186.

5. For a good discussion of this whole topic, see C. LaCugna, 'Placing Some Trinitarian Locutions', *ITQ*, 51 (1985), 17-36, and the same writer's comments, 'Balancing Masculine Language for God', in F. S. Fiorenza and J. Galvin, eds., *Systematic Theology: Roman Catholic Perspectives*, Dublin, Gill and MacMillan, 1992, 180-184.

6. On this issue, see especially: Elizabeth A Johnson, *She Who Is: The Mystery of God in Feminist Theological Discourse*, NY, Crossroad, 1992.

7. For an interesting outline of the implications and applications of trinitarian theology today for various other areas of theological discussion, the reader is recommended to consult Catherine LaCugna, *God for Us*, 377-411.

Epilogue

Reflection on the mystery of the Trinity is not the exclusive preserve of theology. Nor has theology any reason to feel proud of its achievement over the centuries in its efforts to shed some light on the mystery. That, at least, even the summary review of these efforts presented in this book should leave in no doubt. Theology has every reason to see itself as a humble servant, ever engaged in correcting its faults, ever repenting of its sins. Thankfully, the Christian mind gives expression to its faith in many other ways also. The history of the creative efforts of the mystic, the writer, the artist, to image for us the Triune God is an impressive and fascinating one. One thinks immediately here of the great fifteenth century painting of Andrei Rublev, a painting born of deep faith and yet also so thoroughly theologically informed. This is a painting which speaks and moves and rivets the attention of even the untutored eye. The writer would like to conclude his effort at a theological study of the Trinity with a simple acknowledgement of the achievement here of this other, creative side of the Christian mind. To do so, he quotes a poem of John Donne which is explicitly trinitarian and therefore speaks for itself. But he would also like to refer to another poem of Donne's which is not consciously or explicitly trinitarian but which has, to the writer's mind at least, profound trinitarian implications.

A recurring feature of Donne's poetry is his fascination with the theme of relationship. His greatest achievement here is undoubtedly *The Ecstasy*. In this poem Donne is certainly not thinking of the doctrine of the Trinity. But to the mind of this writer the application seems obvious, and deeply moving. The reason why is not far to seek. Theology identifies the distinctions in God as relations, a very human word for a very human experience. We can only hope to probe the meaning of the divine relations by deepening our reflection on the human experience. This poem represents John Donne's deepest reflection on this theme which fascinated him. The application now seems obvious. The poem is too long to quote here. I can only, therefore, invite the reader to read the poem for himself or herself in the light of the comment made here and the connection suggested. They will have to decide for themselves, however, whether the application which seems so obvious to the writer has for them any validity or not. But there is no doubt what is the theme of the following poem.

> Batter my heart, three-personed God; for, you
> As yet but knock, breathe, shine, and seek to mend;
> That I may rise, and stand, o'erthrow me, and bend
> Your force, to break, blow, burn, and make me new,
> I, like an usurped town, to another due,
> Labour to admit you, but oh, to no end,
> Reason your viceroy in me, me should defend,
> But is captived, and proves weak or untrue,
> Yet dearly I love you, and would be loved fain,
> But am bethrothed unto your enemy,
> Divorce me, untie, or break that knot again,
> Take me to you, imprison me, for I
> Except you enthral me, never shall be free,
> Nor ever chaste, except you ravish me.

Discussion Questions

INTRODUCTION

1. 'Tell me your prayer and I will tell you your God.' How do you pray and what does this say about your understanding of God?
2. How has God revealed God-self to us human beings?
3. In what way has the Christian community and its liturgy and worship helped you to expand and deepen your awareness of the presence of God in your life?
4. What is the relation between prayer and theology?

CHAPTER ONE

1. What does the incident at the Burning Bush, as narrated in Exodus 3:1-15, tell us about the God of Israel?
2. What is salvation history and why is it important for an understanding of God?
3. What is anthropomorphism and how does it enter into discussion of God?
4. What implications do the references in the Old Testament (Hebrew Scriptures) to the Word/Wisdom and the Spirit/Breath of God have for our understanding of God?
5. How absolute is the Old Testament statement that there is *one* God?
6. How would you assess the suggestion that revelation of the Trinity was *implicit* in the Old Testament?

CHAPTER TWO

1. Why is the notion of the *completion* of salvation history significant for the Christian understanding of God?
2. What evidence is there that the New Testament maintains and continues the Jewish assertion that there is one God?

3. How is this 'one God' identified in the New Testament?

4. According to the New Testament, how is Jesus of Nazareth related to the one God of Jewish and Christian faith? What significance has this relationship both for the understanding of Jesus and of God?

5. How is there both continuity and development between 'Ruah Yahweh' in the Old Testament and 'Spirit of God' in the New?

6. How do the examples of Christian prayer and early credal formulas contained in the New Testament indicate a triadic understanding of God?

CHAPTER THREE

1. What does it mean to say that the New Testament references to the Trinity are pre-theological?

2. Why did early Christian writers have to express their understanding of God in terms used by Greek philosophy?

3. What tensions arose between the biblical understanding of God and these efforts to express the nature of God in philosophical terms?

4. Some efforts to express the meaning of God were judged by the Church to be deficient. What caused the Church to reject a) Sabellianism, b) Dynamic Monarchianism, c) Patripassionism, d) Modalism, e) Subordinationism?

5. What contribution to the Church's understanding of God was made by a) Irenaeus, b) Tertullian, c) Origen?

6. By the end of the third century, what was the widely accepted general understanding of the nature of God?

CHAPTER FOUR

1. What was the teaching of Arius and why was it judged unacceptable?

2. How did the Church at the Council of Nicaea counter the teaching of Arius?

3. Why did the teaching of Nicaea not settle the issue which Arius had raised? Why did the conciliar teaching itself soon become the subject of dispute?

4. What role did the Emperor play in the controversy? How did this factor influence the course of events?

5. What stance did St Athanasius adopt in the controversy? Why has he been called *Athanasius contra mundum*?

6. Who were the Cappadocian Fathers? What was their contribution to the resolution of the issue at the heart of the controversy?

7. In what way did the Council of Constantinople complete the agenda of Nicaea?

CHAPTER FIVE

1. What are the two understandings of 'the one God' which emerged as a result of the trinitarian controversy?

2. What are the main concerns of St Augustine in his great work on the Trinity? What are the particular emphases which characterise his presentation of this theology? How would you describe the strengths and weaknesses of his position?

3. In what particular way did St Thomas Aquinas influence the presentation of trinitarian theology?

4. What are the basic concepts on which the scholastic Tract on the Trinity is structured? How do these concepts help us to understand the doctrine of God as Trinity?

5. What are the main emphases which characterise the Latin theology of the Trinity? How are these emphases manifested within the system? Does a problem begin to appear here in this theology?

6. What significance does the notion of the Divine Indwelling have for theology? for spirituality?

CHAPTER SIX

1. Karl Rahner maintained that Christians today are 'almost mere "monotheists"'. What does Rahner mean by this statement? What does this situation say about the doctrine of the Trinity today? Why and how has this situation developed?

2. What is Rahner's basic proposal for revising and revitalising trinitarian theology? What difference would this make?

3. Why is the distinction between nature and person important for an understanding of the Triune God? Why is the concept of 'person' a subject of discussion today?

4. What implications has the revision of trinitarian theology, now under way, for the theology of the Holy Spirit?

5. What does 'the social doctrine of the Trinity' mean? Do you think that understanding God as Trinity has such implications?

6. How and why does the doctrine of the Trinity create a problem
   for our language about God? What particular issues are important to bear in mind in approaching this question? What would
   you consider a good solution to this problem?
7. What issue or issues concerning the Trinity, other than those
   discussed in this chapter, do you think merit consideration today?

Recommended Reading

Biblical

Dodd, C.H., *The Apostolic Preaching and Its Developments*, London, Hodder & Stoughton, 1963.

Dunn, J.D.G., *Jesus and the Spirit*, London, SCM, 1975.

Hamerton-Kelly, R., *God the Father: Theology and Patriarchy in the Teaching of Jesus*, Philadelphia, Fortress Press, 1979.

Hengel, M., *The Son of God: The Origin of Christology and the History of Jewish-Hellenistic Religion*, London, SCM, 1976.

Jeremias, J., *The Prayers of Jesus*, London, SCM, 1967.

Lebreton, J., *History of the Dogma of the Trinity*, 1, The Origins, London, Burns Oates & Washbourne, 1939.

McPolin, J., 'The Holy Spirit in the Lucan and Johannine Writings: A Comparative Study', *ITQ*, 45 (1978), 117-131.

Marsh, T., 'The Holy Spirit in Early Christian Teaching', *ITQ*, 45 (1978), 101-116.

Mayes, A., 'The Emergence of Monotheism in Israel', *The Christian Understanding of God Today*, ed. Byrne, J.M., 26-33, Dublin, Columba Press, 1993.

Montague, G.T., *The Holy Spirit: Growth of a Biblical Tradition*, New York, Paulist Press, 1976.

Rahner, K., 'Theos in the New Testament', *Theological Investigations*, 1, 79-148, London, DLT, 1961.

Renckens, H., *The Religion of Israel*, London, Sheed & Ward, 1967.

Wainwright, A.W., *The Trinity in the New Testament*, London, SPCK, 1962.

Historical

Bettenson, H., ed., *The Early Christian Fathers*, Oxford, OUP, 1956.

— *The Later Christian Fathers*, Oxford, OUP, 1970.

Burns, J. Patout & Fagin, G.M., *The Holy Spirit*, Message of the Fathers of the Church 3, Wilmington, Glazier, 1984.

Butterworth, G. W., *Origen on First Principles*, London, SPCK, 1936.

Fortman, E. J., *The Triune God: A Historical Study of the Doctrine of the Trinity*, London, Hutchinson, 1972.

Gregg, R. and Groh, D., *Early Arianism: A View of Salvation*, Philadelphia, Fortress, 1981.

Hanson, R.P.C., *The Search for the Christian Doctrine of God: The Arian Controversy*, Edinburgh, T & T Clark, 1988.

Hill, E., *St Augustine: The Trinity*, New York, New City Press, 1991.

Jurgens, W.A., *The Faith of the Early Fathers*, I-III, Collegeville, Liturgical Press, 1970-1979.

Kannengiesser, C., 'Athanasius of Alexandria and the Holy Spirit between Nicea 1 and Constantinople 1', *ITQ*, 48 (1981), 166-180.

Kelly, J.N.D., *Early Christian Doctrines*, London, A & C Black, 1968 (4th edition).

— *Early Christian Creeds*, London, Longmans, 1960 (2nd edition).

Luibhéid, C., *The Council of Nicaea*, Galway, Galway University Press, 1982.

Murray, John Courtney, *The Problem of God*, New Haven, Yale Univ. Press. 1964.

Pelikan, J., *The Christian Tradition: A History of the Development of Doctrine*, 1, The Emergence of the Catholic Tradition [100-600], Chicago and London, Univ of Chicago Press, 1971.

Prestige, G.L., *God in Patristic Thought*, London, SPCK, 1952 (2nd edition).

Rusch, W.G., ed., *The Trinitarian Controversy*, Philadelphia, Fortress Press, 1980.

Young, F., *From Nicaea to Chalcedon*, London, SCM, 1983.

Watson, Gerard, *Greek Philosophy and the Christian Notion of God*, Dublin, Columba Press, 1994.

Systematic/General

Byrne, J.M., ed., *The Christian Understanding of God Today*, Dublin, Columba Press, 1993.

Boff, L., *Trinity and Society*, Kent, Burns & Oates, 1988.

Comblin, J., *The Holy Spirit and Liberation*, Kent, Burns & Oates, 1989.

Congar, Y., *I Believe in the Holy Spirit*, I-III, London/NY, Chapman/Seabury Press, 1983.

Durrwell, F-X., *The Spirit of the Father and the Son*, London, St Paul Publications, 1989.

Kasper, W., *The God of Jesus Christ*, London, SCM, 1984.

Hill, W.J., *The Three-Personed God: The Trinity as a Mystery of Salvation*, Washington, CUA Press, 1982.

Johnson, Elizabeth A., *She Who Is: The Mystery of God in Feminist Theological Discourse*, NY, Crossroad, 1992.

LaCugna, C.M., *God for Us: The Trinity and Christian Life*, San Francisco, Harper, 1991.

— 'The Trinitarian Mystery of God', *Systematic Theology: Roman Catholic Perspectives*, eds. Fiorenza, F.S. and Galvin, J.P., 149-192, Dublin, Gill & MacMillan, 1992.

— 'Placing Some Trinitarian Locutions', *ITQ*, 51 [1985], 17-36.

Mackey, J.P., *The Christian Experience of God as Trinity*, London, SCM, 1983.

Moltmann, J., *The Trinity and the Kingdom of God*, London, SCM, 1981.

— *The Spirit of Life: A Universal Affirmation* , London, SCM, 1992.

O'Donnell, J. J., *The Mystery of the Triune God*, London, Sheed and Ward, 1988.

Rahner, K., *The Trinity*, London, Burns & Oates, 1970.

Vischer, L., ed., *Spirit of God, Spirit of Christ: Ecumenical Reflections on the* Filioque *Controversy*, London, SPCK, 1981.

Other Works Cited

Barrett, C.K., *The First Epistle to the Corinthians*, London, A & C Black, 1968.

Black, M. & Rowley, H.H., eds., *Peake's Commentary on the Bible*, London, Nelson, 1962.

Denzinger, H.- Schonmetzer, A., *Enchiridion Symbolorum, Definitionum et Declarationum de rebus fidei et morum*, Freiburg im Breisgau, 1965.

Jungmann, J.A., *Pastoral Liturgy*, London, Challoner, 1962.

Kelly, J.N.D., *The Epistles of Peter and Jude*, London, A & C Black, 1969.

McKenzie, J.L., *Dictionary of the Bible* , London, Chapman, 1965.

Neuner, J. & Dupuis, J., eds., *The Christian Faith in the Doctrinal Documents of the Catholic Church* , London, Collins, 1983 (4th ed).

Wolters, C., ed., *Julian of Norwich: Revelations of Divine Love*, London, Penguin Books, 1966.